The Generative Enterprise Revisited

Noam Chomsky

The Generative Enterprise Revisited

Dicussions with
Riny Huybregts, Henk van Riemsdijk,
Naoki Fukui and Mihoko Zushi

With a New Foreword by
Noam Chomsky

Mouton de Gruyter
Berlin · New York

Mouton de Gruyter (formerly Mouton, The Hague)
is a Division of Walter de Gruyter GmbH & Co. KG, Berlin.

∞ Printed on acid-free paper which falls within the guidelines
of the ANSI to ensure permanence and durability.

Library Congress Cataloging-in-Publication Data

> Chomsky, Noam.
>   The generative enterprise revisited : discussions with Riny Huybregts, Henk van Riemsdijk, Naoki Fukui, and Mihoko Zushi, with a new foreword by Noam Chomsky / by Noam Chomsky.
>   p. cm.
>   Includes bibliographical references and index.
>   ISBN 3-11-018001-4 (pbk. : alk. paper)
>   1. Generative grammar.   2. Linguistics.   I. Huybregts, Riny.
> II. Riemsdijk, Henk C. van.   III. Fukui, Naoki.   IV. Zushi, Mihoko, 1964−   V. Title
>   P158.C49   2004
>   415'.0182−dc22
>
>   2004005300

ISBN 3-11-018001-4

Bibliographic information published by Die Deutsche Bibliothek

Die Deutsche Bibliothek lists this publication in the Deutsche Nationalbibliografie; detailed bibliographic data is available in the Internet at <http://dnb.ddb.de>.

© Copyright 2004 by Walter de Gruyter GmbH & Co. KG, D-10785 Berlin (1982 Foris Publishers)
© Copyright for the new interview 2002 by Noam Chomsky and Naoki Fukui
© Copyright for the new foreword 2003 by Naoki Fukui and Mihoko Zushi
All rights reserved, including those of translation into foreign languages. No part of this book may be reproduced or transmitted in any form or by any means, electronic or mechanical, including photocopy, recording or any information storage and retrieval system, without permission in writing from the publisher.
Cover design: Frank Benno Junghanns, Berlin.
Picture of Noam Chomsky: Courtesy of Donna Coveney, MIT.
Picture of Building 20/MIT: Courtesy of The MIT Museum.
Printed in Germany.

Dedication

*To all generative grammarians who,
however far away, however isolated, however minoritarian,
devote their energies to the pursuit of progress
in our joint quest for new insights
into the theory of grammar.*

Contents

Foreword by Noam Chomsky ix
Preface xv
Introduction by Naoki Fukui and Mihoko Zushi 1

The Generative Enterprise
Noam Chomsky in Discussion with Riny Huybregts and
Henk van Riemsdijk

Preface by Riny Huybregts and Henk van Riemsdijk 29

Part I   On Linguistics

Chapter 1   Language and Cognition 33
Chapter 2   Explanation in Linguistics 53
Chapter 3   The Field 63

Part II   On Grammar

Chapter 1   A Historical Perspective 87
Chapter 2   Issues in Formal Grammar 110
Chapter 3   Core and Periphery 131

The Generative Enterprise Revisited
Noam Chomsky in Discussion with Naoki Fukui and Mihoko Zushi

Linguistics in the 21st Century 147

1. Linguistics: The Development of Linguistic Theory
   in the past 20 Years 147
2. Linguistics and other Sciences 170
3. Prospects for the Future 186

Bibliography 189
Index 199

Foreword

Noam Chomsky

As Naoki Fukui and Mihoko Zushi explain in their penetrating review and analysis of the course of generative grammar (GG), the first of the two discussions contained in this volume took place at a time of considerable excitement in the field, as a new approach to the study of language was taking shape: the "principles and parameters" (P&P) framework, which appeared to offer a great deal of promise for empirical inquiry and theoretical insight, for neighboring disciplines as well.

The P&P framework was in significant respects a much more radical departure from the long and rich tradition of linguistic inquiry than earlier work in GG. That work, from its origins, had substantially taken over traditional notions of rule and construction, seeking to discover rules for forming interrogative constructions in English, nominalizations in Turkish, verbal constructions in Hidatsa, etc. It also adopted, at first without acquaintance with the earlier history, the traditional insight that language involves "infinite use of finite means" (in von Humboldt's aphorism). These ideas were reformulated and sharpened in terms of new understanding that had been achieved in the formal sciences, and within what later came to be called "the biolinguistic perspective," which studies language as a component of the human mind/brain alongside of other interacting systems: visual, motor action, circulatory, etc., all "organs of the body" in the informal sense of standard usage in the biological sciences.

The earliest efforts revealed, dramatically, that much of what had been taken for granted was far from accurate. It was commonly assumed at the time that the technology of linguistic description was reasonably clear, and that language variation was so free than nothing of much generality was likely to be discovered. As soon as efforts were made to provide fairly explicit accounts of the properties of languages, it immediately became obvious how little was known, in any domain. Structuralist grammars skimmed the surface of language structure, and the descriptive and analytic technology was by no means as well-founded or comprehensive as assumed. Traditional grammars and dictionaries were valuable for their specific purposes, but they basically provide hints that can be used by people with an intuitive knowledge of the language in question or, for pedagogical purposes, at least a functioning faculty of language (FL). They in effect presuppose what the study of language as a biological system seeks to discover and explain: the knowledge of a language on which its use is based, and the basis in the mind/brain for the acquisition of this knowledge.

As soon as the first attempts were made to fill in the gaps, it became evident that they were enormous. Each specific proposal immediately yielded a mass of counter-evidence, a consequence that was highly productive for research, but soon posed fundamental problems. Even to begin to approach descriptive adequacy, it seemed necessary to postulate complex rule systems, varying widely among constructions and languages. These discoveries gave rise to the serious tension that Fukui and Zushi discuss: descriptive adequacy appeared to require complex rule systems that vary widely among languages, but the most elementary observations led to the realization that this cannot be correct and that languages must be fundamentally cast to the same mold, or explanatory adequacy cannot be achieved: there will be no account of how knowledge of language is attained.

A related tension also became increasingly evident. From the earliest explorations of GG in the late 1940s, I and others concerned with the topic assumed that the theory of FL (Universal Grammar, UG) provided a format for possible I-languages ("grammars," in conventional but misleading terminology) and a procedure for selecting among them. But if so, the format must be highly articulated and intricate to ensure that only a limited number of I-languages will be available for selection, given the experience (primary linguistic data, PLD) available to the child. That conclusion, however, raises both methodological and substantive quandaries. The intricacy of rule systems that seems to be required to deal with the problem of explanatory adequacy is undesirable from a methodological point of view. The substantive problems have to do with the origin of FL in human evolution, apparently about 60,000 years ago, in a small breeding group of which we are all descendants – what some biologists call "the great leap forward" in human evolution. However remote serious inquiry into these issues might have been, it was recognized that the questions are of fundamental importance, and, evidently, they are harder to address to the extent that FL is constituted by complex principles that are specific to it. From the general biolinguistic perspective, then, there were serious methodological and substantive problems, alongside the tension between considerations of descriptive and explanatory adequacy. The problems were frequently discussed at interdisciplinary conferences and elsewhere, but seemed irresoluble at the time.

The P&P approach offered hope for escape from these dilemmas. Relying on ideas that had been developed and widely applied in preceding years, it proposed that traditional concepts of rule and construction be abandoned; or more accurately, that these be regarded as taxonomic artifacts, rather like terrestial mammal, real enough but the result of interaction of more fundamental principles. There is, for example, no question whether the expression "John was expected to win" is a passive or a raising construction. Its form and meaning are determined by interaction of principles that apply more generally, including, perhaps, a principle as elementary as "move anything anywhere" that applies far more broadly to expressions of varied types, possibly principles that are even more general. If the approach is feasible, the tension between descriptive and explanatory adequacy can be considerably reduced: the principles are an invariant component of FL, as is the array of parameters, which must meet the empirical condition that their values can be determined by PLD. Similarly, there are new prospects for relieving, perhaps significantly, the methodological and substantive dilemmas that arise within the biolinguistic perspective. Under the P&P approach, acquisition is entirely divorced from the format for I-languages provided by UG, which in turn reduces to fixed principles and parameters (their values to be set by experience). There is no longer a daunting conceptual barrier to the search for an account of UG that is much more attractive from a methodological point of view and that also restricts the specificity of FL, thus offering at least some hope of isolating the factors that entered into "the great leap forward."

As Fukui and Zushi discuss, the crystallization of the P&P framework led to an explosion of inquiry into a very broad range of typologically diverse languages, at a level of depth not previously envisioned. New and challenging questions came to light, sometimes possible answers. The framework also contributed to reinvigorating related psycholinguistic studies of acquisition and processing, their guiding questions reframed in terms of parameter-setting within a fixed system of principles of UG with at least visible contours. And it became possible to ask to what extent there might be a principled explanation for properties of I-language, reaching beyond FL itself.

For any organ of the body, we can identify three factors that determine its growth: (1) genetic endowment, (2) environment, and (3) general principles of growth and development that are not specific to the organism, perhaps not even to the organic world. Under the P&P approach, (1) fixes the principles and parameters, while (2) sets parameter values. That the third factor is real, and plays a fundamental role in both evolution and morphogenesis, is not controversial, but investigation of it is extremely difficult even for very simple organisms. For many organs, FL among them, the most far-reaching theories we have are computational: we would therefore expect that principles of computational efficiency that are organ-independent (and perhaps deeper still) would enter crucially into their growth and development; in the language case, into acquisition of I-languages.

We can regard an account of properties of I-language as "principled" insofar as it relies on principles of category (3) and on conditions that FL must meet in order to function at all. Specifically, FL must satisfy interface conditions: it must link to the systems of thought, interpretation, and organization of action (the "conceptual-intentional" interface C-I) and also to those that enter into externalization of expressions (the sensory-motor interface SM). Unless FL satisfies the conditions imposed by C-I it cannot be used at all, and unless it satisfies those imposed by SM, it cannot be used for human interaction (including communication).

If we adopt this framework for inquiry into principled explanation, we ask to what extent FL is an "optimal solution" to the interface conditions, where the concept of optimal solution is spelled out in terms of principles of computational efficiency. Some obvious desiderata are minimal search, no look-ahead and backtracking, reduction of cyclic operations to a single cycle, restriction of operations to rearrangement of syntactic objects already generated in the course of derivation, with no tampering, and others that might be special cases of principles that are independent of FL. To be sure, the conditions "external" to FL – interface conditions and those that determine optimal solution -- are only partially understood: we have to learn about the conditions that set the problem in the course of trying to solve it. The research task is interactive: to clarify the nature of the interfaces and optimal computational principles through investigation of how language partially satisfies the conditions they impose. That is not an unfamiliar feature of serious inquiry, in the hard sciences as well. Independently, the interface systems can be studied on their own, including comparative study; and the same is true of principles of efficient computation.

In a variety of ways, then, the P&P approach opened the possibility of inquiry that would both clarify and address some of the basic problems of the biology of language. The second discussion included in this volume considers the course of these investigations since the possibility was opened by the crystallization of the P&P approach, and some of the dilemmas and prospects that lie ahead.

Cambridge, Massachusetts
February 2004

Preface

Generative Grammar was initiated in the 1950s by Noam Chomsky and established itself in a niche in Cambridge, Massachusetts at the Massachusetts Institute of Technology in the largely hostile environment of American structuralism. But, as is to be expected with great ideas and exciting new scientific perspectives, more people elsewhere in the USA and the world became actively involved in Generative Grammar. Some went to MIT, some started working wherever they were. Gradually, Generative Grammar became one of the dominant theories in North American linguistics. Small pockets of generative grammarians also started to emerge in Europe and Japan during the 60s and have since then increased in number and importance.[1]

Visits by Chomsky to various places tended to inject these activities with energy and direction. One of the most pervasive developments of this kind took place when Chomsky stayed at the Scuola Normale Superiore in Pisa in 1979, culminating in his so-called Pisa Lectures that were published in 1981 as *Lectures on Government and Binding*.[2] Even before then, the small group of young generative linguists in Europe had decided to found an organization, Generative Grammarians in the Old Worlds (GLOW) that made it its business to further the contacts among generative grammarians, primarily in Europe, by organizing a yearly conference and by actively supporting the organization of summer schools. In other words, out of the enthusiasm of individuals evolved something like a common purpose.

Recognizing this, Riny Huijbregts and Henk van Riemsdijk decided to ask Noam Chomsky what he thought about the turn Generative Grammar was taking after the Pisa Lectures and to discuss ways in which the emergent Generative Enterprise could and should develop and how it could be made to thrive. In November 1979 and in March 1980 three discussion sessions were held on these topics. This resulted in a book

---

1. For Japan, see Fukui, N. and M. Saito. (1993). For Europe, a similar document does not exist, but see Haider, H., M. Prinzhorn & H. van Riemsdijk (1987). For the history of GLOW, cf. also "The History of GLOW", URL: http://www.meertens.knaw.nl/glow2002/history.html.
2. Chomsky, N. (1981b).

entitled *The Generative Enterprise* that was published in 1982 by Henk LaPorte at Foris Publications, a small publisher who was very supportive of Generative Grammar in the 80s. Due to insufficient marketing, however, that book never got the audience it deserved in the opinion of the few who had seen it.

Generative Grammar has taken many new turns since then, the enterprise is registering successes as well as failures, but many of the ideas discussed there and many of the vicissitudes attending the generative enterprise are as relevant today as they were then. This emerged clearly enough when Naoki Fukui and Mihoko Zushi held another interview-discussion with Noam Chomsky on November 22, 2002 at MIT. In the same spirit of linking past ideas with present ideas, past concerns with present concerns, this interview is now published in Japanese together with a Japanese translation of the Generative Enterprise book.[3]

In order to make the discussions of the post-Pisa-Lectures era optimally accessible to modern audiences, the translation has been supplemented with a set of annotations. And this in turn led to the plan to republish the English version of the Generative Enterprise, together with some annotations and an introduction and with the new discussion between Noam Chomsky and Naoki Fukui/Mihoko Zushi. And this is what you have before you now.

We wish to thank Noam Chomsky for taking the time to write his foreword to this English edition. Thanks are also due to Teresa Griffith for her assistance with editing the 'new' interview. And we would also like to thank Mana Kobuchi-Philip and Jennifer Mand for having helped us translating the Japanese parts into English, and Wolfgang Konwitschny, the production editor.

The authors would also like to express their heartfelt gratitude to their editor, Ursula Kleinhenz (who has compiled the index on the basis of the original index by Sie Ing-Djiang), for doing everything and much more, well beyond the call of duty, to make this project happen.

Naoki Fukui
Riny Huybregts
Henk van Riemsdijk
Mihoko Zushi

---

3. Chomsky, N. (2003).

Introduction

Naoki Fukui and Mihoko Zushi

Translated by Mana Kobuchi-Philip

The two interviews included in this volume discuss diverse scientific topics from a number of perspectives. In all of these discussions, however, the theory of Generative Grammar always serves as a kind of centripetal force. Modern Generative Grammar pursues a scientific investigation of intrinsic properties of the human mind, on the basis of a detailed examination of the human cognitive capacity called language. In this introduction, we will try to provide a minimum intellectual background necessary for properly understanding various topics covered in these interviews, briefly discussing and clarifying the most basic issues in the theory of contemporary Generative Grammar.

1. The Basic Problems of Generative Grammar

Every scientific field has a set of basic problems that determine the "nature" of the field. In the case of modern Generative Grammar, the basic problems can be summarized as follows (Chomsky 1986, Jenkins 2000):

The set of basic problems in Generative Grammar

(1) The knowledge of language
(2) The acquisition of language
(3) The use of language
(4) The physical basis of language
(5) The origin and evolution of language

What we must clarify first is that Generative Grammar consistently defines language as the "linguistic competence that a human being holds inside his or her mind/brain," which is different from a common sense understanding of language. When we use the phrase "language," we are ordinarily referring to a particular language, such as English, Japanese, Swahili, etc., treating it as if it existed as an external object. This assumption of the existence of "language as an external object" is not just found in the common perception of language. It was also the view adopted by (American) structural linguistics, which was very influential in the field of linguistics (at least in the U.S.) prior to the advent of contemporary Generative Grammar in the 1950s. The (American) structural linguists, who were strongly influenced by behaviorist psychology (and indirectly by logical positivism), complied faithfully with the doctrine of behaviorism and focused only on "phenomena that are directly observable" as the object of inquiry. Thus, it was inevitably assumed that the essential nature of language was that it was an entity external to human beings (see, for instance, Bloomfield 1926).

However, as has been widely discussed (Chomsky 1986, Fukui 2001), the assumption that language is an object which exists independently of human beings is very dubious. And it is already a historical fact by now that (American) structural linguistics, which dealt only with directly observable linguistic phenomena, concentrating throughout on the taxonomic (and mostly phonemic) description of language, has failed to capture the essential nature of human language. "Language" simply cannot exist independently of human beings, and "the essential nature of language" resides only within the human mind/brain (henceforth "brain," abstracting away from various issues concerning the slash). In this regard, the study of language is nothing other than the study of (an aspect of) the human brain.

With this in mind, let us consider the basic problems listed in (1)-(5). The problem of "the knowledge of language" stated in (1) is an inquiry into what knowledge the human brain contains when a person is able to speak his/her first language. "Knowledge" here refers, in most cases, to subconscious or tacit knowledge, knowledge that the speaker is not precisely aware of. If this usage of the term invites misunderstanding, we may instead use a technical term, namely "competence." However, this term may also cause misunderstanding. This sort of terminological confusion can be avoided, after all, only by making an effort to understand the relevant term on the basis of the definition given in the field, without being misguided by various other uses of the term in other fields. Thus, we will use the term "knowledge of language" to mean "knowledge of a language that enables a person to speak and understand the language," i.e., the linguistic competence possessed by a speaker of the language. Following the conventional terms (cf. Chomsky 1986), we call "knowledge of language" in this sense "I-language" (where "I" stands for "internalized," "intensional," etc.), as opposed to the concept of language as an external object, i.e., "E-language" ("E" stands for "externalized," "extensional," etc.). I-language is a (relatively) steady state of a certain component of the native speaker's brain. Thus, to the extent that the concept of "human being" has reality, that is, as long as human being is part of the natural world, I-language is also a real thing, having its place in the natural world. We call theories of I-languages "(particular) grammars."

Let us next consider the problem (2). How is the linguistic knowledge of a speaker (I-language) acquired? Some factors involved in this process are relatively clear. First of all, it is impossible to acquire knowledge of a language (an I-language) without appropriate linguistic stimuli from the environment. Since this is such an obvious fact, it has been the basis of the traditional claim that the essential source of knowledge of language was "experience" (in this case, the appropriate linguistic stimuli from the environment). Generative Grammar, of course, does not deny that the appropriate linguistic stimuli from the environment (usually called the "primary linguistic data") are necessary for the acquisition of an I-language.

However, once we examine the materials contained in the primary linguistic data and the contents of the acquired knowledge of language, it becomes fairly obvious that the latter includes much information that is not included in the former. Furthermore, much of the content of an I-language is not likely to have been learned by "general learning mechanisms" (such as induction, generalization, analogy, and the like) applied to the primary linguistic data. Let us briefly illustrate this point by the following example that Chomsky often uses:

(6) John expects to visit him.

In (6), the pronoun *him* cannot refer to *John*. This is a fact that any native speaker of English "knows," and it is a judgment of fact unanimously agreed on among English speakers. Now consider (7), which contains (6) within it:

(7) I wonder who [John expects to visit him].

Here, it is possible for *him* to refer to *John*. The part inside the square-brackets in (7) is identical with (6); thus, it is impossible to explain the difference between (6) and (7) in the interpretation of the pronoun, by using the simple "principle of analogy." (Note that "identity" is the strongest form of "similarity" employed in the principle of analogy.) In

(7), the subject of the verb *visit* is evidently *who*. That is, (7) can be logically represented as in (8):

(8) I wonder for which person x, John expects x to visit him.

Here, x is an element (called a "variable") that refers to an indefinite person (*which person*), and the speaker of English interprets (7) taking this element x as the subject of the verb *visit*, even though it does not have a phonological content (that is, it is unpronounced). On the other hand, in (6) above, the subject of the verb *visit* is *John*. (This is also a "fact" which every native speaker of English agrees on.) Thus the logical representation of (6) comparable to (8) would be as follows:

(9) John expects x (= John) to visit him.

That is, the unpronounced subject x of the verb *visit* is *John* in (6) (as shown in (9)), whereas in (7), the subject is not *John* but the indefinite noun phrase (variable) meaning *which person* (as shown in (8)). Now note that the possibility for *him* to refer to *John* in (7) is parallel to the possibility for *him* to refer to *John* in (10) below:

(10) John expects Bill to visit him.

In (10), the subject of *visit* is *Bill*, which is an element that (as it happens) has a phonological content, unlike the element x in (6) and (7) which lacks a phonological content. For the speaker of English to interpret the sentences in (6), (7), and (10), it does not seem important whether or not the relevant element has a phonological content. Rather, the interpretation of the pronoun is determined on the basis of a more abstract representation.

Bringing together what has been discussed so far, it is possible to attribute all the observed properties of pronoun interpretation to a simple principle which dictates that a pronoun not refer to a noun phrase in the same clause. This principle does not distinguish between pronounced and unpronounced elements and it applies to abstract "logical representations." Speakers of English "know" this principle without relevant experience, and the pronoun interpretation pattern seen in the examples (6), (7), and (10) is common to all speakers of English. It is a clear property of English. Thus, any theory of the knowledge of language describing English (namely a grammar of English) must explain this fact in some form if it is to be an empirically adequate theory. Furthermore, it is also highly unlikely that children can "learn" such complex properties of pronoun interpretation by means of induction or analogy applied to the primary linguistic data. The relevant information is simply not available. Nor is it very plausible that they might obtain the "rules of English pronoun interpretation" in terms of "correction" or "training" given by people around them. If such a claim is to be pursued, one must show how such "learning" is indeed possible. So far, no such claim has ever been made with a concrete proposal, as far as we know. (A similar point has been made by Kuroda 1999, based on a discussion of properties of "head-internal relative clauses" in Japanese. Note also that Chomsky's original argument contains much more complex material.)

Given the facts considered so far, an obvious hypothesis is that the principle governing English pronoun interpretation (and various mechanisms associated with it) is not abstracted from the primary linguistic data via induction, analogy, etc., but rather it is in some form genetically built into the brain of the child learning English. Thus, if we schematize the process of language acquisition as in (11), the middle part (human brain) should supply certain properties of I-language (English) whose source cannot be found in the primary linguistic data (the "poverty of the stimulus" argument).

(11) primary linguistic data → human brain → knowledge of language
(I-language)

If the hypothesis is basically correct, it predicts that the child learning English can automatically predict the complex pattern of the pronoun interpretation discussed above by simply learning (from the primary linguistic data) that *him* is a pronoun. This accounts for the well-known fact that despite the low quality of the primary linguistic data, an I-language is acquired very swiftly within quite a short period of time. In addition, the function of the human brain depicted in (11) is uniform across the human species. As is also well known, any child of ordinary intelligence can acquire, without fail, at least one I-language (no matter which I-language it might be).

Thus, the human species is equipped with a "mental organ" as a biological property that makes possible the acquisition of the surprisingly complex and intricate knowledge of language on the basis of quite limited and impoverished primary linguistic data. We call this organ the "language faculty." The language faculty is one of the modular subsystems contained in the overall human cognitive system. The language faculty is assumed to be an autonomous system that actually exists in the human brain (interacting with other cognitive modules), just as the circulatory system and the respiratory system exist as "(physical) organs" in the body. (We will come back to some issues concerning this claim later.) Given the considerations presented thus far, the diagram depicted in (11) can be revised as shown in (12). (Incidentally, we set aside here the issue of whether the box in (12) contains *only* the language faculty or if it contains something else as well.)

(12) primary linguistic data → language faculty → knowledge of language
(I-language)

If we think of the language faculty as an "organ," then we can interpret the process of language acquisition shown in (12) as a process of what we might call "language growth," i.e., a process in which the language faculty "grows" on the basis of the nutrition provided mainly by environmental stimuli called the primary linguistic data. This is analogous to the growth of various other human organs, organs which grow on the basis of the appropriate environmental (and nutritional) stimuli. We call the language faculty of a newborn human which has not yet experienced any primary linguistic data the "initial state," and we assume that it reaches a "steady state" (or a "stationary state") and completes the process of "language growth" (= language acquisition) after going through various intermediate states. The knowledge of a particular language, namely an I-language, is nothing other than this steady state of the language faculty.

Earlier, we mentioned that we call the theory of an I-language (= a steady state of the language faculty, knowledge of a language) a "(particular) grammar." On the other hand, the theory of the initial state of the language faculty is called "universal grammar (UG)." Given these terms, we can say that the problem stated in (1) (namely the question about the knowledge of language) amounts to a question of constructing a grammar of an individual I-language, and the problem (2) (namely the question about language acquisition) is equivalent to constructing UG. Here, there exists a "peculiar" relationship, which does not seem to be easily observable in other fields, between the theory of an individual I-language and UG. This peculiar relationship arises from the following situation. First, the object of these two theories is different states (the initial state and the steady state) of the same organ (the language faculty). However, while the initial state is truly universal to the human species, the steady state shows a certain degree of variation. It is an interesting question whether the diversity of the steady states is in fact a characteristic that is particular to this organ, the language faculty, and if this is indeed the case, why it is so. At this point of our understanding, however, there does not seem to be enough of an empirical basis to warrant substantive proposals. Thus we will not pursue this question any further. Let us simply observe that a particular grammar and UG are theories of different states of the same mental organ, and that UG is a theory of the truly "universal" state (the initial state) of the language faculty, whereas a grammar is a theory of the language faculty grown into a certain different form through environmental stimuli and experience.

The existence of this peculiar relationship between a grammar and UG gives rise to a situation that is (perhaps) particular to the field of linguistics, i. e., that one theory (UG) "evaluates" (or, ideally, "determines") the adequacy of the other theory (grammar). UG regulates the possible form of an (individual) grammar, on the basis of various factors involved in language acquisition. To use the traditional terminology of Generative Grammar, a grammar attains "descriptive adequacy" when it correctly describes its object of inquiry, i. e., the knowledge of a language (an I-language). On the other hand, we say that UG (which has sometimes been called "general linguistic theory" in earlier literature on Generative Grammar) attains "explanatory adequacy" when, on the basis of the primary linguistic data, it can select a descriptively adequate grammar of a given I-language. We have just used the expression "select." This is because, in the early 1960s (see for example Chomsky 1965), when the notions of descriptive and explanatory adequacy were first introduced, it was assumed that there could be more than one descriptively adequate grammar for a given I-language, and furthermore, that (part of) the role of UG was to provide the procedure for, given two descriptively adequate grammars, selecting a "better" grammar.

This was a quite reasonable and realistic judgment at the particular stage of linguistic theory back in the 1960s. At the same time, this view has become a source of a certain "tension" between descriptive adequacy and explanatory adequacy. To achieve descriptive adequacy, it seems necessary to enrich the format of permissible systems (grammars), whereas the demand for explanatory adequacy requires much simpler systems (grammars). Put metaphorically, descriptive adequacy points to complexities, but explanatory adequacy demands simplicity. This was a hanging and recurrent problem throughout the 1960s and 1970s, but the crucial step towards a real solution to this problem was taken when the "principle-and-parameters approach" crystallized around 1980. Rather detailed discussion is made on this point at various places in the two interviews included in this book.

Of the five problems listed at the beginning of this introduction, Generative Grammar so far has been focusing mainly on the problems (1) and (2). More specifically, it has been trying to obtain a theory of universal grammar that satisfies explanatory adequacy, through serious efforts to construct descriptively adequate grammars of a variety of I-languages. Generative grammarians mainly focused on constructing a descriptively adequate theory of individual I-languages, in the period roughly ranging from the 1950s up to around 1980. With a series of attempts that eventually crystallized as the principle-and-parameters approach, linguists started to look seriously into the internal structure of UG. The direction of the shift of focus that occurred in Generative Grammar, i.e., from particular grammars to UG, is quite reasonable for various reasons, including the fact that directly relevant data about UG (a theory of the initial state of the language faculty) are considerably more difficult to obtain than data on individual I-languages.

Thus, it might be said that Generative Grammar has hardly been dealing with problems (3), (4), and (5) (except for some fragmentary references). This is in a way a logical necessity (although actual research is not always conducted in a logical order). It is obvious that if we raise questions about such issues as "the use of X," "the physical basis of X," or "the origin and evolution of X," without knowing the essential properties of X (i.e., not knowing what X is), then we will only have, at best, very vague and unrevealing "answers" to the questions. It is of course a totally different matter if one denies the existence of "X" (= the language faculty) and instead makes an extreme claim that the essential properties of language lie (only) in its use. (This naturally calls for an empirical justification.) However, it would not bring us much understanding if we ignored the basic properties of the language faculty as they have been discovered by Generative Grammar, and speculated on the "physical basis" of language as "a tool for communication."

This, however, by no means implies that Generative Grammar excludes from consideration issues such as language use or sees them as insignificant. It is an obvious fact that language is "used" as a means of expressing thought and facilitating communication in various social contexts. There is no doubt that we cannot possibly obtain an overall understanding of language without considering the use of language. However, it is another matter to claim that the "nature" of this cognitive capacity lies in its use. Generative Grammar asserts that the language faculty underlies and is indeed the foundation of the use of language, that it is a system that is to a large extent autonomous (we will come back to this issue in more detail later on), and that it can be examined independently of other cognitive systems. The use of language is a result of interactions of the language faculty with other cognitive systems that govern thinking, intention, articulation, sense, and so on.

Given the current situation that so little is known about the other cognitive systems that interact with the language faculty, it is not entirely clear whether a scientific theory of language use will ever be possible. However, even if a genuine scientific theory is impossible (at this point), it does not necessarily reduce the importance of the study of language use. Below we will not discuss matters concerning language use, but it is worth pointing out that interesting results have been steadily accumulating regarding the so-called "parsing" system and in the area of the study of "pragmatics" which deals with interpersonal communications. For the former, see, for example, Phillips 1996. For the latter kind of inquiry, the research within the framework of the "relevance theory" (Sperber and Wilson 1986/1995) and a game-theoretic approach suggested by Rubinstein 2000 seem to point in some interesting directions (needless to say, interesting studies are not limited to the work mentioned here).

With respect to the physical basis of language stated in (4) and the evolution of language stated in (5), it is also very difficult to make any substantive claim at this point, given our very limited knowledge. However, it seems necessary to clarify certain points concerning these issues as they relate to the theory of Generative Grammar. In the following section, we will turn to this.

2. Clarifying Some Basic Claims of Generative Grammar

With regard to some of the basic claims of Generative Grammar discussed in the previous section, certain confusions have occasionally arisen, particularly among researchers outside this field. This has sometimes caused criticisms toward Generative Grammar based on serious misunderstandings. Below we present our view concerning some of the basic claims of Generative Grammar in an attempt to avoid further unnecessary confusions. In doing so, we will touch on the issues of the physical basis of language and the evolution of language (the phylogenesis of human language).

2.1. The Faculty of Language and Its Autonomy

As we have discussed above, the child is provided with incomplete data of low quality (primary linguistic data) and eventually acquires, in a very short period of time, very precise knowledge of a given language (an I-language), knowledge which contains a huge amount of information not included in the input data. Moreover, every human being, regardless of race, gender, and other individual variation, is equipped with this language-acquisition device. To explain this fact, Generative Grammar claims that the distinctive ability to acquire a human language (namely the language faculty) is biologically built into human beings. The goal of Generative Grammar is to understand the nature of this distinctive human feature (the basic problems 1 and 2 in the previous section).

The claim of Generative Grammar that humans are biologically equipped with a "faculty" (= the language faculty) that makes language acquisition possible caused much intense opposition when it was first proposed almost half a century ago. However, it seems to be widely accepted by now, particularly among researchers in the brain sciences. Furthermore, the claim that the language faculty constitutes a "cognitive module" (just like other modules such as vision) also seems to be widely accepted (see Sakurai and Sakai 2000, Sakai 2002). This basic claim is accepted probably because it fits well with classical findings in the field of cognitive neuroscience (starting with the discovery of the Broca Field and the Wernicke Field in the 19th century), and with the rapidly increasing recent experimental results made possible by brain imaging technology. (See Hagiwara 1998 and Sakai 2002 for an introduction to the brain science of language. See Marantz et al. eds. 2000 for more technical presentations.)

Thus, at least one of the specific claims of Generative Grammar, namely the claim that the human species is equipped with a biological property (the language faculty) that makes language acquisition possible, seems to be widely accepted in the general scientific community (but certainly not in the humanities and the social sciences). However, the autonomy of this cognitive capacity is still controversial. Certain disagreements are observed even among generative grammarians as to how we should interpret the autonomy of the language faculty. (The "domain-specificity" of language discussed below is also taken up and discussed in detail in the "Linguistics in the 21st Century" interview in this volume.) The strongest interpretation of this concept is that various essential properties of the language faculty are truly specific to language and cannot be found in any other cognitive domain outside of language. Thus, these properties are simply unpredictable (in comparison to other cognitive capacities). Under this interpretation, studies of other cognitive capacities would not help much in the formulation of UG (a theory of the initial state of the language faculty). At an earlier stage in the development of Generative

Grammar (up to around 1980), when the focus of research was placed on the construction of descriptively adequate grammars for individual I-languages, such a strong interpretation of the autonomy of the language faculty seems to have been the predominant view. This is because, for one thing, attempts were made rather intensively during this period to describe particular I-languages (or even particular constructions) in terms of phrase structure rules and transformational rules, and the theoretical foundations for capturing abstract and more fundamental principles had not yet been established. The goal of explanatory adequacy was often mentioned but was considered by many to be a premature attempt.

With the crystallization of the principles-and-parameters approach around 1980, universal grammar emerged as a much more coherent and articulated system. The principles-and-parameters approach effectively "solves" the paradox caused by the tension between descriptive and explanatory adequacy (one might even claim that the principles-and-parameters approach nullifies the distinction between the two types of adequacy). And just as properties of linguistic phenomena described by the "rules" of each grammar were shown to be deducible from the parametrized principles of UG (as they interact with each other), the principles-and-parameters approach opened up the possibility that by elevating the level of explanation still further, one might derive the fundamental features of human language (which had been assumed to be specific to this cognitive capacity) from more general principles that are more or less independent of language. (Incidentally, Chomsky himself had been occasionally talking about this possibility long before the advent of the principles-and-parameters approach.) This research program was intensified by the proposal of the minimalist program (or minimalism) around 1990.

To give a concrete example, one observed universal property of human language is that it has "labeled hierarchical structures." That is, sentences and phrases in human language have hierarchical structures with categorial specifications. This was represented by means of phrase structure rules (phrase structure grammars) in earlier Generative Grammar, and the relevant aspect of each I-language was described by a distinct phrase structure grammar, i.e., by a distinct set of phrase structure rules. Later developments in linguistic theory showed that such an analysis has (fundamental) theoretical and empirical problems. Thus, the system of phrase structure rules was dismantled under the principles-and-parameters approach, and the regularities which had been described by individual phrase structure rules were explained as the outcome of interactions of the (idiosyncratic) properties of each lexical item and certain general principles of UG. One principle that played a particularly important role in this regard was X-bar theory, which regulates the general principles of phrase structure composition. This theory elegantly captures the parallelism among various categories and the general properties of phrase structure across languages. Yet its form is quite peculiar to language, and it was almost impossible to find any analogous phenomenon outside of human language. (And because of this very peculiarity, many generative grammarians felt that this was a "discovery" of an intrinsic property of the language faculty.)

When minimalism was explicitly introduced in the early 1990s, the view toward the language faculty as a cognitive system embedded within the overall human cognition, and the concepts of economy/optimality came to the fore. Accordingly, the conceptual foundations of X-bar theory itself (as well as various other proposed principles/concepts in UG) came under minimalist scrutiny. As a result, it was shown that all the existing generalizations concerning phrase structure captured by X-bar theory could be effectively represented by "Merge," a very general and highly abstract operation. Given Merge, we can see that the fact that human language has labeled hierarchical structures merely means, after all, that this binary operation does not obey the associative law. As is well known, when a binary operation (o) satisfies a o (b o c) = (a o b) o c for any arbitrary elements a, b, and c, this binary operation is said to fulfill the associative law. Now, if we assume that a, b, and c are syntactic objects and that a sequence a # b # c is created by Merge (designated here by the symbol #), then the claim that a # b # c has a "hierarchical structure" simply means that a # (b # c) = (a # b) # c does not always hold. In other words, the binary operation Merge does not satisfy the associative law. If Merge satisfied the associative law and it is always assured that a # (b # c) = (a # b) # c, then it would not be necessary to assume such a superfluous thing as "hierarchical structure" behind a # b # c.

And if this is a viable conclusion, then it seems that the situation is not limited to language. The operation Merge is a simple and general operation that combines two elements, and there seems no basis to claim that an operation like this is employed only by the language faculty. Rather, it is natural to assume that Merge is just an instance of a basic (cognitive) operation within logic, thinking, and other forms of human cognition. It is not too difficult to find a binary operation within the "logic/thinking module" that also does not satisfy the associative law. For example, the logical conjunction and the logical disjunction satisfy the associative law, but logical implication does not.

Does this then mean that the "autonomy of the language faculty" is denied? Not necessarily. It is true that as the theory of language evolved over the past half century, it has become increasingly clear that fundamental mechanisms employed in language show sufficient generality that makes it possible to realistically look for their analogues in other cognitive domains outside of language. Language no longer looks like a mess. But this situation does not necessarily falsify the hypothesis that the language faculty constitutes an autonomous system. It may well be the case that each of the various elements and mechanisms employed in the language faculty have evolved for some other purpose not directly related to language, and therefore that they each may have applications in other human cognitive capacities as well. However, the language faculty can still maintain its "autonomy" in the sense that it organizes these mechanisms in such a way as to function as a coherent system linking the sensori-motor and conceptual systems (so that each linguistic expression has its sound and meaning). This "weak" version of the thesis of autonomy of the language faculty seems more adequate than the strong version discussed above, given our current understanding of human language. (See Chomsky 2000, p.2, Chomsky 2001, Note 1, among others.)

In fact, an analogy can be made to the notion of a "speech organ," a physical organ which exists in a more readily visible form. In speech production, various organs, such as the trachea, the larynx, the vocal chords, the pharynx, the tongue, the teeth, the lips, and so on interact with each other to make it possible to produce complex linguistic sounds. None of these organs is designed specifically for language, and every one of them must exist independently for other purposes (though the non-linguistic function of the vocal chords is not entirely obvious). It is possible to claim that the term "speech organ" is defined by referring to (a part of) the existing organs such as the respiratory organs and the digestive organs as a system, which are secondarily used for language (speech production). It seems not completely inconceivable to conjecture that the mental organ we're discussing now exists as something similar within the brain.

Now, if this is indeed the case, what are the implications for the problems concerning the origin and evolution of the language faculty? It has been reported in evolutionary biology that, when an organ which has developed for some purpose reaches a certain form (in terms of its size and shape), it starts to be used for other purposes. Once this happens, the process of so-called "natural selection" comes into play, which makes the form of the organ develop further (into the optimal form for the new purpose). (See Kingsolver and Koehl 1985 among many others.) Chomsky (1988) suggests that a similar process might have taken place in the origin of mental organs that govern human cognition. He cites the ability to count (the concept of the natural numbers) as a concrete example. Let us call this the "number faculty." The number faculty seems to be uniformly supplied to every human being. There exist some cultures in which this faculty is not widely used. Yet an adult who has grown up in such a culture does understand the concept of the natural numbers without much difficulty and can acquire the ability to count when put in an appropriate environment. If a child raised in a society which does not widely use the number faculty moves to an industrial society, he or she will be able to use the number faculty as well as any child of the industrial society. The number faculty seems to be a cognitive faculty that exists in every human being regardless of whether it is used or not in actual practice. (Kronecker's famous words "Only natural numbers came from God, all else is Menschenwerk" may indicate some deep truth, quite apart from his original intention.)

The essential property of the number faculty, as clearly shown by, say, Peano's axioms, is its infinite generative power using a recursive procedure, which results in the discrete infinity of the natural numbers. The concept of the discrete infinity (and the mechanism that generates it) is biologically supplied to every human being. Thus, if a child learning natural numbers learns numbers 1, 2, 3, and up to n, he or she does not think that numbers end there with n, but unconsciously infers the existence of $n+1$ for any number n, naturally understanding the "infinity of the natural numbers." Having the concept of the "natural numbers" with the property of discrete infinity seems to be particular to the human species. (Notice that the ability to "count" from one to, say, seventeen and the ability to form a new number $n+1$ for an arbitrary number n, are distinct abilities.)

Exactly how, then, has the number faculty come to existence in the human brain? Given the fact that there exist cultures in which this faculty is not used, as we mentioned above, and, furthermore, the fact that recognition of this faculty is a relatively recent event in human history, it is hard to see how the number faculty could have been "produced" by natural selection. It is also not easily conceivable that the kind of human beings who can understand the concept of the natural numbers have a higher rate of reproduction and that the number faculty has emerged as a result of the higher reproduction rate by natural selection. Although this by no means disproves an account in terms of natural selection, the explanation of the origin of the number faculty by natural selection does not seem very convincing at the moment.

Thus, Chomsky suggests the hypothesis that the number faculty is actually a by-product of some other cognitive faculty. What, then, could this "other cognitive faculty" be? It is the language faculty. We have mentioned above that the essential property of the number faculty is discrete infinity, made possible by the recursive procedure. Indeed, as is well known, this is a property shared by the language faculty. For example, there is no human language that has a principle such that when the number of words in a sentence exceeds n, then it is no longer a sentence, and every language has a mechanism that makes the length of a sentence potentially infinitely long. The property of discrete infinity seems to be found only in the human species. Furthermore, it is a property only found in the language faculty and the number faculty. It is also observed that the origin of the language faculty goes back quite far in human evolution, and it is present regardless of culture. Thus, it does not seem completely implausible to suppose that at the point where the language faculty with its central property of discrete infinity emerged, the number faculty was also formed in the brain, by extracting from the language faculty the very mechanism needed for discrete infinity, and by abstracting away from various other language particular properties of the language faculty (i.e., those properties that are necessary for connecting sound and meaning). The number faculty would then be latent, but ready to be used as soon as appropriate environmental conditions are met. If this account is on the right track, it presents a case where a mental organ (the number faculty) emerged as a by-product of the emergence of another mental organ (the language faculty). (The relationship between the number faculty and the language faculty is also discussed in the two interviews in this volume.)

How, then, did the language faculty itself emerge? With regard to this question, it is not possible to even speculate at this point. This is because, unlike the number faculty, the essential properties of the language faculty are not known yet in detail. As briefly mentioned earlier, when we ask about "the origin and evolution of X," the question becomes rather empty unless we know, with considerable accuracy, what the nature of X actually is. Nonetheless, with the accumulation of empirical studies over the past half century, Generative Grammar has, to a large extent, been approaching a good approximation of the nature of the language faculty. Thus, it is fair to say that any theory about the origin and evolution of the language faculty might turn out to be a rather empty hypothesis if it did not take into account the various properties of the language faculty that Generative Grammar has discovered so far.

We cannot discuss here in detail various properties of the language faculty which Generative Grammar has discovered so far (see Fukui forthcoming, among others). However, as a very general remark about the development of the field, we can say that our field has developed as follows. Earlier Generative Grammar focused on the formulation of descriptively adequate grammars for individual I-languages. At that point, it was not yet possible to make substantive proposals about the language faculty, although there were occasionally some intriguing preliminary suggestions about universal grammar (general linguistic theory). Inquiry into the origin and evolution of the language faculty was then an even less realistic undertaking. Around 1980, the principle-and-parameters framework took shape, and UG was formulated as a modular system consisting of a small number of invariant principles, each of which is associated with certain parameters. As we have discussed earlier, the research focus was clearly shifted from descriptive adequacy to explanatory adequacy under the principles-and-parameters approach. We might say that this is the period in which, along with the shift of research focus just mentioned, the level of attention to the origin and evolution of the language faculty gradually increased among generative grammarians. The theoretical transition during this period is vividly discussed in the interviews in this volume.

The development of empirical and theoretical research under the principle-and-parameters approach throughout the 1980s can be described as explosive. Due to the cumulative effect of the enormous amount of technical research at this time, certain general characteristics of the language faculty started to emerge by the end of the 1980s as overarching principles behind various individual properties of UG. Generative Grammar thus started to take further steps towards the goal that goes "beyond" its original goal of explanatory adequacy.

Given a certain object of inquiry X, let us call a theory stating what the components of X are and what kind of mechanisms are at work in X, etc. a "descriptive theory" of X. Let us then call a theory explaining "why" X has such a structure and such mechanisms an "explanatory theory" of X. In these terms, earlier Generative Grammar mainly looked for descriptive theories of individual I-languages (with due attention to UG), while Generative Grammar after the advent of the principle-and-parameters approach realistically attempted to construct UG, namely an explanatory theory of individual I-languages. The terms "descriptive adequacy" and "explanatory adequacy" established in the literature of Generative Grammar reflect the state of affairs of this time. To use the terms just introduced, although UG is an "explanatory theory" of individual I-languages, it is still a "descriptive theory" of the language faculty in the sense that it only describes the essential properties of the language faculty, and never addresses the question as to "why" it has the properties it has (rather than other properties). It should be pointed out, however, that given the enormous difficulty of obtaining direct and relevant data concerning the language faculty, it is amazing that Generative Grammar has come to the point where it brings into sight a prospect for a descriptive theory of the language faculty within such a short period of time.

With the proposal of the minimalist program in the early 1990s, Generative Grammar makes a bold step forward towards the construction of an "explanatory theory of the language faculty." The thesis that the minimalist program puts forth is that human language is a computational system that connects the sensori-motor system and the conceptual system in an optimal way. Therefore, the various properties of the language faculty ought to be either imposed by the two "performance" systems linked through language, or else a result of optimality principles governing language itself. The minimalist program is an attempt to explain all the core properties of the language faculty just in terms of these two types of factors. To the extent that this attempt is successful, we will come closer to an explanatory theory of the language faculty. (See "Linguistics in the 21st Century" for details.)

Of these two factors, the requirements placed on the language faculty by the two performance systems (the so-called "interface conditions") have clear origins. (This is of course not to say that the various properties of these two performance systems are already well-known.) On the other hand, the origin of the other factor, the optimality principles, is not clear. However, the optimality requirement does not necessarily have to be a mysterious property of the language faculty that rejects all explanations. It can be explained as a reflection of general laws that govern the origin and form of organisms. In this connection, Chomsky often refers to the pioneering work of Turing and Thompson (Turing 1952, Thompson 1942) and suggests that it may turn out to be an effective approach to the question of why the language faculty shows the property of optimality. See Fukui 1996, Uriagereka 1998, Jenkins 2000, among others, for relevant discussion. See Stewart and Golubitsky 1992 for a concise explanation of the Turing-type research. For a more technical discussion, see Maynard Smith, et al. 1985 and the references cited there. Kondo and Asai 1995 is a recent attempt to apply Turing's reaction-diffusion model to the formation of the stripe patterns of the marine angelfish, which strongly suggests the correctness of the Turing-type approach to morphogenesis.

Full-scale applications of the Turing/Thompson approach to human language remains to be done.

More discussion of the origin and the evolution of the language faculty will lead us merely to a list of uncertain conjectures, at least at this moment. An important point, however, is that when we consider why and how the language faculty has emerged in the history of human evolution, we should always keep a firm grasp of its essential properties as discovered by, say, Generative Grammar. Without understanding the essential properties of the language faculty, the problem of its origin and evolution cannot even be addressed in a meaningful way.

Many of the theories of the origin of language that are floating around in the general scientific community seem to completely lack a proper understanding of the very point we have just made. We will not obtain any deep answer to the question of the origin of language if, instead of taking into consideration the intricate internal properties of the language faculty discussed in Generative Grammar, we merely assume that "language is a tool for social communication" (although this is one of the important functions of language). There seems to be no one (including Chomsky, who is often mistaken to be an extreme anti-Darwinist) who believes that natural selection has played no role in the evolution of the language faculty. But those who claim that it is possible to explain the origin (and the properties) of the language faculty purely on the basis of natural selection have the burden of proof, i.e., they have to demonstrate exactly how the essential properties of this mental organ can be explained by natural selection. On the other hand, one of the tasks of approaches like minimalism is to give enough substance to the claim, which is still quite vague at this point, that certain physical and mathematical laws of nature, which define the "channels" through which natural selection works, are reflected in the core properties of the language faculty.

Only by a shared perception of these points can the common grounds be made for constructive intellectual collaborations of researchers in linguistics, evolutionary biology, and the brain sciences on the problems of the origin and evolution of the language faculty. We hope that such work as an article co-authored by Chomsky and evolutionary biologists (Hauser, M. D., et al. 2002) mentioned in "Linguistics in the 21st Century," will be a good starting point for fruitful future intellectual collaborations.

2.2. Linguistics as a Natural Science

The "Generative Enterprise," as we have discussed so far, is a collective effort to explore, in the manner that has been exercised in modern science, the nature of the language faculty, a mental organ that actually exists as a system (mainly) in the human brain. If this is indeed the case, Generative Grammar ought to be regarded as a branch of the natural sciences (see Anderson and Lightfoot 2002, Chomsky 2000, 2002, Jenkins 2000, among others), particularly given the "methodological naturalism" it assumes, according to which mental phenomena such as language should be studied in the same way as other phenomena in the natural world. (For relevant discussion, see Chomsky 2000, Quine 1992, and references cited there.)

Now, if Generative Grammar is indeed a field that studies a part of the brain (the language faculty) in the way carried out in the natural sciences, then how does it relate to the so-called brain sciences? In this connection, it is instructive to note that Maynard Smith points out that there are (at least) the following three possible approaches when we consider the relationship between behavior and the brain (Maynard Smith 1986, Chapter 7). One is an approach that treats the brain as a black box, given that the material substance of the brain itself does not tell us much and that we cannot directly observe it, and this approach tries to figure out how behavior depends on experience, by observing the input (the experience) and the output (the behavior), both of which are directly observable. The second is an approach that examines the material substance of the brain itself and tries to find out how exactly the numerous neurons in the brain function. The third is an approach that constructs a model of the contents of the "black box" (= the brain) on the basis of the input and the output.

Maynard Smith defines the first approach as the behaviorist method, and the second as the physiological/neurological method. He then suggests that the heredity laws of Mendel are a classical example of the third approach. As is well known, Mendel proposed, on the basis of the artificial cross-fertilization of sweet peas, that genetic characteristics are governed by "factors" that follow a certain set of general laws. Mendel proposed this hypothesis as a kind of abstract model of heredity. Given this abstractness, exactly what the model consisted in at the biological level was irrelevant. Rather, only formal relations were described. It was only after several decades that Mendel's work was "rediscovered" and scientists found that the "factors" were a part of a chromosome. And we had to wait for the development of molecular biology in the 20th century in order to discover that it was indeed a DNA molecule. (See Jenkins 2000 for much relevant discussion.)

Among the three approaches, the relationship between the behaviorist method and the other two approaches is not quite clear. But Maynard Smith claims that the physiological method and the "abstract model" approach are in supplementary relation with each other. If, on the one hand, there is an elegant abstract model of how a certain behavior (phenomenon) occurs, then it should be easier to study the physiological foundation for the model, because the model guides the physiologists as to what they ought to be looking for. If, on the other hand, we have a clear physiological/neurological understanding of the phenomenon, then that must surely help us construct a viable abstract model.

Given Maynard Smith's characterizations of the three possible approaches just mentioned, the relationship between the brain sciences and modern Generative Grammar is exactly the same as the relationship between the physiological/neurological approach and the "abstract model" approach. Generative Grammar attempts to discover the fundamental properties of the language faculty by constructing an abstract model, whereas the current brain sciences investigate the properties of the language faculty mainly at the physiological level. From this point of view, it may be misleading to talk about the "relationship" between Generative Grammar and the brain sciences of language. Generative Grammar is indeed a subfield of the (theoretical) brain sciences, adopting an abstract model approach just mentioned which is different from (but complementary to) the standard physiological/neurological approach widely assumed in other domains of the current brain sciences.

The brain is made up of very complex circuits of neural cells and it has a sort of layered structure. The bottom level is perhaps the level of genes. Chemical reactions and neural communications create the cellular functions, and then intricate connections of the cells form circuits. Furthermore, the various circuits interact, in a modular fashion, in such a way as to create systems like the cerebellum, the cerebrum, the brain stem, and so on. Only when we have gained a clear understanding of the brain at every one of these levels, can we claim that we have come up with a general picture of the human brain. Of course, the current level of our scientific understanding of the brain is far from it. Rather, the situation of the brain sciences seems to be that individual researchers conduct their research only within a given domain, mostly at the levels of genes and/or neural cells. As is clear from our discussion so far, Generative Grammar attempts to construct a computational model of one of the neural circuits of the brain, i.e., the language faculty. Given the current situation that we are far from being able to gain a complete and clear understanding of the various circuits of the brain, it may be almost impossible to interpret various discoveries made within Generative Grammar as substantive findings about the brain circuits. This has led the brain scientists to the attitude that (almost) completely ignores the results of Generative Grammar.

Thus, it is hard to say at this point that Generative Grammar and the brain sciences successfully communicate, offering insights to each other. However, as we have emphasized above, it is never the case that these two fields are incompatible, but rather, that they only adopt two different approaches to the common object of inquiry. It is clear from the relationship between Mendel's work and modern genetics, or as is epitomized by what happened to chemistry and physics when Bohr's model was proposed (and then accepted), the insights obtained in abstract models often offer important suggestions as to the directions for research on the "physical basis" of the phenomena under consideration. Mutual understanding and healthy interactions are quite difficult to achieve between academic fields that have developed in distinct academic traditions and research cultures. There are obviously various differences in research conventions, for example, the method of data presentation and experimentation. A field must have the attitude of making a serious effort to learn about the accomplishments of other fields and not be bound too much by its own research conventions. In the case of linguistics and the brain sciences, this is absolutely necessary in order to build a collaborative research enterprise in which, on the one hand, the brain scientists working on language can learn from the insights and discoveries accumulated in Generative Grammar, while, on the other hand, Generative Grammar, when grammatical models are to be constructed, can take into account various neuro-physiological processes unveiled in the brain sciences.

When such cooperative research becomes widespread and, as a result, the integrated brain sciences develop to the point where a substantial portion of the research results of Generative Grammar can be explained in the terms of the brain sciences, then Generative Grammar will be truly "unified" with the brain sciences. It is of course premature to conjecture how such a unification could take place in the distant future.

3. Situating the Two Interviews in the History of Generative Grammar

As we have mentioned earlier in this introduction, the history of the development of contemporary Generative Grammar can be (roughly) divided into three major phases. The first phase can be characterized by extensive efforts to achieve descriptive adequacy, with due attention to general principles governing mechanisms in particular grammars. The beginning of the second phase is marked by a significant shift of focus, i.e., the shift from descriptive adequacy to explanatory adequacy (as these terms were defined above). During this period, Generative Grammar started seriously looking for a viable theory of (the initial state of) the language faculty, UG. In the third phase, attempts are made to address the question as to "why" the language faculty has the properties it has, i.e., why UG provides a certain set of principles but not others.

The first phase begins in the mid-1950s when contemporary Generative Grammar was first put forth, facilitating in retrospect the creation of the modern cognitive sciences. This is the period when the fundamental issues of Generative Grammar were first raised (though naturally in a somewhat preliminary form). One of the most salient characteristics of Generative Grammar in this period, i.e., approximately from the mid-1950s to the mid-1960s, which attracted much attention from researchers in other sciences, seems to have been its formal rigor. Generative Grammar presented a grammar as a well-defined rule system, adopting and modifying the mechanisms developed earlier in the 20th century in the study of formal systems (recursive function theory, in particular). In doing so, Generative Grammar revived as an explicit and falsifiable claim the important (and long-forgotten) insights about human language of von Humboldt and others, that the nature of human language is its infinite creativity. It was the Generative Grammar of this period that presented a convincing case to the general scientific community that human language can in fact be studied successfully in terms of formal models. In addition to a vast amount of empirical research, Chomsky went on to study the properties of formal systems themselves, and, in collaboration with a few other researchers, obtained very important results concerning the "hierarchy" of various types of grammars, languages and their recognizers (automata), leading to the creation of a subfield of applied mathematics called the formal language theory.

In the mid-1960s, the focus of Generative Grammar shifted toward more empirically-oriented research, in an attempt to construct descriptively adequate grammars based on the developed formal system (for example, a transformational grammar with a context-free phrase structure grammar as its base). Numerous intriguing linguistic analyses of English and other languages were carried out in this period. As descriptive research accumulated, however, a fundamental vexing problem started to emerge. This was the "tension" between descriptive and explanatory adequacy which we discussed earlier in this introduction. In a nutshell, the tension stems from the fact that it seems necessary to enrich the format of permissible systems (grammars) for the sake of descriptive adequacy, whereas the demand for explanatory adequacy requires much simpler systems (grammars). It was research on the general conditions on grammatical rules (and representations) which played a crucial role in resolving this tension (or paradox). The research along these lines was successful in abstracting various common properties of grammatical rules (phrase structure rules and transformations) and attributed these properties to invariant principles of UG, with the result of reducing the parts that need to be stipulated in particular grammars. Sustained efforts in this direction started with some preliminary proposals in early 1960s, and after some epoch-making works in the mid-1960s to the mid-1970s, finally crystallized in the late 1970s forming a completely new model of UG, called the principles-and-parameters approach. This model fundamentally transformed the traditional view of language and grammar (largely carried over to contemporary Generative Grammar, though in a much more sophisticated form), and its significance for the development of our understanding of human language was almost equivalent to, or even surpassed in certain respects, the significance of the birth of contemporary Generative Grammar in the 1950s.

The first interview contained in this volume ("The Generative Enterprise") was conducted almost at the very time when the principles-and-parameters approach was taking shape. The narrative voice of Chomsky, who candidly talks about virtually every aspect of linguistic theory, is overwhelmingly powerful, reflecting his excitement about what was happening in the field at the time of the interview, a major theoretical breakthrough that cannot be expected to occur very often in any science.

The birth of the principles-and-parameters model brought about, more than anything, an explosion of theoretical and empirical research on a wide variety of languages. Diverse types of languages, including a number of languages whose properties had not been looked into before, were taken as an object of serious research. Descriptive research directly connected to linguistic theory rapidly accumulated and close and fruitful interactions were (re-)activated between linguistics and those fields that have a close connection with language, in particular psychology, the brain sciences, and computer science.

While leading such a dramatic development of theoretical and empirical research, Chomsky continued to pursue the research program that had been around for some time (the point is also touched on in "The Generative Enterprise"). The goal of this program was to pursue a way to simplify the (stipulated) content of UG, trying to deduce the effects of the general principles of UG from something even more general, perhaps "language-external" principles. This change started to materialize in the late 1980s as the pursuit for the "principles of economy" of human language. Investigations of economy principles, coupled with the (renewed and serious) recognition of the fact that language is embedded within other cognitive modules (at least those having to do with "sound" and "meaning"), eventually led to the emergence of minimalism in the early 1990s. (Incidentally, minimalism should not be regarded as a rejection of – or an alternative to – the principles-and-parameters model, but rather, it is simply a specific development within this model.) At this time, it may be hard to say that minimalism has had the same magnitude of impact on the (empirical research of the) field as the (earlier forms of) principles-and-parameters model once had, due perhaps to the fact that minimalism has an intrinsic property of depriving us of the "tools" for linguistic descriptions. However, we can see that this research program has had a significant and important influence on the whole field of linguistics in the following sense: It demands deeper and principled explanations for linguistic phenomena. This has a very positive effect of eliminating pseudo-explanations, which have much too often been inadvertently accepted in linguistics. Furthermore, it takes UG not as an "ultimate" theory, but as an explicandum whose properties call for further explanations. This move opens up a possibility of integrating the study of the language faculty and that of other cognitive systems, and furthermore, it suggests tighter connections between linguistics and other sciences dealing with the properties of organisms in general. In the past ten years or so, the number of linguists has been increasing who have serious interest in the relationship between linguistics and the natural sciences. This seems to be related to the fact that minimalism indicates the possibility of transforming the nature of the field of linguistics.

The second interview in this volume, "Linguistics in the 21st Century" was carried out in the fall of 2002, twenty years after the appearance of the principles-and-parameters approach, and about ten years after the (explicit) emergence of minimalism. Chomsky discusses a number of topics, including his characterization of the development of linguistic theory in the past twenty years, some of the major empirical issues in the theory of Generative Grammar, the nature of two kinds of minimalism, the role of the Galilean/Newtonian style in modern sciences, the relation between Generative Grammar and various other sciences such as mathematics, the brain sciences, the evolutionary theory, etc. One might perceive that the tone of his voice here seems to differ from that in the previous interview. He rather calmly looks back over the history of Generative Grammar, and seems to discuss the future of the field rather "objectively," keeping his distance from it.

It is in a way obvious where this difference, if any, comes from, given the twenty years of time that has passed between the two interviews. In the face of what is discussed in the two interviews in this book, it is up to us whether we want to be optimistic or pessimistic about the future of the field. In these interviews, Chomsky discusses his major intellectual concerns in great detail, and in doing so, he offers an inspiration that is never easy to obtain for one who is seriously interested in a science dealing with human nature. It is again up to us to decide how to respond to his inspiration.

(This Introduction was originally written in Japanese for the Japanese edition of *The Generative Enterprise* and was later translated into English in an abridged form.)

The Generative Enterprise

Preface

Riny Huybregts and Henk van Riemsdijk

The present text is the result of a series of discussions with Noam Chomsky, held in November 1979 and March 1980. We have edited the tape transcripts and rearranged the material into the format in which it is presented here. However, we have deliberately kept the style somewhat informal to convey the atmosphere of informal exchange of ideas in which the discussions were held.

Why another interview with Noam Chomsky[1]? We felt that there are a number of issues which had not been hitherto addressed, which nevertheless deserved attention, and which by their very nature, are most easily treated in the form of discussions. These issues are of two kinds. On the one hand they concern the role of linguistics, and generative grammar in particular, within the academic institutions and in society. On the other hand, the Pisa lectures, which Chomsky delivered in the spring of 1979, gave rise to a wholesale rethinking of many aspects of the theory of grammar; and some of the debates which characterized the period between the Pisa lectures and the publication of *Lectures on Government and Binding*[2] are taken up in our discussions.

The preparation of *Lectures on Government and Binding*, which naturally had to take precedence over the editing of the present text, caused the delay between the time of the discussions and their appearance. Nevertheless, we feel that even though some of the more technical questions and answers are somewhat dated, they are illustrative in a useful way of the post-Pisa-lectures period. As for the other material, it is largely new ground that was covered and has lost nothing of its relevance.

Perhaps the single most important motive for the general thrust of our questions was the following. Since its inception in the mid fifties, generative grammar had known a number of clear intellectual landmarks,

---

1. Cf. Chomsky (1977c), which deals with linguistics in a fairly general way and with political issues.
2. The Pisa lectures were presented in the spring of 1979 in connection with the GLOW conference at the Scuola Normale Superiore, Pisa. A much expanded version of the theory presented there appears in Chomsky (1981b).

among them *Aspects*[3], the debate with generative semantics[4], and the publication of "Conditions on transformations"[5]. In each case there have been perceptible influences on the social and scientific organization of the field of generative grammar. Though some of these developments have meanwhile, by a felicitous coincidence, been insightfully dealt with in Newmeyer's *Linguistic Theory in America*[6], there has been little or no reflection on the social structure of generative grammar. While it may be very dangerous to adopt the attitude of the philosopher of science vis-à-vis the present state of affairs, it is also an undeniable fact that linguists spend just as much time debating the vicissitudes of the field as they do discussing new analyses, theoretical problems, and conceptual speculations. Yet it is only the latter, but rarely the former topics which find their way into the publications. We believed that the time had come to attempt a joint presentation of some issues of both types. And as the questions dealing with the social organization of the field and its role in society are perhaps of a less rigorously scientific nature than the usual tightly structured arguments of the generative "normal science", we decided that the format of informal discussion would be most appropriate to tackle some of these aspects of the "generative enterprise".

In preparing our questions, we have benefitted from discussions with and suggestions from Arnold Evers, Chris Halvorsen, Jan Koster, Jean-Roger Vergnaud, Edwin Williams, and many others. In addition we would like to acknowledge the fact that the library of the Utrecht University Linguistics Department has been an invaluable tool in the preparation of the footnotes and the bibliography. We alone are to blame, however, for those questions that we raised as well as for those that we failed to bring up. All we can say is that we hope we have succeeded in conveying a sense of the main type of issues that generative linguists talk about with each other almost every day all over the world.

Tilburg/Utrecht
June 1982

---

3. Chomsky (1965).
4. See the articles in Chomsky (1972), Lakoff (1971), Newmeyer (1980), Postal (1972), and references cited in these publications.
5. Chomsky (1973).
6. Newmeyer (1980).

Part I
On Linguistics

Chapter 1
Language and Cognition

Let us start by trying to locate the field of linguistics within a somewhat wider intellectual context. You have defined the field as a part of psychology, or, to use a more modern terminology, of cognitive science. Part of your writing has also touched on philosophical issues. In addition, of course, there are ties between your work and biology. There has not been all that much reaction from those related fields to these "territorial claims" of generative grammar. But let us try to review some of these. Take philosophy, for example, which has perhaps been the most fertile point of contact. Would you say that in general when philosophers comment on generative grammar they understand the issues?

Of course, the interactions with philosophy are very tight and many-layered. They occur in all sorts of places. I think one can roughly distinguish several strains. On the one hand there are people who have looked to linguistics to try to answer philosophical questions. Take the work of Zeno Vendler, for example.[1] If he is interested in philosophical questions about cause and effect, he will want to ask how the word "cause" is used in English and try to find out what linguists can say about this. This is a natural expectation, if you come out of ordinary language philosophy. You would expect that the field that deals with ordinary language ought to say something about the philosophically significant questions you are interested in. The chance of extracting answers to those questions from linguistics seems to me very slight. I cannot imagine why linguistics would offer any particular insight into the specific topics that happen to interest people like Zeno Vendler. Maybe it could be of some help, but it is pretty far-fetched.

There is another level of contact, where philosophers are really just doing linguistics, like the tradition that comes out of John Austin's work.[2] Austin himself, I think, would have been perfectly happy to regard himself as a linguist, except that I think he was more of a philologist. He felt that some essentially philological work was perhaps the most important work

---

1. Vendler (1967).
2. See Austin (1962).

to be done in what he called philosophy at that time, and that by doing it one could lay the groundwork for answering, maybe even answer, or lay to rest at least, major philosophical questions. That kind of work, and other work that comes out of it on speech acts and performatives[3], one can think of as a type of linguistics. Maybe the people who do it are interested in different questions, but there the connections are obvious.

Other points of contact have to do with work in semantics. For some reason philosophers regard semantics as part of philosophy. Maybe rightly, maybe wrongly, but insofar as they do, they are dealing with questions which linguists also deal with. This is certainly true, for example, for model theoretic semantics of natural language.[4] One can say it is a point of convergence and people will be interested in each other's results. And then there is another connection in which philosophy is concerned with the methodological problems of the sciences. So if somebody discusses the question of what explanation in linguistics is, he is doing philosophical work pertaining to linguistics[5] which can relate to it the way the work on explanation in physics will relate to physics, and could be more or less close to it, in fact. In physics, this kind of work is often done by physicists.

All of these are obvious points of contact, but there is another one in a totally different domain, which I think myself is the most interesting, or which interests me most, and that is thinking about what the study of language has to say about questions of epistemology. That is, one can conceive of the study of language as being one possible paradigm for the investigation of the nature of knowledge, the nature of human knowledge, and the problems of a priori knowledge.[6] In my view, here is where the most interesting connections lie, but only a very small number of philosophers are interested in these questions.

Now you have outlined where the points of contact with philosophy are, but again, we should also ask ourselves to what extent the core issues come across correctly instead of just some peripheral questions. For example, take the last two points of contact that you mentioned as being the most important ones: epistemology and methodology. Aren't those also the ones where misunderstanding is most likely to arise?

---

3. Cf. Searle (1969).
4. See Part II, Chapter 2 for a more extensive discussion.
5. See, among many others, Dougherty (1973) and Katz and Bever (1976).
6. For discussion, see Chomsky (1968, 1975, 1980a).

No, it depends on the person. Some people, I think, understand the issues very well and have interesting things to say. I do not necessarily agree with them. For example, I disagree with Steve Stich[7] on many things, but I think he certainly understands the issues he is talking about. There are other people who are off the wall, but I think that among philosophers, especially younger ones, fortyish approximately, there are a fair number who really have a good understanding. I presume it is always a dated understanding. However, it is a serious understanding of the kind of work that has been done and continues to be done. In fact I often think their understanding is better than that of many professional linguists.

When scientists from such fields as biology write or speak about generative grammar one sometimes wonders whether they have a true understanding of the fundamentals of our work. Take, say, the writings of Monod or Jacob, or, from another angle, Wilson.[8]

I do not think Wilson did, judging by the comments that he had in the last chapter of *Sociobiology*, which, I thought, showed really farreaching misunderstanding. I think Jacob and Monod understood as much as was relevant to their purposes. The same is true for Gunther Stent, Salvador Luria, and other biologists too, who also wrote about generative grammar in the same context.[9] They are all interested in the question, but they have not tried to find out much about the details. When you read their comments, it is worth knowing that there is a systematic misinterpretation of the use of the phrase "deep structure". By and large they use the phrase "deep structure" the way we use "universal grammar". We must have done something to contribute to that misunderstanding, I guess. But once one reinterprets the phrase "deep structure" as "universal grammar", then it seems to me that their accounts are perfectly reasonable and, at the level of their discussion, appropriate.

Let us narrow the scope of the question somewhat and concentrate on MIT, that is to your own everyday academic institutional environment. What are your contacts with other disciplines like, say, in the natural sciences? Which links are the most fruitful ones?

---

7. Cf. Stich (1972, 1975, 1978).
8. See, e. g., Monod (1970), Jacob (1973), Wilson (1975).
9. Cf. Luria (1973), Stent (1973).

I think the answer will be misleading. The fact is that my contacts are slight, but the reason is that I am just so involved in other activities that my contacts with anything are slight. Twenty years ago I was teaching joint courses in other departments, for example in the engineering department, a course that had contacts with mathematics and other fields, but that is all finished. I had to drop that because I did not have the time. So for personal reasons my actual contacts are more limited than I would like. The remaining ones are with philosophy and psychology, where I teach joint courses, occasionally. Also, for example Salvador Luria and I ran a seminar a couple of years ago on the biology of language, and that is the kind of thing we would certainly pursue, at least I would certainly pursue. I suspect he would too if we had the time for it. And I have talked with David Hubel[10] about teaching joint courses on brain and mind, which would bring together neurophysiology and language. We might very well do that one day. I think it would be the intellectually responsible thing to do at this point. I think there is enough interest around to make it work. The problem is there is not enough personnel or time to do it. I think the network of connections loosely around the cognitive sciences, reaching from biology to computer sciences, from psychology to parts of mathematics, from engineering to philosophy, form a pretty natural nexus. My own guess, frankly, is that if the kind of linguistics I am interested in survives in the United States, it may very likely be in that context, rather than in linguistics departments.

That would have quite drastic repercussions, institutionally-speaking, but it might not be so bad for the field if that happened.

No, in fact I think it would be a very reasonable thing. I think that is where linguistics belongs anyhow. But yes, it is administratively and institutionally difficult.

At MIT some quite exciting work seems to be going on within the context of cognitive science that you mentioned. For example the article by Marr and Nishihara that you distributed to your students recently[11] clearly suggested that there is a basis for discussion. But apparently you don't get to talk to such people much.

---

10. The author of, among others, Hubel (1978) and Hubel and Wiesel (1962).
11. Marr and Nishihara (1978).

Not much, no. We get together when we can, but that happens rarely. That is just a personal thing. I would like to, we have things to talk about, but there is no time. The best thing would be if the students would have contacts. That is where the contacts really ought to be. So, for example, when I was a student myself at the University of Pennsylvania, I was able to be a contact between people like Nelson Goodman and Zellig Harris, who had never talked to each other, because of my joint interest. I think that is what really ought to happen, and to some extent it does. For example, when Craig Thiersch was a student in our department, he kept alive important contacts between computer science and linguistics just through his own activities. Good things came out of those contacts, for example Mitch Marcus' work,[12] and more recently, the very interesting work of Bob Berwick of the artificial intelligence laboratory, who has been working with Amy Weinberg of our department. Yukio Otsu and Alec Marantz, also students in our department, keep contact at some level between psychology and linguistics. I think such contacts are really going to be fruitful in the future.

Another reason for the lack of contacts might be that much work in so-called artificial intelligence appears to be addressing somewhat different questions, questions that from our perspective are the wrong ones. That reduces the prospect for fruitful cooperation, presumably.

Take that paper by Marr and Nishihara that you mentioned, their work on vision, which is within artificial intelligence and connected with neurophysiology and psychology, that is exactly the way artificial intelligence ought to be done.

Yes, but the work by Marr and his colleagues seems to be quite exceptional within that field, doesn't it?

It may be unique. But it is real science. What has been developed in artificial intelligence is very flexible and effective techniques for using these monsters. They really know how to do very fancy things with complicated computational systems. Then the question is what do you do with a technique. Marr may be the first person – the first one I know of at least – to use that technique in the way a serious scientist would. He studies problems that require this kind of fancy computational system to test out his models. What he and his group are trying to do is somewhat analogous to

---

12. Marcus (1980).

what we are doing. They are interested in developing systems of representation and levels of representation which will on the one hand have a basis in physiology, if they can find it, and on the other hand will account for important perceptual phenomena. For example, why do you see an object in motion as being that object and not some other object, when you get several presentations of it. What they want to do is work out mental models and computational models that will give representations that will account for these phenomena and their properties. They do discuss artificial intelligence in a critical fashion. What they are doing is, in a sense, artificial intelligence, but what we are doing is in the same sense artificial intelligence, except we do not use computers, but rather type papers on typewriters. What they point out is that there are a number of different levels of investigation that you might imagine. First there is a level at which you deal with particular elements like diodes and neurons, and that is biochemistry, or physiology. Second, there is a level at which you talk about bigger units, assemblies or groupings of these units, and that is more abstract. Third, there is a level at which you talk about algorithms, actual procedures, parsing procedures, etc. And finally, there is what they call the theory of the computation, where you try to abstractly characterize the general properties of the system and how it functions and what its nature is. Given a theory of the computation there can be many algorithms that may solve the problems formulated and established within that theory. They argue, plausibly I think, that the theory of the computation is the most crucial and also the most neglected level of research, and that the fundamental work, conceptually, will be at the level of the theory of the computation. They criticize work in artificial intelligence for beginning at too concrete a level, for beginning with efforts to construct algorithms to solve particular problems. So, for example, people will construct a system to answer questions about human behavior, to answer questions about what happens in a restaurant[13], and that is much too concrete a level to expect any answers. Maybe there ultimately will be such systems but I doubt if there ever will be. Certainly it is not the level at which you are going to reach any understanding of the nature of the systems.

So one kind of critique that they level against artificial intelligence, which I think is a valid one, is that it is much too concerned with algorithms to deal with specific questions, as compared with an effort to discover the real systems and their nature. Another, independent, critique which they give of the field, also valid I think, is based on their observa-

---

13. Cf. Schank and Abelson (1977).

tion that one can roughly divide problems into two types. There are two criteria by which you can classify problems. One criterion is whether humans can do it or not: there are some things humans can do very well and some things they do very badly. Proving theorems in propositional calculus they do very badly. On the other hand, recognizing the shape of an object in motion they do very well, understanding sentences they do very well, etc. And then another sort of dimension is whether we understand the theory of the problem or not. For example in the case of propositional calculus we understand the theory perfectly, we have got it worked out. In the case of the study of an object in motion, we do not understand the theory very well. And what they suggest is that most of the work in the field has tended to gravitate towards things whose theories are well understood but that humans are very bad at. But judging just by these two dimensions, the obvious thing you want to do is find areas where people do well and where you understand the theory. But then the way to proceed is to take areas where people do well, and to try to develop the theory, that is the theory of the computation, in the first place. That suggests a direction for artificial intelligence, and it is a direction in fact which they follow, and which is very close to what we try to do in linguistic research. I think that these are very sensible comments about artificial intelligence.

But take something like behavior in a restaurant. We seem to be quite good at it and we don't understand the theory well at all.

Behaving in a restaurant is something that people do well but it is doubtful that there is any relevant theory. It is not that the theory is not understood, it is that it is not clear why there should be a theory in the first place. It is just a particular piece of knowledge. So that is different. It just seems to me inconceivable that the kind of work done by say Roger Shank's group could ever have any results at all.[14] Of course what they are describing are real things. It is perfectly true that if somebody goes into a restaurant, orders a hamburger and then leaves a big tip on the table, we would assume that he probably ate the hamburger. If he walked out and did not leave a tip, we might assume that he did not eat the hamburger. And no doubt you can get a machine to duplicate those judgements. But what conceivable interest could there be in this. There is a feeling among the artificial intelligence people that they are somehow capturing the notion of understanding, because if they could get a machine to answer

---

14. Schank and Abelson (1977).

questions about restaurants as we answer them, then perhaps they would grasp what understanding is. John Searle[15] pointed out an obvious problem: you could imagine a human who is following formal instruction in Chinese. He does not know anything about Chinese, but he has English instructions which tell him how to manipulate symbols in Chinese. That human could be programmed, he could have English instructions telling him that when certain Chinese symbols come in he should push certain Chinese symbols out. And the program could be one which gives the answers to those restaurant questions for Chinese. But we certainly would not say he understands Chinese (or anything about restaurants) because he is pushing the right symbol out. So whatever understanding is, it is not following this program, it is some other thing.

What is it that makes work at this level, at the level of the algorithms, the work on processes rather than on the underlying principles, so appealing to so many people? Is it because it is easy?

No, I do not think that it is easy. I think it is hard, and grubby. But you sort of feel you have your feet on the ground. There are people who are worried about abstraction and want to keep close to the data. It is like doing descriptive phonetics or descriptive semantics, I think. If you look at intellectual activity in the humanities and the natural sciences, with very rare exceptions, it is highly data-bound. There are only a few areas of intellectual endeavor where people have really gone beyond to develop theoretical work which is not a kind of data arrangement, in the humanities as well as in the natural sciences. I think constructing algorithms feels safe. How far wrong can you go?

This is speculative psychoanalysis or something, but I think many people would like to believe that there is not much to discover, that everything is going to be pretty close to the surface, that there are not going to be complex, maybe even frightening things. It is possible that they do not want to have to discover those things. And as long as you keep to constructing algorithms to parse sentences and the like, then you do not seem to be getting into areas where there may be far-reaching and abstract principles, theories with a complex deductive structure, and questions of what could be the physical nature of these mental objects. I think much of the impulse behind behaviorism and descriptivism in linguistics is of this nature, but that, as I say, is amateur psychoanalysis.

---

15. Searle (1980).

The appeal of processing models and the like might also be related to the quite widespread interest in finite state transducers and other automata.

Back in the fifties, many people were interested in finite state automata because there was great faith in recent technological developments and because the theory of finite state automata was beginning to be understood. It related in obvious ways to information theory. If you look back to Shannon and Weaver's book, *The Mathematical Theory of Communication*[16], or George Miller's book *Language and Communication*[17] in the early fifties, there was really a feeling of breakthrough. There were these technical tools, like information theory, and finite automata, and Markov sources, and sound spectograms, and so on. People thought that they were on the verge of extending the natural sciences to include the phenomena of the human mind and human cognition. And that was very exciting. It was extremely naive, but maybe it was worth trying. As a student it seemed perfectly obvious to me that it was never going to work, and in fact it collapsed very quickly. I do not think anybody believes anymore that you can construct finite automata to represent the characteristics of human cognition. Nonetheless people try to develop finite automata to model certain processes. And from a certain point of view that is not absurd. After all, processing involves a finite brain, so it is representable by a finite system. But still, I think it is by now understood pretty well why it is the wrong approach.

Why is it the wrong approach?

It is the wrong approach because even though we have a finite brain, that brain is really more like the control system for an infinite computer. That is, a finite automaton is limited strictly to its own memory capacity, and we are not. We are like a Turing machine in the sense that although we have a finite control unit for a brain, nevertheless we can use indefinite amounts of memory that are given to us externally to perform more and more complicated computations. A finite automaton cannot do that. So the concept of the finite automaton is OK, as long as we understand it to be organized in the manner of a control unit for a much bigger, unbounded, system. The control unit of a Turing machine also is a finite automaton, but what makes the Turing machine not finite is the fact that

---

16. Shannon and Weaver (1949).
17. Miller (1951).

the control unit interacts with something outside, namely memory, to enable it to carry out its computations with access, in principle, to an unbounded memory. At this level of description, we are like that. If we were really finite automata, then we could understand sentences up to, say, three levels of embedding, but when they got up to four levels of embedding, we would have nothing, zero, because they would simply be outside our capacity. But obviously that is false. We can go on indefinitely, if we just have more and more time, and memory, and so on. We do not have to learn anything new to extend our capacities in this way. This means that we are not finite automata in the sense of the fifties.

Would you say that it is impossible to gain insight into linguistic problems through work in automata theory?

I would not say so necessarily. I think what happened is that there was a period of fairly fruitful contact between automata theory and linguistics in the late fifties and the early sixties. It mostly had to do with the properties of context-free grammars. Things turned up which are quite interesting. I do not know how much linguistic interest they have, but maybe they have some. In fact there was one result[18] which had linguistic interest, namely the fact that you can think of a context-free grammar as a certain kind of automaton that takes symbols from left to right and prints out tree structures for them. You can make this precise but intuitively that is what it is. A context-free grammar has interesting automata-theoretic properties, in fact; it has the properties of a pushdown storage automaton.

And what is the significance of that for linguistics?

Well, it means that to the extent that context-free grammars represent properties of languages pushdown storage automata can yield reasonable processors for language. That extent is not zero and is not a hundred percent. Certainly context-free grammars represent some of the properties of languages. This seems to me what one would expect from applied mathematics, to see if you can find systems that capture some of the properties of the complex system that you are working with, and to ask whether those systems have any intrinsic mathematical interest, and whether they are worth studying in abstraction. And that has happened at exactly one level, the level of context-free grammar. At any other level it has not hap-

---

18. Cf. Chomsky (1959a,b).

pened. The systems that capture other properties of language, for example transformational grammar, hold no interest for mathematics. But I do not think that that is a necessary truth. It could turn out that there would be richer or more appropriate mathematical ideas that would capture other, maybe deeper properties of language than context-free grammars do. In that case you have another branch of applied mathematics which might have linguistic consequences. That could be exciting.

Talking about mathematics, that is not really a field that we would generally interpret as part of cognitive science. Yet, on the basis of the classification of levels of inquiry that we discussed before in connection with Marr, one might approach arithmetic in a similar way. And after all there is a branch of mathematics, intuitionistic mathematics[19], which might be interpreted along such lines.

In a way, that has to do with the question of the theory of the computation and the theory of the algorithm, in Marr's sense. Actually I think it also has to do with taking a Platonistic view of language. Let us compare the study of language to the study of arithmetic. We might say that in the study of arithmetic there are just the arithmetical truths, there are the properties of the numbers. So the fact that the square root of two is irrational is just like the fact that the sun has helium in it. And if we take a classical view of mathematics, then the truths of mathematics are just truths on a par with the truths of physics even. They are truths that are independent of our ways of thinking. So the theory of mathematics in a sense is independent of any particular techniques that we use for carrying out arithmetical computations or making mathematical constructions. For example we have an understanding of the notion "number" that may be distinct from the algorithms that we use in carrying out computations. That is all OK if you take a classical view of mathematics. On the other hand, if you take an intuitionist view of mathematics, which is a serious position, and one that some working mathematicians as well as people interested in the foundations of mathematics regard as essentially correct, then mathematical objects do not have the existence imputed to them in the classical view. Instead, there are mathematical objects because we have succeeded in constructing them. From this perspective mathematics becomes the study of mental constructions of a certain type. Then the whole story that I just told collapses. If you have a formal proof

---

19. See mainly Brouwer (1913), Heyting (1956), Dummett (1977).

but the things demonstrated in the proof are proven in a nonconstructivist way, there is no sense to saying that the results are established, from this point of view. And the properties of the numbers are just the properties that a constructive approach to the analysis of numbers can demonstrate, not other properties that they may have quite apart from our capacity to carry out computational description and analysis. One could perhaps take the intuitionist view of mathematics as being not unlike the linguistic view of grammar. That is, grammar does not have an independent existence apart from the functions of the human mind, but they are in fact precisely systems of principles that the human mind is capable of constructing, given the primary linguistic data.

If we return now to the first question, let us take another look at the "adopted mother" of linguistics: psychology. It has been more than twenty years now since you wrote the Skinner review. Do you feel that psychology has undergone a dramatic change since then?

Yes, it is true that in the late fifties cognitive psychology in our sense was more or less beginning to take hold. You cannot say it was invented but it was beginning to take hold, at least in the United States, at about that time. The stranglehold that behaviorism had over thinking and research in psychology was beginning to be broken and that has now taken place to a large extent. There is still plenty of behaviorist psychology, but it does not have anything like the prestige or power that it had, or the ability to constrain research and teaching. You will find universities in the midwest where it is still dominant but it is not a general phenomenon. So I think, yes, there has been a big change.

So there must also have been a profound intellectual crisis.

I think behaviorism collapsed very easily. At that time it was taken very seriously not only by people that worked on training pigeons. Now it is still taken seriously by the people training pigeons, but I do not think anyone else pays much attention. Sometimes you can get humorous things, for example you may have seen this article in the *New York Times* a couple of weeks ago about pigeons who were trained to carry out symbolic communication. It reported on an article in *Science*[20], an amusing article by Skinner and some of his students, in which they succeeded more or

---

20. See Epstein, Lanza, and Skinner (1980).

less in duplicating with pigeons what had been done with some apes. That looked like the most spectacular achievement so far in training for symbolic communication. They said we can do it with pigeons, and they did. The pigeons did the same thing that apes did. Then they concluded that this shows how humans work. If you look at what actually happened, if you look at the details of the experiment, it should be obvious to anyone that it is about as interesting as a circus trick. One pigeon is trained to peck a key whenever it sees red or green, and then the key makes some kind of signal and the other pigeon is trained so that when it sees the signal it pecks at some other thing, and so on and so forth, all very straightforward. If you put that whole system together, you get the impression that the pigeons are communicating. You give information to the first pigeon that there is food here because that is the way the signal is interpreted. And then the second pigeon does something which maybe helps it to get the food, it is told the food is over there. It is only when you take the set-up apart that you see that it is just a trick. As I say it may be that some psychologists are still misled by this kind of thing. I suppose Skinner is, but I think it is generally true that it is treated as the joke that it is.

So, apparently psychology has overcome the behaviorist heritage. Nevertheless, to us as outsiders it does not look like a very productive field. Is that due to certain aspects of behaviorism that have not been successfully overcome?

First of all, there are parts of psychology that were never too much tainted by behaviorism, that were and still are productive, like perceptual psychology. But cognitive psychology is not productive. Maybe it is just hard. Nobody has really found the way to a breakthrough. Behavioral psychology provided many techniques and good experimental designs. You can use them but they do not seem to solve hard problems.

You briefly mentioned the work that has been done with primates, chimp language and the like. It has been a big discussion which is pretty much concluded now, it seems, after the publication of Herbert Terrace's work.[21] It has been quite an emotional discussion too. In fact, one felt that there was something more at stake than just finding out and settling the issue of whether primates have a language faculty. Should we in some sense be happy, for example, now that it has turned out that human grammar is rad-

---

21. Terrace (1979).

ically different from what primates appear to be able to acquire? Does it make sense to say that this result is a direct consequence of the findings that we have learned through our linguistic work?

Well, my own feeling is that the reason for the belief that there is going to be no close similarity between, say, the human language faculty and anything in the ape brain, really lies elsewhere. It lies in the fact that it is just extraordinarily unlikely that a biological capacity that is highly useful and very valuable for the perpetuation of the species and so on, a capacity that has an obvious selectional value, should be latent and not used. That would be amazing if it were true. But if it turns out to be true, then I do not think anything much would change. All the problems would be exactly where they are. Now you have to explain something even harder, namely how this capacity developed without ever having been used or selected or anything like that. It would just make the mysteries deeper, but I do not see any reason to believe that the mysteries are that deep, that something like this capacity could have evolved without any selectional pressure.

As to why we would not expect it from the point of view of those things that we are discovering, what we are discovering is very specific principles which do not seem to have any obvious application in other cognitive domains. If principles or properties of that kind were already present but latent in an ape's brain, I think we would be extremely surprised. As to why we should care, basically I do not really care very much. Humans are obviously radically different from any other organism around. I think there would not be any possible question about that. For example, it is superficially obvious that humans are the only organism that has a history. The concept of history does not exist for any other organism; there are no changes other than biological changes, except in the most trivial respects. For humans that is just not true. The question is what this has to do with, and it does not seem unreasonable to suppose that it has to do with the ability to express a vast range of thinking. The elementary materials that enter into thought may very well be primitive and available for other animals. That is, it is perfectly possible for example that perceptual categorisation or object identification is similar among a lot of organisms. They have all more or less the same perceptual world and they have the same problems to deal with. So it could very well be that a lot of notions like individuation and predication could be if not identical, perhaps related across species. Hence something must be lacking in the other species and what is it? Well, what it is, it appears to me, is the computational aspects of the language faculty. It is interesting to think about the other things that seem to radically differentiate humans from other primates. For example, one result that apparently has come out of Dave Premack's work[22], is that he seems to have run up against a blank wall in two areas. One: language, and the other: the number faculty. He can not seem to get the apes to do anything at all with numbers; and that is kind of interesting too, because it is just conceivable that the same thing is involved in both cases. What is involved is some kind of capacity to deal with discrete infinities through recursive rules which from one point of view give you the number faculty and from another point of view, together with different principles, give you the capacity to construct an unbounded range of expressions. And when that is linked to the conceptual system, which could be more primitive, then you get crucial elements of the capacity to have free thought. That could be what enters into the uniqueness of human life. So in this sense what seems to be a plausible account, and the only one I can think of as to why humans are really so radically different from anything else, could very well turn on these things. That would be interesting and it would make linguistics a very central field.

If the crucial evolutionary difference between apes and humans in this respect centers around the basic computational capacity, could we go further and say that this capacity constitutes our main selective advantage over primates?

The conceptual capacity permits us to perceive, and categorize, and symbolize maybe even to reason in an elementary way, but it is only when linked to the computational capacity that the system really becomes powerful. I think that the great step in human evolution could have been that two things which had a quite separate evolutionary origin happened to interact in a fantastically fruitful way. One is the basic elements of the conceptual system, object identification and perceptual constancies and other things which may go beyond that such as planning and the attribution of intent to other organisms. That is one kind of system which may be shared in part with other primates. And then, imagine that for some unexplained reason a computational capacity developed, maybe as a consequence of some change in brain size or whatever. Of course, parts of this have been latent throughout all of human history, like, say, the capacity to deal with the properties of natural numbers. That is a capacity that could not have been specifically selected, because it was never overt

---

22. See in particular Premack (1976).

until human evolution reached essentially its present stage. That just developed for some reason, maybe in relation to the capacity to form an infinite range of logical forms and syntactic structures. When that capacity links to the conceptual system, you get human language, which provides the capacity for thought, planning, evaluation and so on, over an unbounded range, and then you have a totally new organism. It seems to me that something like that could be what is involved in the qualitative differences between humans and other organisms. So you do seem to find symbolic behavior at very primitive levels, it appears, maybe prior to language for all we know. Some of the ape studies seem to indicate at least some rudimentary ability for some kind of symbolization. But what appears to be totally lacking is anything analogous to the computational facilities, which means that the conceptual capacities are more or less mute. Maybe they are there, but they can do very little with them.

If the computational capacity is so central to both the language faculty and the human mastery of the number system, wouldn't we expect both types of knowledge to be acquired or to "grow" in essentially the same way? But at first sight at least that doesn't seem to be the case.

It depends on what level of mathematics we are talking about. For example the ability to deal with the properties of natural numbers is acquired just like languages, it seems. If you are presented with the relevant materials you immediately know it all. Maybe you have to memorize the multiplication table, but, for example, the fact that you can add one indefinitely, does not have to be taught. You teach kids numbers and very shortly they understand that they can keep on adding them forever. And the properties of addition are going to carry over to the big numbers as well as the small numbers. It takes a lot of training to learn how to do it accurately, but that is beside the point. We are not built to be arithmetical computers but we have the concept of number.

For example it is very easy to teach people concepts like prime number. In fact, most of the history of mathematics is based on a very limited class of intuitions, intuitions about number and intuitions about visual space. Those things just seem to be inherent to humans. I am told that when you introduce aboriginal people into a market economy they very quickly develop the facility for all this, so that at least the rudiments of the system are latent, just waiting to be used. That raises a question, akin to the question that would be raised if people did find language capacity in apes, namely what is it doing there, what was it doing there up until may be the Greeks?

Why was no one ever using it? The answer to that must be that, again miracles aside, it is a concomitant of something else which was being used. Maybe it is a concomitant of elements that enter into language. It is striking that these are the two systems that seem to involve the notion of discrete infinity, which is, I think, very rare in the biological world, if it exists at all elsewhere. If you look at biological and animal communication systems, as far as I know there are none that have the property of discrete infinity. People say that they are more impoverished, but that is not quite true. Many of them are richer in a sense because they are based on notions of continuity. If you think of the weak generative capacity, these are richer systems, vastly richer systems. Of course in many ways they are more impoverished, but what is strikingly obvious is that humans do not acquire finite languages, which is a surprising fact if you think about it. Why don't children assume that there is only a finite number of integers, and why don't they make a grammar which has only a finite number of sentences? These are not obvious points. In fact we would think it very odd if the numbers stopped at, say, 183, but it is not obvious why we would think that odd.

Somehow the evolutionary leap which we are talking about seems to be quite a big one. Yet, the period of differential evolution has been comparatively short.

It could turn very heavily on this one fundamental change, namely the development of the capacity to deal with discrete infinities. It just could be that much of it turns on that. We do not know, but that might reflect a small change in the brain. It could, for example, be a consequence of the increase in brain size or complexity. And if that system develops and links to a conceptual system, it really offers a total new world. For all we know that has happened once in the history of the universe. There is no particular reason to believe that it has happened elsewhere, so those possibilities and in fact even likelihoods make this a very important central issue.

Do you find it likely that this fundamental evolutionary leap should have been the result of random genetic drift? If not, why should it have developed?

It does seem very hard to believe that the specific character of organisms can be accounted for purely in terms of random mutation and selectional controls. I would imagine that the biology of a 100 years from now is going to deal with the evolution of organisms the way it now deals with the evolution of amino acids, assuming that there is just a fairly small space of physically possible systems that can realize complicated structures. It is not that you try every possible combination and certain big molecules happen to be useful, so they work. There are only certain kinds of big molecules that have the right property and it could very well be that if we understood more about the way organisms are put together, the way they function and the laws they have to observe, we would find that there are not many kinds of possible organisms. There is some work already that goes in that direction. For example, there is work by Mandelbrot in his book Fractals[23]. He has tried to show that many phenomena in the natural world, totally diverse phenomena, like for example the distribution of lake sizes, the length of coast lines, the shapes of organs, and many other things follow from some extremely simple, conceptually simple, but mathematically intricate, principles of organisation in terms of statistical models and the like. It is in a way related to things like d'Arcy Thompson's[24] attempt to show that many properties of organisms, like symmetry, for example, do not really have anything to do with a specific selection but just with the ways in which things can exist in the physical world. Evolutionary theory appears to have very little to say about speciation, or about any kind of innovation. It can explain how you get a different distribution of qualities that are already present, but it does not say much about how new qualities can emerge. It could be that the answer to the puzzle is similar to the answer to the question of why after the big bang you went from hydrogen to helium, not to something else. It was not because a lot of things were tried and helium worked, but just that that is what the world is like under particular conditions of cooling and so forth. It could be that when the brain gets so complex, it simply has to encompass systems of discrete infinity. Nothing that simple could be true, but perhaps something like this will prove to be part of the truth.

Recently you seem to have adopted the terminology of classical genetics. Nevertheless, it seems that there is a difference in outlook: classical genetics aims at reducing at least some intraspecific variation to genotypical variation, whereas generative grammar idealizes to the genotypical invariance of universal grammar. Whatever variation there is within universal grammar, such as parametrized constructs, for example, is environmentally induced.

---

23. Mandelbrot (1977).
24. D'Arcy Thompson (1961).

What kind of genetic theory of language acquisition is generative linguistics then? You are not seriously looking for subjacency mutants, after all.

This is more the way in which, say, a developmental biologist would deal with such a question, I think. For example, suppose that a developmental biologist is interested in the factors that enter into the specialization of organs. He would also abstract away from genotypic variation. It could enter somewhere, but it is not the main topic. The main topic is the uniformity of development. As you mention, it could ultimately be an interesting question whether there is genetic variation that shows up in language somehow.

But you are not very keen on looking for it?

Well, I would be keen on looking for it if we could do it. In fact, it has been very seriously suggested. For example, Salvador Luria has suggested that we ought to be looking for this, and I do not think it is out of question. There are some apparently hereditary traits that show up in language. Since nobody has looked very hard it is very speculative, but, for example, some clinicians say that things like extraordinarily late language development seem to run in families. There are kids who do not start learning language until they are four or five and it turns out very often that the same is true for one of their parents. That is very gross, but you might find something. There is some rather suggestive work by Maureen Dennis[25] on infantile left hemispherectomies. It has been assumed that such children achieved complete language recovery, and it looked like that. They talk to people and seem very normal. But she started doing some research with quite simple structures, looking at passives and the like, and it turned out that there are differences between the normal child and the child with the left hemisphere removed. They apparently do not have a normal right hemisphere, a fact that is related to the condition that requires the surgery. And they have a different brain as a result of the operation. It could be that that slightly different brain is doing things a normal brain would not. Of course that is not genetic, unless the condition that requires the surgery is in part genetically determined. Another area which might be worth looking at from this point of view is schizophrenic language, since there apparently is some evidence of genetic elements entering into schizophrenia. A good place to do this

---

25. Cf. among others, Dennis and Whitaker (1976).

would be countries like Denmark or Holland, where they have a social service system which is very advanced. They keep track of everybody and everything, and they must have cases of twins, where one is schizophrenic and the other is not. If there are genetic elements in schizophrenia, and if strange things are showing up in schizophrenic language, you would very much like to know what is happening in the non-schizophrenic twin. This type of research does not seem to me totally outlandish and it might be interesting to do it. Nevertheless, I think it makes a lot of sense to proceed the way we do, that is to abstract away from variation, for the same reasons that hold for developmental biology in general. There are major phenomena that have to be understood, and those are almost the same wherever we look, so you can forget about the variation.

Chapter 2
Explanation in Linguistics

Since the beginning of transformational grammar many things have changed and many things have remained the same. But the most fundamental change, perhaps, has to do with the explanatory goals that generative linguists have set themselves. The standards of comparison for linguistic theories are drastically different now from those most popular thirty years ago. This is perhaps also the change that many have not been able to appreciate, the move that has alienated linguists and non-linguists alike. Yet to us it appears that a completely new dimension has been added to linguistic research by insisting on far-reaching ideals of explanation. What exactly is the relevant dimension along which linguistic theories should be evaluated?

The most interesting linguistic dimension, I think, is the one that is mentioned at the end of the first chapter of Aspects[1]. The basic concept, it seems to me still, is explanatory adequacy, thought of in terms of the projection problem, the problem of explaining how a particular grammar is selected on the basis of certain data. If that is the fundamental problem, then you can develop the notion of explanation in those terms.

Much work still remains to be done in this area, but at least you can see how it could be done. What you want is a function which is going to map small amounts of data uniquely onto grammars, and that function will be an explanatory theory in the sense that it will explain the phenomena predicted by the grammars on the basis of boundary conditions given by the data. How do we get to that function? Well, the only way we get to it is by a theory which reduces the number of grammars that are accessible given fixed data.

That has got to be the empirically significant criterion. It could very well be that linguistic theory permits a grammar for every recursively enumerable set, maybe even beyond. That would not change the basic point at all. What is required in linguistic theory is some notion of accessibility. We need a scattering of grammars in terms of accessibility, so that not many of them, in fact maybe only a few or only one, are available

---

1. Chomsky (1965).

given small amounts of data. That seemed to me the basic problem of explanation and hence that seems to me the empirically relevant dimension along which theories should be evaluated. Very highly structured theories which have very strong generative capacity are good candidates. For example, suppose you have a very strange way of coding Turing machines, which sort of scatters them in a very strange fashion, with regard to fixed data. There will be infinitely many such systems compatible with any choice of data that you have, but almost all of them are way out in terms of their complexity by some measure. That could be the right theory. On the other hand, standard notations for Turing machines are no good, because everything is too easily available. There is no scattering of systems with regard to data.

What you suggest is that the hierarchy of formal languages is not the right dimension. And notions such as weak generative capacity, and even strong generative capacity, are also not central in characterizing this dimension. Is there any way of formalizing the dimension of explanatory adequacy that you have just outlined?

I do not think that these are problems that lend themselves to formalisation now. It is a matter of finding theories of universal grammar which in the crucial cases, namely natural languages, do not allow many possible grammars.

Do you envisage that the next step will be to characterize the parameters of Universal Grammar along which individual grammars may vary, and then to establish the interdependence among the parameters, their ranking, their relative accessibility, the paths through networks of parameters etc.?

Right. If you could work out a highly constrained parametrized theory, then you know how to proceed. You would say, well, the principles are fixed, here are the parameters, here is the ranking and the ordering of the parameters and there is the path through them. It could turn out that there is some path that gives you ultimately a grammar for every recursively enumerable set. If it does then it means that with unbounded experience people could learn a grammar for every recursively enumerable set. That is irrelevant to the problem of explanation, because in fact the problem has to do with the rich systems that are developed on the basis of restricted data. That is the real problem of explanation. I do not think it is going to happen, because it looks to me as if in the more plausible theories there are only a finite number of grammars anyway; I do not know if these questions are going to arise; but if they did arise, it would not necessarily show that anything is wrong.

Many people feel, of course, that something is indeed very wrong, that what we should be looking for is not formal explanations of this type at all. Many linguists get much more excited about functional explanations. In answer to such proposals you have argued that functional explanations can be relevant at the level of evolution, but not when we are seeking to characterize the system of Universal Grammar that the human species is endowed with now. In light of this, what is the status of the argument in "Filters and Control"[2] to the effect that several filters interact in such a way as to ensure that the multiple base forms of infinitival relatives correspond to a single surface realization. Isn't that a functional argument?

Assuming that it is correct, I would think of it as being an evolutionary explanation. That is, to put it very concretely, the question is: does the child learn these filters because his mind discovers that it reduces a large number of base forms to a small number of surface forms? That seems to me very unlikely. It doesn't seem to be a plausible ontogenetic mechanism. But you could ask: do the languages have these filters because they serve the function of reducing ambiguity; did either the language or the species evolve in such a way that this should be the case? In general it is very hard to offer plausible functional explanations at an ontogenetic level. I think the same is true for physical mechanisms. It doesn't make much sense at that level. It is not that it is logically impossible. For example it could be that the embryo developed a circulatory system because it figures out that that is the only way to get oxygen to all of its parts, but nobody thinks that those are plausible explanations. And I don't see why they should be here either. This has a great deal to do with very popular speculations about language and communication. John Searle is somebody who has argued that it's just perverse and pointless to discuss structure without thinking of the functions that it allegedly serves.[3] Also a lot of the work on child language acquisition is now guided by the feeling that if you really study the way in which communicative intention develops, then everything else will fall out.

---

2. Chomsky and Lasnik (1977).
3. Cf. in particular Searle (1972).

Again, pursuing the matter of explanatory theories, there seems to be a certain tension between richness and elegance. As a realist, you know there has to be a mentally represented Universal Grammar which is rich enough to account for language acquisition, and from this perspective you are perfectly happy to postulate really complicated and intricate mechanisms as part of Universal Grammar. On the other hand, as a scientist you pursue the ephemeral goals of optimally elegant theories, ultimately of beauty. Do you feel that there is an inconsistency between the two points of view, perhaps even a paradox?

In physics, one might ask the same question: why look for elegant answers? Everybody does, but you might ask: why do it? The reason they do it is an almost mystical belief that there is something about our concept of elegance that relates to truth, and that is certainly not logically necessary. Our brains might have been devised in such a way that what looks elegant to them is totally off base. But you really have no choice but to try to use the resources of your mind to find conceptual unification and explanation and elegance, hoping that by some miracle that is the way the world works.

Up to a point it's been successful. But when you study biological systems, like language, it is not at all obvious that it is going to be successful, because while it could be that elementary particle theory is some sort of magnificent realization of abstract mathematics, it's very unlikely that the circulatory system is. The reason is that that just developed in too much of an accidental fashion. The way that the circulatory system developed had to do with biochemistry and ice-ages and running away from predators and all sorts of other things, which are just too accidental. There isn't any particular reason to believe that the way it ends up is going to be a reflection of beautiful mathematical ideas, the ways in which you might imagine that elementary particles are going to be. The same could be true of language. That is, it might be a fundamental error to search for too much elegance in the theory of language, because maybe those parts of the brain developed the way they did in part accidentally. For example, what has been so far a very productive leading idea, trying to eliminate redundancy, could be argued to be the wrong move, because in fact we know that biological systems tend to be highly redundant for good reasons. Suppose it does turn out that biological systems are messy, either because of historical accident or maybe because they work better when they're messy. They may provide many different ways of doing the same thing. If something fails, something else will work. To the extent that that is true, the theory of these systems is going to be messy too.

If that would be the case, it might be a really fundamental error to be guided too much by an effort to eliminate redundancy in developing explanatory theories. I think that is something to bear in mind. In this sense this paradox, if you like, may be a very real one. I think, with all due caution, we can just judge by how productive it is. So far it seems to me to have been reasonably productive, to pretend that we're doing elementary particle physics. Yet, I think we ought to bear in mind that we might be going quite in the wrong direction, and that might show up, sooner or later. It would be unfortunate. I don't know about others, but for me it would mean that the field would lose a lot of its interest.

Another way of getting out of the paradox might be to take just the simple way out and to abandon realism. But is it possible to be a good generative grammarian without at the same time subscribing, at least implicitly, to some genetically based version of Universal Grammar, to the interpretation of grammar as a mental organ. Concretely, do you feel that a position such as Milner's in his reply to the GLOW-manifesto[4] is a coherent one?

I think a linguist can do perfectly good work in generative grammar without ever caring about questions of physical realism or what his work has to do with the structure of the mind. I do not think there is any question that that is possible. It just seems to me to indicate a certain lack of curiosity as to why things are the way they are. You might argue that even if you turn to the question of biological realism you are not really answering these questions. You are getting an answer, but it is not a helpful answer. You say: things are the way they are because of the genes. But we do not know how to proceed from there. That is true, I think, but still it is worthwhile to try to establish what may even be premature connections with other fields that ought to be interested in these topics. For example, it seems to me that we should be on the lookout for interesting results from physiology and genetics and so on. Why should we be on the lookout? I think we certainly should be, and we should encourage such contacts, and expect that sometime in the maybe not too remote future they will really be important. The point is that there is no point in looking for those contacts if you do not accept the realist point of view. If you think that generative grammar is just an interesting game people play with linguistic materials, you can probably do what most linguists do, but then of course there would be no reason whatsoever for anything discovered

---

4. GLOW Manifesto (1978) and Milner (1978a).

from any other point of view to have any bearing at all. In fact, it is not clear to me what is the point of the game, but that is another matter.

There has been a continuous series of attacks against the realist point of view in linguistics. For some reason realism in linguistics appears to be much harder to accept, both for linguists and non-linguists, than realism in the other sciences. Why is that so?

That is a much harder question, in many ways. There are some real questions. What do we mean for example when we say that the brain really does have rules of grammar in it. We do not know exactly what we mean when we say that. We do not think there is a neuron that corresponds to "move alpha". So we are talking somehow about general structural properties of the brain, and there are real nontrivial questions about what it means to say that the brain, or any system, has general properties. It is like saying, what do we exactly mean when we say this computer is programmed to do arithmetic? We say that, and we understand it – it certainly has some meaning. But we do not mean there is a neuron in there that says "Add 1" or a diode or something that says "Add 1". I think there are really serious questions here that people should investigate, trying to get a better grasp of the notion of "true statements" that attribute general abstract properties to complex systems. And in fact I am far from the only one who has thought about it – there is a lot of work on such question. For some reason these questions are thought not to arise in physics, because by now we are trained to accept a realist point of view without any further question, which is not so obvious. It was certainly not obvious, for example, what a wave was in the period in which these things were being sorted out in physics for the first time. We can easily comprehend, and it is useful to imagine, why the Cartesians were unable to accept Newton because he was talking about things that did not seem real, and could not be real. And it is a true intellectual breakthrough to be able to accept those things as real. That is now commonplace in the sciences. So if somebody says there are quarks, or for that matter that water has hydrogen in it, we have come to an understanding, or at least an acceptance, that that has a realistic interpretation, and we have a vague understanding of what it means. Yet, in detail, it is not obvious what it means. What are we in fact referring to when we refer to hydrogen? We are not referring to any particular thing. Maybe we are referring to something abstract. But that does not bother people much. They are willing to accept that degree of lack of understanding and to proceed, leaving the problem – philosophical or conceptual – to be settled somewhere or sometime in the future. In the study of language that intellectual breakthrough has not been made. People are unwilling to accept the idea that statements about the structure of some system could be true statements, that is that there could be properties of the system that correspond to what is attributed to it in the theory. The question then is, why people feel that psychological tests shed light on psychological reality. That I simply do not understand. I have no explanation as to why anybody thinks that a reaction time experiment tells you more about psychological reality than a fact about synonymy. It just seems to me totally irrational.

Aren't there analogues in physics, for example? Couldn't you say about physics that it is not about physically real systems out there in the real world, but just about photographs, computer printouts of sophisticated measuring machinery, and, in particular, about the human interpretation of these. From the same perspective you would then maintain that linguistics is not really about psychologically real systems at all, but is merely a study of introspective judgments.

Many people say that, but to say that linguistics is the study of introspective judgments would be like saying that physics is the study of meter readings, photographs, and so on, but nobody says that. Actually people did say that during the heyday of operationalism, but that did not have a pernicious effect on physics, because even the people who said it did not really believe it at any relevant level, and they did their work anyhow. At any rate, it did not make any sense and was rapidly discarded. Not only does that not make sense, but it also does not make sense to call linguistics the study of introspective judgments. Why should we restrict our data to that? Suppose there is some data from electrical activity of the brain that bears on, say, word boundaries. Why should that be irrelevant to word boundaries? It just seems absurd to restrict linguistics to the study of introspective judgments, as is very commonly done. Some philosophers who have worked on language have defined linguistics that way. And many textbooks that concentrate on linguistic argumentation for example are more or less guided by that view. They offer special sets of techniques for dealing with particular data and thus reduce the field to problem solving, defining the field in these terms. That is perhaps the natural definition if you abandon any realist conception of the field.

When you talk about mental representation, you very often say that some principle, some grammar, or whatever, is represented "in the mind, ultimately the brain". What does that formula mean? Can there be any sense in which the brain could be said to be more real than the mind, for example? Are you consciously leaving the options for dualism open?

Well, I think that there is nothing that we are doing that leads you to dualism, but there is nothing that disproves it either. We can simply understand all this talk about the mind as talk at an appropriate level of abstraction about properties of some physical systems of the brain. So it seems to me that mental talk is not inherently dualistic any more than talk about programs and computers is dualistic. I am really using that phrase to head off the assumption that since we are talking about the mind we are committed to dualism. We are not committed to its negation either; we are not committed to monism. Maybe it will turn out that there is a mind but that it is a separate substance. In fact I do not think it would be surprising if we found out that the whole question of dualism is tainted by a fatal unclarity, which is not often recognized. In the discussion of dualism it is assumed that the notion of body is well understood, and that the problem is to find out what the mind is. But in fact – at least if the history of science is any guide – this is very far from clear. The notion of body is continually changing, and it is continually expanding to deal with new phenomena that were not thought to fall within it before. It could be that the apparent problems of mind will be settled not by reducing mind to brain, but by expanding brain to mind, as Newton expanded the notion of body to include the phenomena of the motion of heavenly bodies, which was not incorporable within the early theory of body. Maybe you need new concepts to deal with mental phenomena, in which case you could resolve the mind/body problem the way the problem of the heavenly bodies was resolved, by changing the theory of body. The reason for such comments is to try to avoid entanglement in what are probably non-questions, like those about dualism. They are non-questions because for example the notion of body is not clear enough for there to be any question.

But if that is so, wouldn't it be better to say "the mind or the brain" or "the mind/brain" rather than "the mind, ultimately the brain"? It still isn't very clear what "ultimately" is supposed to mean in this context.

Well, I guess I am tacitly assuming that there will be no dualism, either because we already in principle have the right physics, or because richer physics must be constructed to incorporate mental phenomena. But if either of those two things is correct, then talk about the mind is talk about the brain at a certain level, just as, to make an analogy, talk about the orbits of the planets is talk about physical entities, at a certain level.

You just mentioned the notion of body. And since we are talking about the human mind/brain, what about the notion of human body. You recently said in a talk[5] that the concept of human body is a fairly useless one.

Well, I would not say it is a useless concept, it is a very intricate one. It is extremely interesting to try to work on what our concept of the human body is. But that is a different enterprise of course.

In that talk you compared the concept of human body to the concept of human intelligence, saying that both are too intricate and ill-understood to be of any scientific use. Does that have any bearing on the allegation that being committed to innate ideas entails being committed to the claim that intelligence is innate?

There is no reason to believe that "intelligence" refers to anything specific. What you talk about as intelligence is apparently some vast kind of amalgam of all sorts of abilities and capacities. I would imagine most of them, if not all of them, have innate components just like everything else does. You can perhaps construct an intelligence test that will predict pretty well how people do in school whatever the point or nonpoint of that may be. It is true that talk about innate structures of whichever kind leads people to the conclusion, which many of them find unwelcome, that there could be, in fact probably will be, differences in innate capacity. And it is a very interesting question why people should find that bothersome. Nobody finds it bothersome that there are differences in innate capacity with regard to physical growth. Nobody finds it bothersome that if your parents are tall then you are likely to be tall, and if your parents are short, then you are likely to be short. It does not seem hard to assimilate that. So why should it be difficult to accept that if there is something in your genes that makes you a good violinist you are different from somebody who does not have that in his genes. Generally it is liberal progressive types who find this unpleasant but I think that they are only revealing their own deep commitment to inegalitarian ideologies, and the physical analogy ex-

---

5. A talk presented in the Independent Activities Program (IAP) at MIT, January 1980.

plains why. After all, the reason why many decent, honest people find it unpleasant to imagine that there might be differences in mental capacity that are biologically determined is that they have a residual belief that the way people ought to be treated or what they deserve, somehow reflects some kind of intrinsic merit. Nobody believes that the way salaries are determined should reflect your height (except maybe in basketball). Once you drop the very pernicious assumption that humans should not be treated as humans but in terms of their capacities to solve certain problems, then the question of innate ability, mental ability, is on a par with innate physical properties. You ought to be delighted that there are differences. If the whole world consisted of people who looked identical, it would be a pretty boring world. If the whole world consisted of people who were mentally identical, it would be intolerable.

The problem appears to be that the differences lead to inequality.

It leads to inequality only because of our social systems, there is no other reason why it should. You could have inequality based on height too. In fact in sufficiently primitive societies you may find inequality based on physical strength. But those are things to be overcome. However, I still think that we should be pleased by virtually all the variety there is in the human race, pathology aside.

Chapter 3
The Field

Within present day linguistics the position of generative grammar is of necessity somewhat antithetical in that we try to revolutionize the field. But on the other hand, you have always been interested in finding links between your work and ideas in earlier periods of linguistics and philosophy. Recently, however, you have not worked so much on the history of ideas. Is that another one of the domains that you have sacrificed to your political work?

I have not really done anything extensive since the mid-sixties except with regard to some of the philosophical issues which I have been interested in pursuing, but not the more linguistic ones.

What about the more philosophical ones?

Well, I have read more about some of the seventeenth century origins. For example, I have recently been looking at some of Descartes' physiology and have been interested in the physiological or quasi-physiological arguments that are offered for a kind of representational theory of neural coding that enters very much into the nature of innate ideas and so on. That is worth pursuing some more, and I have some ideas about it. There has been a tremendous amount of work, during the last ten years or so, on earlier linguistic traditions, and some of that I think would probably be worth studying; I do not think much of it has been done particularly well, frankly, but there is a lot of work coming out.

There is a journal now too, Historiographia Linguistica.

There is the journal and there have been some publications of primary sources. A lot of the original material is now available, which really was not ten or fifteen years ago, when it was very hard to find this material, even such works as the Port-Royal Grammar. But now, a lot of the primary sources have been made fairly well accessible. Also there are commentaries, and there have been a number of publications, some of them with interesting material on the origin of universal grammar, some on medieval and renaissance grammar, and so on. I would think it should be possible now to do a much more careful and comprehensive piece of work on this. I have not done it myself for a number of reasons, but I think somebody ought to. One reason is, I have been sort of put off by the field, frankly. For one thing, there is such a fantastic amount of misrepresentation in the field that I have kept quite remote from it. I refuse invitations to conferences and so on. My own work has just been wildly distorted, in the most amazing ways. For example there is a whole literature devoted to my distortions of Locke. I could hardly have distorted Locke, since I did not discuss him at all, apart from a few innocuous and uncontroversial references that have never been challenged. There are also numerous references to the alleged fact that I overlooked the renaissance origins of Port-Royal Grammar, although I did in fact mention this the very first time I introduced the Port-Royal Grammar in Cartesian Linguistics.[1] Work of this sort is so ridiculous that it is hardly worth discussing. It is unfortunately rather typical of the intellectual or, in a way, even moral level of the field. I just did not want to have anything to do with it. But now there is so much more material available, much of it very interesting, that I think that a really significant field could develop. And there are a few quite serious people working in the field, so perhaps this will happen.

Why is it that there is so little interest, especially from linguists, in this type of question?

Perhaps it has to do in part with the tradition of intellectual history, the field of history of ideas, which is often much more concerned with history and less concerned with ideas. There have been some exceptions, but in particular in branches like the history of linguistics there is a tremendous concern with connections and borrowing and that sort of thing, and very little concern with the nature of the ideas themselves, which are not taken seriously. When you begin to take them seriously, I think you get a rather different picture of how things develop. But you know, an awful lot of this work is a very barren type of scholarship. Many scholars are missing major elements in the intellectual structures that have developed, and are just not taking them seriously. For example, I discovered when I started working on these questions myself, years ago, that there was not very much in the literature, and furthermore that practically none of it took the materials seriously. They would almost always regard

---

1. Chomsky (1966).

an idea as some sort of exotic object that one could study in some field of arcane scholarship but which could not possibly have any interest.

You have had relatively little to say about the principal ideas behind 19th century linguistics, the German tradition in particular. Yet, couldn't it be, that discussing those ideas in a modern context might help bridge the gap between our work and present day philology?

Yes. Partly I did not discuss them because of my own linguistic limitations. It is just too much trouble for me to read German, and most of the material is in German. I can do it, but I would have to work at it and I did not have the time; I was willing to struggle through von Humboldt, just because it was so interesting, and boy, it was a struggle, believe me. But it would take somebody with greater facility and ability to do it. However, for my own personal satisfaction, if I had time to go back to this, what I think I would go back to more intensively is the period between Descartes and Kant. There are a lot of interesting questions about the origins and the backgrounds of Kantian conceptions and earlier ones in psychology for example. There is a very good secondary literature in this case and that is something I have to work on as well. I think that whole period has great relevance really, but I agree with you that somebody, not me, should work on the nineteenth century. Another thing is, it seems to me, that this kind of work should really be done by people with a much deeper grounding in historical and comparative linguistics than I have.

In terms of the history of ideas our field has had a rich history, in terms of the history of science, on the other hand, its past is relatively poor. In particular if we focus on generative grammar there is virtually no sense in talking about a long series of major discoveries. Nevertheless, precisely because the field is so young, the assessment of the structure, the health, the progress of the field is among the favorite discussion topics among generative linguists. In some sense we have all turned into amateur historians or philosophers of science. Inevitably, the situation is evaluated in terms of Thomas Kuhn's work[2], or at least his terminology. Whatever the merit of Kuhn's theory, it would appear that it has been quite badly misused in characterizing the ongoing linguistic revolution. Now that Kuhn has

---

2. In particular, Kuhn (1962).

joined your department, perhaps this is an appropriate time to comment on the field from the point of view of the philosopher of science.

You talk about the misuse of Kuhn's work. I think it is wildly misused outside of the natural sciences. The number of real scientific revolutions is extremely small: two maybe three if you press it, or perhaps a few more. To find one outside the natural sciences is very hard. There just are not enough interesting and significant ideas around, but it is curious if you read the sociological or linguistic literature, that people are discovering revolutions everywhere. I read a paper by C. J. Bailey[3] once in which he had an accelerating rate of linguistic revolutions, I think they were coming once every six months by the end. Every time somebody writes a new article or something. The point is that real conceptual changes in the significant sense are very rare. My own feeling is that linguistics has not even reached anything like a Galilean revolution. Its first revolution is maybe somewhere on the horizon. So I think that Kuhn's notions do not really apply outside the fields in which really significant intellectual progress takes place.

One of Kuhn's notions which may be worth considering in this context is that of normal science. While it is exciting to be in a prerevolutionary or revolutionary phase, eventually normal science is what we are striving for. Do you feel that normal science in generative grammar is very remote?

My feeling is that normal science in linguistics is still basically natural history. I think myself that the level and the scope of descriptive work has very greatly improved in the past 25 years, but it is still largely descriptive work. Our first revolution will come when normal science becomes work that is involved in deepening explanatory theories and that is still a pretty exotic enterprise in linguistics. It is for this reason that I just do not think that linguistics has undergone any kind of intellectual revolution. For example, it was very striking to me when transformational grammar first gained a certain small degree of popularity in the early 60s, to notice that primarily it was just used as another descriptive device. There are things that you can describe in that way more easily than in terms of constituent structure, but that is not a fundamental conceptual change, that is just like adding another tool to your bag.

---

3. Bailey (1981).

Don't you think that the situation has begun to change since your Conditions on Transformations[4]?

My own personal feeling is that that is the first work that I have done that may lead to the possibility of a conceptual revolution, if you like. Most of what preceded seems to me pretty much common sense, though I did find it hard and exciting at the time. But I am very hesitant because there are a lot of problems with it. It also has to be emphasised, as you know very well, that this framework is only taken seriously by a tiny minority in the field, certainly in the United States. For example I very rarely give a talk in a linguistics department on any work of the past ten or fifteen years. If I talk about such things it is in philosophy departments or to literary people, but those are not technical talks. A lot of this material can be presented in a fairly informal and accessible fashion, and often I do. But I rarely go into the technical details with linguists, because there are very few who are interested. So in two respects I think hesitancy is in order. For one thing, I think one obviously has to be sceptical about whether his ideas are going in the right direction. I think they are, but it is certainly not obvious; I can easily understand that somebody would say they are not. The second is that it does not represent a major tendency within the field in statistical terms.

When did you realize for the first time that you were creating a new field rather than pursuing progress within the existing field?

As I have said, I do not really believe it now. My own feeling is that all of this work of the past twenty-five years is preliminary to a future conceptual revolution which I think we can begin to speculate about the vague outlines of. Although it is true that this work is quite remote from what was called "linguistics" twenty-five years ago. That is why I am at MIT, not at a university that had a tradition in linguistics. And it is why my first book was not published until twenty years after it was finished, in 1975.[5]

But still it is a fact that sociologically something is happening. There is a group of people who believe very strongly that they belong to this new scientific enterprise, and you are in the middle of that group.

---

4. Chomsky (1973).
5. Chomsky (1955).

To put it kind of crudely, it seems to me that normal science in linguistics still remains descriptive work of increasing sophistication. There is a tendency which one can discern, and that is the one that you are talking about. Some people are beginning to be concerned with the foundations of a truly unified explanatory theory. There are a lot of ways which you can go and lots of alternatives to be pursued, but it seems to me that you can begin to see pieces of it coming into focus. It seems to me that all of this is anticipatory. We will have a real major conceptual revolution when this kind of work reaches a sufficient degree of success and depth and comprehensiveness so that it simply becomes absurd not to pursue it. There may still be natural history and maybe even most people may be doing it, but that will be peripheral to the mainstream of the field. Now that has happened a couple of times in the sciences. For example, I suppose if you go back one hundred years, biology was overwhelmingly concerned with collection and arrangement of data and taxonomy and so on; and in fact statistically it is probably a small part of biology that has really assimilated itself to the natural sciences and become part of a really explanatory theory. I think linguistics has the best hope of moving in that direction of any subject outside of the core natural sciences. I think there is encouraging progress, particularly in the last ten years, but it certainly has not reached the level necessary to carry conviction among researchers, which is an interesting test, I mean not necessarily one that one should take too seriously, but an interesting test.

It appears that there is a real problem regarding the number of people who constitute the field. As you say the basis is very narrow and represents statistically only a small minority within linguistics. At the same time you are losing people very fast as you push the field forward. Is that good policy?

For one thing, I am not so certain about that. I think that that is a bit of an artifact. At least as I look back over my own relation to the field, at every point it has been completely isolated, or almost completely isolated. I do not see that the situation is very different now. In fact, I think it is hardly less true now than before. It seems to me that what is different now is that a good deal of the field from which I feel isolated happens to be comprised of former students, or their students, whereas previously it was just other linguists. But I cannot think of any time when the kind of work that I was doing was of any interest to any more than a very tiny fraction of people in the field. For example, there were people who felt that they could use transformations as another descriptive device, and that was popular if you like; but that was irrelevant to my interests. At least, just speaking very personally, my own interest has always been almost solely in the possibility of developing an explanatory theory. That was already true in *The Logical Structure of Linguistic Theory*.[6] The things that interested me in that book were for example the possibilities of getting explanations of properties of the auxiliary system and showing that the interaction of a few simple rules can account for the properties of complex embedded structures, passives, what is now called "control", and things of that kind. Those aspects of that work very rarely interested anyone. I think Morris Halle was the only linguist in the 1950s who I can remember who thought it was even worth pursuing. Until the late 1950s I was really working on it almost completely alone. By that time Hugh Matthews, Bob Lees and Ed Klima were working on it, later Paul Postal, Jerry Fodor, Jerry Katz and a few others. There were maybe twenty people in the world interested in doing this kind of thing. Well, you know, a few years later the overwhelming mass of linguists interested in transformational grammar at all were doing some kind of generative semantics and again the work that I was interested in was done by a very small minority. That carries you through the 1960s and then the 1970s. It has not really been that different. So I do not see any real change in this respect, the change is simply that the number of people working with more or less similar devices, or with a more or less similar target if you like, is much larger. In fact, I feel much less isolated now than I have in the past. There is far more material that I read with interest than was ever true in the past. Most of it comes from Europe, in fact, but there is a lot coming out that I am really eager to read which I did not find true in the 1960s.

The last full-scale opposition was from generative semantics, but that is virtually dead now. The rest of linguistics today doesn't define itself so clearly in terms of opposition to generative grammar, a few individual exceptions and a general emotional resentment aside, of course.

I am not sure that there is any such opposition now. At the time generative semantics offered, right or wrong, a different approach to similar problems. In its more recent versions I do not see that it is even dealing with the same problems. There are people who are, for example, lexical theorists who are dealing with many of the same problems. There, there is much common ground for discussion.

---

6. Chomsky (1955).

The situation is somewhat different in relation to the large number of people working on Montague grammar. They are doing a kind of descriptive semantics. Personally, I am not much interested in descriptive semantics. But I do not see any real issues in dispute. As far as relational grammar goes, I do not know what to say at this point, because I just do not understand it. I thought I understood it a couple of years ago, or at least understood some of the main ideas, but the work that I have seen recently, I cannot say that I understand very well. My general feeling about it, which may very well be incorrect because, as I say, I do not understand or follow it closely, is that it is informed by a rather pessimistic view of what can be done, the feeling that there are not going to be any far-reaching principles, and that therefore a kind of elaborate structure of basically descriptive generalizations is the most we can hope for.

Generative semantics has virtually disappeared, but if you take a look at the people who were generative semanticists, most or at least a large number of them are, as far as I can see in their work, committed to the idea that things are just too chaotic to expect any far-reaching explanations. I feel myself that there is a lot of hostility with regard to, say, a "Conditions"-like framework.[7] There is in the first place just a lack of interest or skepticism as to whether it is on the right track, which would certainly be reasonable. But what strikes me most, what has always struck me, is a kind of resentment, often rather unpleasant. I think it boils down to the point that many people do not believe and do not want to believe that there could be any far-reaching principled explanations for complex phenomena. There is a paper with a beautiful title, "The fall and rise of empiricism".[8] I think that the title of the paper captures a rather significant point about the nature of the field. There is a strong opposition to the idea that there might be abstract theories and principled explanations and deductive chains of arguments from principles that do not look like descriptions of phenomena. The almost inevitable tendency of people in the field when any such proposal is made is to try to shoot it down not to try to improve it or fix it or something like that. That is usually pretty easy, there is just so much unexplained data. Even if somebody came up with the absolute truth it would be easy to "demonstrate" that it is wrong because there are all kinds of data around that do not seem to fit, there is too much that we just don't understand. You can really divide linguists into two different types with regard to the way they

---

7. Chomsky (1973).
8. Katz and Bever (1976).

deal with ideas that are intellectually interesting, maybe wrong, but at least intellectually interesting, far-reaching, or bold, or something like that. There is one type whose immediate intuitive reaction is to look for counterexamples because they do not want to believe in such ideas; they are the overwhelming majority. There is another group, and it is a very small group of people, who see, what is usually true, that it does not work, and then try to either reanalyse the material, or change it, do something with it so that it will work in some domain. Take Luigi Rizzi's paper on *wh*-movement[9], there is a typical case. You consider the *wh*-island constraint and you look at Italian and it just refutes it, period. It seemed to me that it refuted it, and I was confused and surprised, but it just looked like a correct refutation. You could stop there, and most people would have, but he did not. He showed that, if you modify a few things, not only did Italian not refute the constraint and the proposed explanation for it in terms of subjacency, but in fact it supported it. Rizzi proceeded also to explain other things that nobody had thought of. That is a very rare attitude, and unless that attitude becomes a dominant attitude in the field, it still will not have undergone its intellectual revolution, because we can be certain that for a long time in the future it is always going to be possible to apparently refute any adventurous or bold ideas with unexplained data.

It is quite clear from what you say that you are pretty skeptical about the rate of progress within generative grammar and its acceptance within linguistics. For some reason you also think that the situation in Europe is better, in that respect, than that in North America. You suggest that the intellectual atmosphere in Europe is healthier. For us as European generativists who occasionally spend some time in the United States, that point of view is somewhat surprising. Could you be more precise?

It seems to me that there has been something strange happening in the United States which has aborted potentially constructive and creative work in the field. It is not that serious work is not being done; certainly it is. But I think it is not being done, by and large, in what seems to me at least to be the most important directions. One could say that that is my problem, but then again it is my judgment. Why that has happened I don't know. You can think of particular reasons that contributed to it. For example, take generative semantics. Generative semantics was a very

---

9. Rizzi (1978b).

appealing idea, especially to people who did not understand it very well, because if you did not understand it very well it seemed to be saying something very simple and intuitive, namely that there are meanings and there are sounds and there are rules relating them, and what could be more obvious than that? Of course, when you actually looked at technical Generative Semantics it did not have that property at all, because it had global rules[10] relating certain structures and other powerful devices. But at least at a superficial enough level it seemed to be saying an intuitively obvious thing: meaning is mapped onto sound. And for whatever reason it engendered a great deal of enthusiasm. For example, in the late sixties the overwhelming majority of young linguists working in generative grammar were working in generative semantics. When it collapsed, as it did almost totally, many people were greatly disillusioned, feeling that nothing could be done, because this was the only thing that could be done, and it collapsed. There were exceptions, but many people were caught up in that, and were, in a sense, paralyzed. Many people who had made a big commitment to it, and felt that it was the right way to work, came out with the conclusion that linguistics was just a game, that you could do anything you liked. That has been one of the factors that probably led to the situation in the United States.

There are others. For example, it is interesting to me to observe the popularity of Montague grammar, which I would call a type of descriptive semantics except that I think it is not semantics really, in the sense that it does not deal with the classical questions of semantics such as the relation between language and the world. In any event it is a technology we can learn to use and do many things with. It does not lead very far into the frightening area of general explanatory principles, and therefore it has a lot of appeal, as descriptive phonetics does. If people find that interesting, that is their privilege, but it does not seem to me to have any hope of leading to general explanatory principles. They have not been interested in work which I think does have that hope. As for the reasons, I have noticed a tendency, maybe this is characteristic of other places too, for a large proportion of the students who leave here to become very much divorced from any further work that goes on here. That has led to a feeling over the years, that anything goes.

There is not in linguistics a widespread understanding of what is taken for granted in the natural sciences, namely that theory is going to change if it is to stay healthy. I know for a fact, and you can find it in the litera-

---

10. Cf., among many others, Lakoff (1970, 1971), Postal (1972).

ture, that there are linguists who feel that they had to abandon the field because it changes all the time. That is an attitude that is unimaginable in the natural sciences. However, it is not uncommon in linguistics, and as long as you have that attitude, you cannot understand how it could be that a theory that was proposed, tested, and transcended was a contribution to the field. Many linguists feel that if a theory is proposed, tested and abandoned, or modified that shows that there is something wrong with the field.

One of the differences between Europe and North America is that in Europe we have GLOW.[11] *Is that symptomatic of the difference that you have in mind?*

I think what GLOW is doing is exactly right. GLOW has succeeded in bringing together the people who are doing the most active and exciting work in the field. It is a stimulating group with the right kind of internal contacts, lively meetings and so on. That is what a field ought to have. These things develop out of an objective need and they can't go further than the objective situation allows them to go. I would like to see an equivalent of GLOW in the United States, but I don't think the field is ready for it now, unfortunately.

Why not?

Well, because the kinds of topics that the GLOW-linguists tend to work on are not very lively in the United States. One thing about GLOW is that there is a sense of common purpose. People may have different ideas and approaches and so on, but one has a feeling from reading the papers and knowing the people that they think they're working towards a common goal, that they could learn from one another, that there has been progress, there could be more progress, that they can learn from somebody who is trying to make progress. There is a sort of a common enterprise.

---

11. GLOW, which stands for 'Generative Linguists in the Old Worlds', is an international, but largely Europe-based, association of generative grammarians. It was founded in 1977 during a conference on the issue of bounded vs. unbounded rules at the University of Amsterdam. Since then, its main activities have been the organization of an annual conference and the publication of a biannual newsletter.

The generative enterprise?

Yes, obviously some parts are going to be thrown away, and maybe the foundations will be thrown away, but still there is a detectable common enterprise.

We feel that the present situation in Europe has been partly brought about by GLOW. It is true that the active portion of GLOW shares a sense of common enterprise. That awareness of a common goal is partly spontaneous, but partly created by the existence of GLOW. The existence of GLOW forces people to decide where they stand, whether to actively participate or not. Couldn't one introduce something like GLOW in the United States as a similar type of catalyst?

When I think through the Universities here, I wouldn't know who to invite to a GLOW-type conference. There is a very small number of people working within something like the GLOW framework.

All of this doesn't go very far towards characterizing the difference in intellectual atmosphere between Europe and here.

Maybe it is a "grass is greener" phenomenon, but I think there is a difference. I just think that the quantity and the quality of work is different. There are several major centers where interesting and important work is going on: Italy and Paris and Holland. And in each area there are a reasonable number of people working together.

But the biggest group of them all is right here at MIT: you, some of your colleagues, and the students who work with you.

Our students are always very actively engaged in whatever work is going on here and contribute to it in important ways. What has struck me very much over the years is that former students are rarely engaged in the kind of work that is being done here after they're students. They are doing their work, we are doing our work, but they only partially relate. Now exactly why that is, is unclear. It is in this respect that there has failed to develop a notion of common enterprise. Actually, I think some other areas of generative grammar, or whatever you want to call it, have developed that, for example generative semantics. I think that the group of people around the Chicago Linguistic Society had a sense of common enterprise in the sense in which GLOW does. I don't think that is true anymore, probably not, but I think at one time they did. I don't know, I look at it from the outside, but it seems to me that it is also more or less true for Montague grammarians that there is a sense of common enterprise. They work on the basis of each others' results, at least a very large number of them. That field has those properties, but roughly the extended standard theory in the United States has not had those characteristics.

There is another recent phenomenon with respect to the way the field functions at the moment, and one, incidentally, which is common to Europe and the United States, viz. the large Sloan- and Max Planck-funds that flow into cognitive science. But most of the money goes to areas that are quite tangential to the interests of generative grammar.

It has been two or three years that the Sloan money here has been directed to cognitive psychology. There is a difference among people involved as to how they conceive of the field. I have always felt that work in linguistics is simply work in one domain of cognitive psychology, but that is certainly not the way the field is usually understood. Rather psychology, in particular cognitive psychology, is understood more as a study of processes than as the study of systems of knowledge and the growth of such systems. Some useful things have been done through the Sloan impact, but I don't think that has very much to do with linguistics.

You haven't tried very hard to convince them of your interpretation of cognitive psychology and of the way it ought to be done in your view.

I haven't tried very hard. I guess one of the reasons is that I don't think even my own colleagues are convinced, and in this sense I don't feel I have any right to try to convince the people with the money. I think that the only responsible thing for them to do is to support work as understood by the professional community. My own position is rather idiosyncratic in that. So I'm perfectly willing to express it; but I haven't tried to launch a big PR campaign about it.

But that is certainly not a logically necessary conclusion to draw from being isolated, is it?

Well, frankly I did not feel that way twenty-five years ago. Maybe it is age, I don't know.

At least you don't feel it is an ethically necessary point of view.

No, we used to do a lot to try to create some atmosphere in which we could work and our students could work.

Then what has changed?

You mean why don't I want to do it now? I guess I am just following other directions. Some of the ways in which the Sloan money has been spent seem to me very questionable. For example I don't see any point in all these conferences which just interchange the same people over and over again in different parts of the country. Also, while I think it's a good idea to have visiting scholars, I believe that the emphasis on that has been misplaced. My own feeling is that the most important thing that the field needs now is support for graduate students and the expansion of opportunities for young post-doctoral students. The field just needs that desperately, and compared to that, conferences are a very low priority. Paying senior people to visit another university, that's ok, but there are other ways to arrange a sabbatical.

One of our favorite games is the 'ideal department game', in other words pursuing the fantasy of being able to create a totally new department. Let's play the impersonal variant, because it wouldn't be fair to mention any names. What about the structure of an ideal linguistics department? What disciplines do we absolutely need, for example?

I've never felt myself that coverage of every aspect of what falls into the field is terribly important. It seems to me better to get a group of people who can create a research atmosphere of common enterprise. I think that's much more important than touching on everything. It's extremely hard for students if there is one person who is working intensively in some area and who is more or less disconnected from what other people in the department are doing. That makes things very difficult for the students, and also, I think, for the faculty themselves. You need a kind of interchange to work, most people do.

What do you consider to be the ideal training for a beginning graduate student in linguistics?

My feeling is that linguistics can be taught and should be taught for professionals at the graduate level. So what would be the best training to come into it? There are many different possibilities. For example, I think training in the natural sciences and mathematics is a very good background. Philosophy has for some people been a good background, and depending on what kinds of things you want to do, literature, or anthropology has been a good background, or psychology. I don't think there is a simple answer. It seems to me that people ought to have other interests, that linguistics is just too specific an interest. Maybe some of the best linguists in the world are just interested in linguistics, and if people go that way, well ok, it is a personal thing. It just seems to me that, at a kind of human level, one ought to have a broader range of concerns, of which a specialisation in linguistics would only be a part.

But that is true for most other fields too, isn't it?

This is a rather personal view. I wouldn't attempt to justify it, and don't see why others should take what I'm saying seriously. But since you ask, it seems to me that it would be rather strange just to work in some area of anthropology or history and nothing else. Also, I don't think our field is hard enough to require that. Maybe in some fields you just have to, I don't know, I doubt it. The really topflight scientists or mathematicians I've known don't seem to be that narrowly specialized, even in those fields where a firm grasp of an extremely difficult field is required.

Our field isn't hard?

It is hard but it need not be all encompassing. Again, these are matters of personal choice pretty much. I don't doubt that I would do better work in the field if I knew more about it. One makes one's choices about what is important.

When we were students, about ten years ago, it was very easily possible to have read virtually all of the literature; not everything on exotic languages, of course, but all the basic texts in generative grammar. There was a small number of books and a few articles, and that was it.

Yes, you can see the difference in teaching. It used to be possible, not too long ago, to teach from zero to current research, within a term or a year or so, but I don't really think that can be done anymore, which is very good, that's the way it ought to go.

But in most linguistics departments you simply can't give people that kind of training for purely practical reasons.

We have found here that even though most of our students do come with a fair linguistics training, we have to have a very heavy series of required courses. Very few students come through the program in less than four years, practically nobody, and that means more than two years of solid coursework which is only in linguistics. They don't take other things, and I don't think that there's redundancy. In fact there are other things that they ought to be taking, but they are not.

Is that why more and more students come to MIT after fairly extensive training in linguistics at the undergraduate level?

I think we are getting too many of our students from linguistics programs. I have been objecting to that in the department, but I think I may be a minority of one.

Your department gets lots of applications. Is it that there are too few applicants from other disciplines?

By now, very few; partly because there is a strong tendency to take people who have done virtually all of their work in linguistics. I think that is wrong, but that is what is happening. In the past, mathematicians and scientists were some of the very best students. And one thing that I'm a little bit disturbed about myself is this tendency for specialisation in linguistics at the undergraduate level in the USA. So, for example, many of our students, let's say fifteen or twenty years ago, were coming from other fields. But by now, most of them, I'd say almost all of them, come with a very extensive undergraduate training in linguistics, which seems to me very dubious really. The world is just too rich for people to spend both their undergraduate and graduate careers studying linguistics. I would say they should concentrate on other things as well.

So you are skeptical about having linguistics as an undergraduate major. But do you see any reasons for introducing linguistics at the high school level?

Actually, Wayne O'Neil and Ken Hale had some ideas about that at one point, even at the elementary school level. They were trying to use linguistics not so much to teach linguistics as to offer a way of teaching children a scientific method, that is ways of handling problems rationally, in a science-like fashion. They were arguing quite plausibly that in this case linguistics has an advantage over, say, chemistry in the sense that, first of all the data is more or less available to the kids and that they can get a good deal of insight into the data, and can learn something about what an explanatory theory is, or what explanation is, what research is, something of that kind. It certainly seems to me that the material is easily formulable at the level of high-school students. I've occasionally given talks for junior-high-school students. One can't do the most complicated and sophisticated things, but many of the basic ideas in the field can certainly be grasped at that level.

My only hesitation about it would be somewhat different. I think it might be a good idea to have material of this sort taught at the high-school level. On the other hand as I said, I'm very skeptical as to whether it ought to be an undergraduate major. I may actually be a bad person to say that, because I'm one of the very few people of my age who has an undergraduate degree in linguistics, although I didn't take many courses in it, in fact.

As far as linguistics in high school is concerned, might that not be premature in much the same way that the introduction of 'new mathematics' at the high school level may have been premature?

I think the partial failure of new mathematics had other roots, and that is that, in a certain sense, new mathematics tried to teach the ideas of modern abstract mathematics at an introductory level. Perhaps that can be done, but it's a very misleading way to approach mathematics. There's something right about the history of mathematics. Mathematics did develop out of certain kinds of concerns or interests, such as for example the nature of three-dimensional space, the nature of the number system and so on. Many of the ideas of modern mathematics are abstracted from those in a certain fashion. And I think that some of the "new math" undercut the intuitions, including the physical intuitions, that lie behind mathematical reasoning to a certain extent, perhaps to a greater extent than many active mathematicians would recognise. I saw examples of that with my own children, when they were learning Boolean algebra and things like that in elementary, school. It was very striking to see how they made the results come out by inventing completely wrong and even ridiculous concrete images. They would invent concrete models that happen to work in some cases as instances of the abstract system that they were being taught. I don't think that this shows that complicated materials can't be taught at an elementary level, but one has to be careful. I think, in a way, that "new math" – at least what I saw of it – reflected a somewhat superficial approach to mathematics in this respect. There has to be a connection between physical intuitions and some abstract ideas and I think if that can be done, then it can be taught successfully.

Going further and further away from the universities and teaching, let us think about the 'general public'. So far, it seems to us, generative linguistics has been sparsely and inadequately popularized.

There are various levels. For one thing, as far as the general academic or intellectual public is concerned, that's the type of popularisation that involves professional presentation of ideas at a fairly advanced level. As you know, I have tried many times to do that myself with whatever success. I think that at that level there is some interest and knowledge, but also some misunderstanding. It is certainly true that it could be done better than it has been done. As far as the general public is concerned, as you say, there's essentially nothing. I think that is unfortunate because I think that there are important things here, and there's an obvious and tremendous interest in language. All kinds of crazy nonsense about language gets tremendous publicity. I don't know what it is like in Holland, but here there has been a big fad about the decline of the language which has been going on since Shakespeare or whenever.

Weren't you invited once to the Dick Cavett show to talk about that topic?

That is a case in point.[12] That's the kind of thing that gets enormous interest, on television and in popular books. Everybody is worried about the decline of English. That reflects a type of interest in linguistic phenomena which is taken up in the most absurd ways, quite often. Or take all the talk about "ape language" which again has been a tremendous media hit although there's very little worth talking about as far as I can see. Again that shows that there is interest in the topics, and I don't see any reason why the interest couldn't be stimulated and responded to by the presentation of material that makes more sense. It's hard to do, however. There are some people who have tried to do it. Sometimes it has come out badly, I think. For example there were some attempts in the early

---

12. The invitation was declined.

1960s to teach transformational grammar at the school level. Paul Roberts did a series on that[13], I thought it was rather dubious. It was more or less a matter of teaching formal tricks. That's not the point really. What's very hard to get across is the question of why there is any point in any of this. That's the part that's hardest to explain, but the most important part.

In the popularization of the established natural sciences this question hardly ever arises, because the importance of those fields is taken for granted.

I suppose the question might arise if you talk about, say, high energy physics, and it does in fact, but you're right, in the natural sciences it's taken for granted by now that we are learning to understand something. However, outside the natural sciences, it is rightly not taken for granted. It's simply not so clear what the point is of a lot of work.

Can you successfully explain to the general public what your work is all about, why it is worth doing?

Much of the speaking that I do is actually more or less to the general public, I mean to the general educated public, and that does not seem too hard really. I think it's possible, even in an hour's lecture. I think I'd like to try some day, in fact, to do something more comprehensive along these lines.

Suppose someone like Asimov were to do a book about generative grammar, wouldn't that be in some sense the ultimate recognition of the field?

Just to give an indication of the market for it, British publishers have been putting out this Modern Masters series and the books that have to do with language apparently sell very well. For example, John Lyons' book[14] keeps being reprinted, I'm told. Clearly people want to know about such things. I think that's a kind of responsibility that the field ought to be more concerned with. I have no one in particular in mind, but somebody ought to be thinking about it. I think it is healthy for the field to ask whether what we're doing does have some point. And if it does,

---

13. Roberts (1967).
14. Lyons (1970).

then it should be possible to make it clear to people outside the field that linguistics is not just a series of arcane arguments, more and more involuted and internally directed, but that there really is some point to it. I think that's a question that professionals often don't ask, in many fields. In fields where it is sort of obvious, say molecular biology, you don't have to ask it, but in fields like ours, I think you really should.

For better or worse, the field of generative grammar is still centered to a very large extent around you and around your work. Hence, what you do and do not do has a very direct impact on the functioning of the field. Would the field be different today if you had decided not to devote a substantial part of your time and energy to political issues? And how would it be different?

What would the field have been like? I would have done different things. For example, there were things that I very consciously gave up at the time. In the mid sixties, I thought very seriously about how deeply to get involved in political activism, knowing that if I did, I would have to give up many things. I thought about which things I would give up, it did not happen accidentally. And this relates to several of your questions. I consciously gave up phonology and mathematical linguistics, and I virtually gave up anything in the history of ideas. I felt that those were topics that were more peripheral to my main concerns. But at the time I was very much interested in all of them. I do not know where it would have gone, but I certainly would have tried to keep up a more active involvement in them. I really abandoned them up to the point of barely reading about them.

Why is it that you retained syntax?

If I have to rank the topics that I would like to work on, that comes out first.

But you still wanted to do work on mathematical linguistics, for example.

Yes, there were a lot of interesting things. I am not sure it would have been productive. Maybe it was a good idea for me to drop it because what was happening was that the work was getting more and more remote from linguistics. But I was learning many things, and I found them intriguing. Take for example the work that appears in the *Handbook of*

Mathematical Psychology.[15] I have not been thinking about it since then, really, and I do not think it connects to linguistics much, but, at least personally, I would have been interested in keeping it up. However, I probably would have found that I am not a good enough mathematician to do the kind of work that had to be done. I really have no mathematical background. I never even took college courses. I literally never had anything beyond an elementary calculus course until graduate school.

So, one of the things I enjoyed about it was that I was learning some mathematics on my own. I am not sure that would have been useful, it was an expenditure of time and energy, but I think I would have done it anyway.

What will the field be like in the more distant future? Given your dominant position in the field at present, do you think it will be able to sustain itself without you, for example?

First of all, the field, any field, ought to be largely in the hands of younger people. That is where the interesting ideas are going to be coming from, and that ought to happen here too, and to a large extent that is what is happening. However, as I think I said before, my own sense of the field is that contrary to what is often said, it has not undergone any intellectual or conceptual revolution. It is only beginning to approach them. I think we are working in the preliminary stages of what might really be an important conceptual revolution. But someday it will happen, and I think we will know when it does. A test for when it happens is when these centrifugal forces, the pull towards descriptivism, lose their attraction. That will be the sign that the intellectual revolution is taking place.

---

15. Cf. Chomsky (1963a,b), Chomsky and Miller (1958), Chomsky and Schützenberger (1963).

Part II
On Grammar

Chapter 1
A Historical Perspective

Looking back on the history of the field one might roughly divide the development of transformational grammar into four successive periods each of which is introduced by an important piece of work presenting increasingly more general and unifying theories on the form and functioning of grammar: the LSLT-period, the Aspects-period, the Conditions-period, and finally the Government-Binding-period.[1] *One general pervasive line of thought throughout these successive theories was finding ways of constraining the transformational power, once it was shown in The Logical Structure of Linguistic Theory that linguistically significant grammars for natural languages needed devices whose power exceeded that of Phrase Structure Grammar. This program of research eventually led to a very impoverished and restrictive theory of transformational rules, the "move alpha" theory, where general and unifying conditions on form and function interact in a modular conception of linguistic structure to allow optimally general application of grammatical rules. As a starting point, let us take Aspects of the Theory of Syntax, perhaps the least spectacular of the four. What were its main contributions to this program?*

The things that seemed to me important in the Aspects-type framework were on the one hand developing a framework for a selectional and subcategorizational theory, that is a feature framework for categories. That was important and it was missing. It was a step towards X-bar theory[2] and led to some significant improvements in the theory of the base and the theory of the lexicon. The attempts in *Syntactic Structures* and *The Logical Structure of Linguistic Theory* to incorporate the lexicon as part

---

1. The intended references are as follows: *LSLT* = Chomsky (1955), *Aspects* = Chomsky (1965), *Conditions* = Chomsky (1973), *Government-Binding* = Chomsky (1981b). The more easily accessible and more widely known work characterizing the *LSLT*-period is Chomsky (1957).
2. The X-bar-theory seeks to formally incorporate the insight of the endocentric structure of phrasal categories in terms of notions such as head, complement, specifier, and projection. See in particular Chomsky (1970). Other important works on the subject are Emonds (1976) and Jackendoff (1977).

of the categorial component, which led to fantastic complications, could not have been right and that was rectified in the *Aspects* framework.

A second thing that seemed to me important was to notice, which I had not noticed before, that the T-markers of the LSLT-type theory in fact had the property of the strict cycle.[3] I guess it should have been obvious, but it had not been obvious to me. In fact, it was suggested by work of Fillmore's.[4] That led to the possibility of eliminating generalized transformations and developing a theory of the cycle to account for it. That whole structure, which again is a big simplification of the theory and made it look more like things in phonology too, raised the question of how general the principles are. Of course Aspects also incorporated some earlier work (in *Current Issues in Linguistic Theory*[5]) which later underwent quite a significant development, on conditions on rules: the A/A condition, recoverability of deletion and so on.

And then I think it was worth exploring the consequences of the Katz-Postal hypothesis[6], some of the consequences of which I think are correct. I think that the standard theory overstated them, but it overstated something that was in part true, namely that thematic relations are closely associated with base-generated structures. And then of course there was the whole methodological discussion of the first chapter. If I ever rewrote Aspects, I do not think that I would rewrite that discussion in almost any respect.

You would not rewrite it now, but could you have written it ten years before Aspects?

That chapter was basically written in the late 1950s, in fact in 1958–1959, around them. I spent a lot of time trying to rewrite *The Logical Structure of Linguistic Theory*. In fact I did rewrite about the first 7 chapters of it

---

3. Once a simplex sentence to which the singular transformations have already applied is embedded into another structure by a generalized transformation, no singular transformation can 'return' to that embedded simplex sentence. This is in effect the strict cycle property which, much later, plays an important role, both in syntax (cf. Chomsky (1973), Freidin (1978)) and in phonology (cf. Kean (1974), Mascarò (1976)).
4. Fillmore (1963). See also Chomsky (1965) chapter 3, p. 146.
5. Chomsky (1964).
6. See Katz and Postal (1964) and Fodor and Katz (1963). In essence, the Katz-Postal-Hypothesis says that deep structure is the only level of representation which determines meaning. In other words, if two surface structures differ in meaning they must have different deep structures associated with them. A strong version of this hypothesis leads directly to generative semantics.

completely. That revision never got published for various reasons. I completely rewrote the background parts and also redid many of the technical parts, improving them considerably. When I was asked to publish it in 1975, I thought for a while of using the revised version, but that was very hard to do because I had never gotten around to redoing the last two chapters along those lines. It was sort of obvious how to do it, but I had not done it, and I just could not fit them together and so I used the early version.

But then you hardly have any discussion of mentalism in Syntactic Structures. There is virtually no mention of, for example, the "faculté du langage", the projection problem in language acquisition, or competence systems of mature native speakers.

You know what *Syntactic Structures* was. It was course notes for an undergraduate course at MIT. Van Schooneveld[7] showed up here once and took a look at some of my course notes from the undergraduate course I was teaching and said I ought to publish it. Since it had not been published anywhere, I said, why not, and that is what *Syntactic Structures* was. In fact, *Syntactic Structures* is a very misleading book. What is misleading about it is the role that the discussion of automata plays in it, which, I think, has misled a lot of people. There is a natural progression there from finite automata to context-free grammars to transformational grammars, but it is a very misleading progression. In *The Logical Structure of Linguistic Theory* there is no talk about finite automata or weak generative capacity at all. In fact that discussion was put into *Syntactic Structures* because of the MIT-context. When I came to MIT in 1955 after finishing LSLT, I discovered that people really were euphoric, if that is the right word, about Markov processes. There was a tremendously strong feeling about this among engineers and psychologists and other prestigious types. Markov processes are an even narrower class (probabilistic features aside) than finite automata; they are K-order systems where you go back at most K symbols to determine, probabilistically, the next output. That was the special case that was being considered. The notion of finite discrete source seemed to offer a break-through. It was felt that these were going to be the fundamental concepts for the study of language and mind. And it was only for this reason that I ever started

---

7. A Dutch linguist who was associated with Mouton, the company which published many influential linguistics texts in the early period.

working on their formal properties. In *Syntactic Structures* this becomes a more or less central topic, because of the local MIT context – the notes were for MIT students – but it was really a very peripheral one.

What you are saying is that irrespective of the mathematical properties of these finite automata you decided that something along the lines of transformational grammar had to be pursued in order to arrive at the types of explanation that you were after. But then, what made you take an interest in finite automata?

I became interested in finite automata after LSLT was finished, because of the remarkable claims that were being made with regard to the relevance of finite automata and Markov sources for the study of language and psychology more generally. In fact, it was pretty clear that one might reasonably think of finite automata as constituting something like the outer limits of what might be called "a behaviorist theory" (something of the sort was proven by Patrick Suppes about 10 years later[8]) and they could even incorporate ideas offered in critique of narrow forms of behaviorism for example Lashley's[9] critique. So it was of some interest to determine the properties and intrinsic limits of these systems. By the late 50s I did some work which produced some results in mathematical linguistics that I think may be of some linguistic interest, that is, the work on the relationship between context-free grammars and push-down storage automata. What that in effect shows is that anything you can do with a context-free grammar, which is, if you are interested in just covering data, virtually anything, you can also do with a left-to-right automaton with a pushdown memory. In a sense that leads to a principled answer to the parsing problem. That is not very interesting. It does not answer any of the real questions at all, because neither of these two strongly equivalent systems offers any hope, as far as I could see then or now, for dealing with the real problems that have to be accounted for, for example, to take a simple case, why interrogatives and negations break up auxiliaries in the same way. I am sure you can describe it in these terms, but why does it happen? Or why do you get the funny distribution of gaps that we now call control in embedded clauses, for example?

---

8. Suppes (1969).
9. Lashley (1951).

Still there are people who seem to be attracted to the idea that context-free grammars suffice to deal with the properties of natural language, both along the dimension of weak, and along that of strong, generative capacity. Gazdar, for example, in some of his recent papers expresses this line of thought.[10]

I have not read Gazdar's dissertation[11], so maybe I do not quite understand what he is doing. What I have seen of his work on context-free grammars seems to me to be based on a misunderstanding. People often say, I have noticed this in recent papers,[12] that if you can get down to one transformation, say 'move alpha', then an even better theory would be to get down to no transformation at all. Superficially, that sounds right, but it is completely wrong. It is only right if other things remain constant, and in fact in Gazdar's theory other things definitely do not remain constant. He vastly increases the number of possible grammars up to a class of grammars that generate context-free languages, which is a radical enrichment of the theory hence a huge step backwards. His theory does not seem radically different from what was in my *Morphophonemics of Modern Hebrew*[13] back in the late 40s. That was a phrase-structure grammar with a lot of indices, which you could recode as a context-free grammar if you wanted to. What is sometimes not recognized is that such devices vastly increase the class of grammars available. They may have the weak generative capacity of context free grammars, but that is a fact of almost null significance. I think that the reason that that is not seen is because people are misled, as I said before, by the hierarchy of weak generative capacity of grammars. If finite automata have narrowest weak generative capacity, and if context-free grammars have more generative capacity, and if transformational grammars have a still greater one, and if you think that gives you the hierarchy or preferability of grammars, then it will seem a step forward to move from transformational grammars to the lower level of context-free grammar. However, it is not if you think in terms of the class of accessible grammars in the sense we discussed earlier, the sense discussed in *Aspects*.[14] That is the only relevant question. If you allow yourself the class of contextfree grammars, including those coded with indices, then that is just a huge mass of possible systems as

---

10. See Gazdar (1981), Gazdar (forthcoming). For a recent reaction, cf. Williams (1981b).
11. Gazdar (1979).
12. See, for example, Bresnan (1978), Brame (1978), Brame (1979).
13. Chomsky (1951). Cf. also Harman (1963).
14. Chomsky (1965), chapter 1, pp. 60–62.

compared with for example X-bar theory with 'move alpha' added to it. Therefore, the conceptual basis of that approach is wrong to start with, quite apart from the fact that we discussed earlier, namely, that theories of the sort that we have been considering for the past 10 years or so allow only a finite number of possible core grammars anyway (apart from the lexicon), so that all of these questions dissolve.

Suppose someone claims that knowledge of language can be adequately represented by a subclass of finite state transducers which in addition deal satisfactorily with troublesome phenomena in some domain of performance such as multiple center-embedding. Would that not be an interesting position that could have a bearing on some conception of the competence-performance dichotomy? The claim would be then that finite state transducers absorb the whole of linguistic competence?

Well, that has been known for a long time. What was known by the early 1960s was that you could account for this in terms of a finite state device with a single push-down tape.[15] In fact it gave you qualitatively the right results; that is, if you put any finite bound on the push-down tape, you will get a finite bound on the amount of intelligible center embedding, which is more or less right. As you get more time, more space and so on, you can go on more or less without limit. In fact that was known in essence by the late 50s. One could think of the push-down storage automaton as a representation of some kind of competence, and of the finite bound as reflecting some variable performance constraint. But this has very little to do with serious problems in the study of language.

You claim, then, that these approaches are not likely to give interesting insight into the properties of anaphora, control, or movement the way transformational grammar does. So you argue in effect for the priority of studying systems of knowledge over the study of systems of performance. What possible linguistic interest would you expect that the study of finite state parsers holds?

It is obvious, in some sense, that processing systems are going to be represented by finite state transducers.[16] That has got to be the case, and it is

---

15. Cf. Miller and Chomsky (1963), Miller and Isard (1964).
16. For a recent argument, cf. Krauwer and des Tombe (1981). See also Langendoen (1975, 1979).

possible that they are represented by finite state transducers with a pushdown tape. That is a plausible sort of memory: maybe you need two pushdown tapes, which carries you up to Turing machines, as in an augmented transitional network (ATN) system.[17] But then, that leaves all the questions exactly where they were. That just says, we can now explain what kinds of things are always going to be filtered out, whatever the parsing system is like, namely center embedding. But that leaves quite open the question of what is the internal organization of the system of knowledge. It just says whatever it is, it is going to have to be passed through a finite state device with a certain kind of memory and therefore it will have certain properties.

Let us turn now to the surface-oriented approaches to problems of language. These do away with transformations altogether.[18] *Instead, they base-generate all grammatical sentences of the language, making crucial use of the filtering function of the lexicon and some operations on lexically encoded functional structure. It is their claim that they offer real explanations for linguistic problems. Do you feel they do?*

I think not. Let us take VP-analyses for example. It seems to me that the question is how impressed one is going to be by the fact that the kind of VP that can appear without a subject is exactly the kind of VP that can appear with an overt subject that obeys conditions on anaphora, the conditions on reciprocals and pronouns. If one is not impressed by that fact, then we can have VP-complements with some rule to determine subjects. On the other hand if one is impressed by the fact that the set of structures which allow empty elements is exactly the set that allows overt elements which have anaphoric interpretations of varied sorts, disjoint reference and the like, and if you are impressed enough by that fact to look for an explanation then you will pursue a different direction. More generally, the question is how impressed we are by the fact that the properties of gaps can be explained if we take them to be anaphors, pronominals, and namelike expressions of the sort corresponding to their semantics. So it seems to me again that the choice is between the belief, if you like, that there are going to be explanations for patterns that are alike in different parts of the language, which leads you directly to postulate an empty cat-

---

17. See Kaplan (1972, 1975), Wanner and Maratsos (1978), Woods (1973, 1978).
18. See the references given in footnotes 10 and 12. Cf. also Koster and May (1982) for a recent critique.

egory which is an anaphor, pronominal, or variable, or alternatively just the belief that these phenomena are accidental, and that they are just not interesting. It could be that people who are just giving a description are correct. Maybe there is no explanation, maybe the patterns are just historical accident. That always could be. The real question is, where are you looking, what kind of commitments are going to guide your research? For me the field would completely lose interest, I would see no point in studying grammar, if it did not turn out that there were a unifying, rather abstract explanatory theory. My feeling is that for many linguists that is completely untrue and in fact the opposite is true.

It seems to us that these surface approaches have one interesting characteristic in common: they are all claimed to be more 'realistic' models of mental representation. Do you understand why they should be?

Well, I think that reflects a parallel tendency in psychology, parallel to what we have been talking about in linguistics. My feeling is that it runs through all of intellectual history and that the Galilean revolution and its consequences in the natural sciences are perhaps the unique exception. By now they are so important and powerful that we tend to think of them as the norm, while in fact a very natural tendency in scholarship and science and so on, is to taxonomy. The same is true with regard to the work on intellectual history that we were talking of before.[19] The easiest way to be a scholar is to learn a lot of facts and to investigate connections, instead of trying to understand what people are talking about, what they are driving at, which often they do not express clearly and do not have the terms or concepts to express, and trying to look at ideas because of their interest or their potential interest given the way they might have developed, trying to imagine how these very same persons might have developed their ideas with better tools. That is hard, it is not considered scholarship. In fact it is considered as some kind of imaginative literature. Very much the same has been true in the sciences for a long period and it probably still is in most of them. The hard descriptive work where you have fairly clear data and you arrange it, and so on, that is in a sense intellectually easy. I do not mean to say it is not hard to do; you have to work hard. It is only since the revolutions in the physical sciences in the 17th century basically, that there has been something really different in the world of ideas. Psychology is a case where it simply has not happened very broadly.

---

19. Cf. the beginning of Part I, chapter 3.

In fact it is very interesting to observe that in textbooks on psychology, for example, or in the literature in general, even the technical literature, people distinguish psychology from linguistics in terms of whether it deals with performance models or with the structure of a system of knowledge. So if something deals with performance models, then it has to do with psychology, with psychological reality and so on. If it deals with the structure of systems of knowledge, that is systems of competence, then it is some other field, linguistics or whatever. If you can extract yourself from the tradition, it is a very weird idea. It is as if you were to say the way a bird flies is biology but the structures that permit flight are not biology, that is some other field. It is absolutely suicidal for a field to define itself the way psychology of language almost invariably does, as dealing only with processes but not with the structures that might enter into them, or to deal with the observed stages of growth and development, but not with the systems that underlie them. I think that the reasons for this absolutely suicidal tendency are probably the same as the ones we have talked about before. The alternative requires a leap of the imagination, being willing to contemplate systems that are not overtly displayed, and that is just not a move that many psychologists are willing to make.

It is very interesting to look at what has happened in the study of language acquisition in the last ten or fifteen years for example. Again we find the same drift, the fall and rise of empiricism. By now most of the studies, at least the ones I see, are concerned with phenomenology, with surface effects, what you can observe in interactions between parents and children, or speech acts, all sorts of things that have no structure beneath the overt manifestations. That is considered a major innovation and revolution in the field. Well, it is in fact again a drift back towards the norm. There was a slight tendency to go away from it, it was very hard. The earlier experiments probably did not work, you could not expect them to, and they were not going to, and the theories were too weak and so on; then the natural thing is just to drift back towards the norm which is description, some kind of description, and also description that does not idealize. For example, a very strong tendency in all of these fields, I think, is to say that it is a mistake to study systems in abstraction. I just happened to look into a book, one of the thousands of books that are sent here by publishers, which happened to have a laudatory comment by Jerry Bruner on the backcover. So I opened it, and looked at it. It was a book about the growth of the mind of a child, or something like that. It was very critical of language acquisition device (LAD) type approaches to language acquisition because it said that they dealt with the child as if it was an abstract entity, there was no blood flowing through its veins, as if it was just a mechanism, so it was very heartless. That represents an extreme form of anti-intellectualism that holds that if you try to abstract to a system with certain properties, and you do not look at the whole complexity of reality, there is something fundamentally wrong with what you are doing, and that it is just the phenomena of the world that we ought to be studying and that it is wrong or immoral to look for explanatory theories and systems, abstract systems that enter into them somehow.

By now all competing approaches of theoretical linguistics seem to agree on one goal: reduction of transformational power. This has been a pervasive characteristic throughout the history of transformational grammar, resulting in the "move alpha" transformational schema. Some linguists seem to have been overzealous in carrying out this program to the limiting case, reduction to zero of transformations. Is the total elimination of transformational theory the logical conclusion of this program, or is this last move one step too far?

As for the reduction of transformational power, as I see it, what is actually happening is that there has been no reduction of the scope of transformations. Some changes have occurred over the years, but fundamentally very little, as far as scope is concerned. It is just that the available descriptive apparatus for formulating transformations has been very sharply reduced. Not the phenomena for which they are relevant, but rather the available rules have been radically restricted. The range of possible transformational grammars has been sharply reduced, rightly or wrongly, by abstracting conditions and principles which don't then have to be formulated in rules.

I think there have been a couple of misunderstandings connected with this. Two I may mention specifically. One is that when you move to trace theory, then there is an immediate alternative to transformational grammar, or an apparent alternative to the use of transformations, namely a system with base-generated gaps (trace) plus an interpretive rule which relates an item to its trace in the manner in which the movement rule would move the item from its trace position to the antecedent position. In fact that possibility was noted in my 1973 paper "Conditions on Transformations".[20] It is sort of obvious that as soon as you have trace theory, there's going to be this apparent notational variant. Then the question

---

20. Chomsky (1973).

arises: is it more than a notational variant? I don't think that is clear. The difference between these two theories is probably rather subtle. It's not easy to find empirical differences between them. They may exist, you can think of possible differences, but the most important fact is that the movement rules, or maybe equivalently the interpretive rules that do the job of the movement rules, appear to have significantly different properties from other interpretive rules. That seems to me the crucial point, and that seems to be true. That's true whichever of the two variants you pick.

At the end of "Conditions on Rules of Grammar",[21] there is some speculation that it could be that these two models that we are working with are too concrete for the data at hand, that transformational grammar or this alternative are just two ways of working out the same more abstract system, in the sense in which the rotations of a figure in a plane constitute one of a number of ways of realizing the principles of group theory. We always have to ask what the proper level of analysis for a given field is. If you are studying, say, the development of physical organs, the proper level of analysis is one that disregards atoms and electrons. If you are looking at the level of atoms and electrons, you wouldn't be able to say that there are things like arms, because you couldn't find them in those terms. So every field of study must identify its proper level of description somehow, which is not a trivial question by any means. And it's harder to do it when you don't have physical intuitions to guide you. We don't, and it could be, for example, that a theory like transformational grammar is at too low a level of abstraction, and that the proper theory is at the level at which you identify the properties of movement rules like subjacency in contrast to the properties of interpretive rules that violate subjacency, and various other properties. That could very well be true. If that's right, then the two theories we were just talking about, transformational grammar and the interpretive theory, are really equivalent. They would be as equivalent from the point of view of linguistic theory as rotations in a plane and addition of numbers are equivalent from the point of view of group theory. They are just two ways of working out the same principles. On the other hand one should not very quickly jump to that conclusion, I think, because there are possible differences. It is possible to imagine that someday we will understand exactly what those differences are. Well, that is one kind of misinterpretation, there's an apparent way to eliminate transformations, which is not a

---

21. Chomsky (1976), reprinted in Chomsky (1977b). For further discussion, cf. Koster (1978), Chomsky (1980: chapter 4). Chomsky (1981b: chapter 2.4; 6).

real way; it's just a way of calling a transformation something else, you're calling transformations interpretive rules that meet subjacency etc.

Another misinterpretation is a more serious one, which I've seen in a number of papers, and which I believe is implicit in a lot of recent work. That is that if you can reduce the number of transformations to one, why not reduce them to zero? And wouldn't that be even better? Well, *prima facie* it sounds as if it ought to be better. It is obviously better to reduce them from many to one, the reason why it is better being that it reduces the class of grammars. So then if it's better for that reason to reduce them from 100 to 1, why isn't it still better to reduce them from 1 to 0? And the answer is: yes, it would be better if everything else remained constant. That is, if you go from 100 transformations to 1 transformation, while enriching the interpretive part of the theory, that is allowing more alternatives there, then you haven't achieved anything. The only reason why it would be an achievement to go from a hundred to one is that you're not increasing the variety of grammars in some other part of the theory. And here we have to be careful about the notion "enriching". It is OK to enrich the rest of the theory by adding more principles. In fact, that's fine, as long as the enrichment doesn't increase the number of grammars accessible given fixed data. But any enrichment that does you want to avoid, for explanatory adequacy at least. So the reduction from large numbers of transformations to small numbers, maybe one transformation, is progress if the theory of grammars doesn't enrich variety in some other way. And the same would be true for the reduction of one transformation to no transformation. On the other hand the actual proposals that have been made, like Gazdar's for example, vastly increase the number of grammars available. They increase it in fact to a collection of grammars with the weak generative capacity of all context-free grammars, a huge increase in the number of possible grammars, for reasons we have already discussed. I think that the reason for this misunderstanding is that there is much confusion about the significance of the notion of weak generative capacity. It has almost no linguistic significance. From the point of view of the mathematical theory of phrase structure, context-free grammars have a very natural place in some kind of a natural hierarchy, but that is almost irrelevant in these discussions, since the class of context-free grammars is far too broad a class to be considered seriously as a candidate for linguistic theory. And the much more highly organized, and specialized grammars of, say, the EST type, with an X-bar base, the rule "move alpha", various principles on rules and interpretations and so on, form a far narrower class in terms of the only dimension that counts, namely the availability of grammars for fixed data.

Frankly, my expectation is that the study of enriched phrase structure grammar will run its course through the rediscovery of a form of X-bar theory and transformations (perhaps through the device of "metagrammar") and of conditions on rules and representations, with something like a convergence with earlier work, before too long.

But now one could present the following argument. Since it would be ideal to limit the class of accessible grammars to a finite set, and since the lexicon can be argued to be finite for maybe uninteresting reasons, a model of grammar that consists of only a lexicon would be optimal from the learnability perspective.

I don't think that the issue of finiteness arises because the class of grammars incorporating "move alpha" is also finite in the same sense. It is only the lexicon that may permit unbounded variety in principle. Other questions arise. One kind of question is how the alternatives fare in dealing with problems of explanatory adequacy. For example the question of why you have infinitivals without subjects but not tensed sentences without subjects in English-type languages. Why is that? And is that more than fortuitously related to the fact you have infinitivals with anaphoric subjects but not tensed sentences with anaphoric subjects, and so on? Those are the real issues to look at.

In Current Issues it was argued that general conditions would allow only one application of wh-movement per sentence. Aspects gave you the generalized base marker with the notion of the strict cycle. It seems therefore, that everything was there already to connect the 'one-wh-movement-per-S-condition' with the 'Comp-to-Comp' corollary of Subjacency. That is, the theory of island-conditions might arguably have been skipped. Still it took the field six years to realize this. Was Ross's island theory[22] an indispensable catalyst in bringing about the Conditions-framework?

He started off by looking at deficiencies in the conditions that were proposed in the 1964 paper and then went on from that to develop the island theory, which was a very important step, I think. Ross's work made it possible to rethink conditions, to see whether one could deal with the kinds of phenomena that he was working on in a unified way. His disser-

---

22. Ross (1967).

tation is a little bit like Kayne's book[23], in that every time you look at it there is more material, new ideas, new data and so on.

What Ross's dissertation really did, and which was not done in *Current Issues* was to make it very clear that there was going to be a theory of conditions. *Current Issues* contained some proposals about some weird things, but Ross's work, I think, made it very clear that these were not just some weird things but that these were going to be the essence of the field, and that the main problem would then be to explain them. I think Ross's dissertation was a tremendous step forward in bringing in a vast range of materials and giving a rational analysis of them. Well, I think it is a real classic.

Earlier in this conversation we mentioned some of what could be considered major landmarks on the road to truth since The Logical Structure of Linguistic Theory. We discussed Aspects of the Theory of Syntax, Current Issues, Constraints on Variables in Syntax, and it was argued that this last work served as a precursor for the Conditions-theory. What is the next important landmark?

I think Richard Kayne's book should be specifically mentioned. It was a far-reaching and comprehensive analysis of a language, on the basis of very interesting ideas. It is almost unique in that respect, and had a major impact on subsequent work.

Conditions on Transformations clearly introduced a new era of linguistic theorizing with notions such as conceptual unification and deductive depth being keywords. How do you feel about the Pisa -framework?[24] *Is that a major break-through, comparable to Conditions?*

I have a sense myself that it is a qualitative improvement, although I think that it is maybe too early to tell, because there are too many things that have not fallen into place yet. It is in part an attempt to try to develop the kind of deductive structure for the binding theory that the *Conditions*-framework tried to do for the bounding theory.[25] Thinking of the

---

23. Kayne (1975).
24. See the explication in the preface, including footnote 2.
25. 'Binding theory' refers, essentially, to the set of principles incorporating the specified subject constraint and the tensed S constraint of Chomsky (1973) and revisions in Chomsky (1976, 1980b). 'Bounding theory' represents the subjacency condition of Chomsky (1973), with further elaboration in Chomsky (1977a).

period from *Conditions on Transformations* through "On *wh*-movement"[26] at least, the theory developed, right or wrong, a limited deductive structure, with some principles like subjacency that had interesting consequences. The binding theory on the other hand, was more or less descriptive. The Pisa framework is an attempt at further unification, deriving properties of binding from simpler principles and extending a more unified theory to new domains. This is only a bare beginning.

Take for example Kayne's recent work which further tries to relate the theory of government and the bounding theory: to relate subjacency and the Empty Category Principle[27]. If that worked out, that could be a further step in a similar direction. Or take Jan Koster's effort to bring together subjacency and elements of the binding theory,[28] if that works out in some fashion, that would be a further step. I am not convinced it works out, but there is something to it. There are unexplained similarities and overlaps between subjacency, the whole notion of bounding, and elements that are showing up in the binding theory, and some of these redundancies are probably an indication that something is wrong. Much of this has yet to be understood. For example Guglielmo Cinque has very interesting material on extraction from noun phrases in Italian which seems to show that, descriptively, *wh*-movement out of noun phrases is governed by something like the specified subject condition.[29] That is, if you pull out something which is in the domain of something which it is reasonable to call the subject, although it is not structurally obvious that it is one, then it is no good. But that should not happen, according to the current theories at least, because *wh*-movement leaves behind a variable which should act like a name by the binding theory, and that is paradoxical since variables are not constrained by the specified subject condition. These paradoxes have been very fruitful in the past, and I imagine this one will be when it is understood and it may indicate some way in which these theories are to be deepened.

---

26. Chomsky (1977a).
27. See Kayne (1981b). The Empty Category Principle (ECP), developed in Chomsky (1981b), is a principle restricting the distribution of empty elements in syntactic representations.
28. Cf. Koster (1978).
29. Cinque (1980).

Yes, that is very weird. One would naturally have expected wh-movement to be subject to subjacency-like conditions, but not to the conditions that NP-movement is subject to.

It is not quite working out that way, which I think indicates that there is something to be understood. But what we are waiting for is more unifying principles that will bring together things like subjacency and the binding theory and the empty category principle and so on. For example, the empty category principle stands out a bit like a sore thumb in this framework. I suspect that is what motivated some of Kayne's recent work. What ought to be dealt with is this hazy feeling that is beginning to emerge that a lot of these principles serve to uniquely identify certain items, particular empty items but also overt ones. So we have unique thematic role, unique case assignment, unique proper government, and so on. All of that probably reflects some kind of principle yet to be discovered. I think that this aspect of that framework is a very promising one, but one has to wait to see how the pieces fall into place. I feel about it pretty much the way that I thought about Conditions in 1970, when it was written, though by now the theory is considerably more advanced and successful. As it turned out then, a lot of the initial suggestions were wrong. I mean, the scope of the conditions was wrongly identified. I tried to cover too many things in them that did not belong and left out things that did belong. I would imagine that that is going to turn out for this framework too.

You suggested that from Conditions to On Wh-Movement was one coherent step, and now in a sense you are anticipating that the Pisa-theory will initiate another such coherent line of research. On Binding was presumably the trait-d'union between the two.[30] However, the Filters and Control paper[31] stands out like a sore thumb, doesn't it? People think of the Filters theory in a very different way than they do of the Conditions-framework or of the Binding-theory.

Personally, I think the whole filters business was an important stage for me for a number of reasons. For one thing – let us not discuss the control part of it and just talk about filters – it is a fact that they could apparently reduce properties of ordering, interaction, and complex structural de-

---

30. Chomsky (1980b).
31. Chomsky and Lasnik (1977).

scriptions of transformational rules to just a property of the output, and in fact one that was sort of localized and had to do with complementizer structure. That, I think, was an important step forward towards what was an obvious objective, namely a general rule schema "move alpha" for the transformational component. Secondly, one of the most interesting parts of that paper I thought, was the discussion of the *that*-trace filter which provided an explanation for some version of Perlmutter's generalization.[32] And thirdly, the NP-to-VP filter which in a rather intriguing way accounted for the properties of infinitival relatives and other structures.

Now as far as the *that*-trace was concerned, I do not think it stands up as it was formulated. It seems to me that it was the right move for the time and it set off extremely interesting work by Taraldsen and Kayne and Pesetsky and some other people.[33] By now I think that this work has become an interesting subfield in itself, trying to figure out which properties cluster together. I think that the formulation of the *that*-trace filter essentially did its work, namely it raised a question that had to be answered: how does this relate to the nominative island condition?[34] Maybe Taraldsen was the first person to take up the challenge really. That work has been very productive. Much of the Pisa framework, for example, originated in a reconsideration of Taraldsen's ideas on the *that*-trace filter and the nominative island condition.

As far as the NP-to-VP filter is concerned, its effects could be explained in terms of case theory, as Jean-Roger Vergnaud suggested in correspondence proposing ideas that turned out to be very fruitful.[35] It was not obvious; I did not see it until he pointed it out. It was something that emerged directly from the way in which material was being presented in the *Filters*-type-framework. I think it was an important stage, and a clarifying one. What the ultimate story will be with regard to filters

---

32. The generalization, which Perlmutter formulated in his (1971) book, was that the *that*-trace effect (exemplified by the contrast between *Who do you think that left* vs, *who do you think left*) typically shows up in languages that require a lexical subject, but not in languages that don't, i. e. so-called PRO-drop or null-subject languages.
33. Cf. Taraldsen (1980), Kayne (1981a), Pesetsky (1982).
34. The nominative island condition, a reformulation of the tensed S constraint, states, essentially, that a nominative NP, i. e. the subject of a tensed clause, is unavailable for transformational or interpretive relations. In other words, it cannot be extracted from its clause and it cannot contain anaphors that require an antecedent. The *that*-trace filter says something very similar, viz. that extraction from the position right next to a lexical complementizer such as *that* is not possible.
35. Originally in an open letter to Chomsky, dated April 17, 1977. Cf. also Vergnaud (forthcoming) and Rouveret and Vergnaud (1980).

I do not know. It is striking that conditions on output appear to have a powerful effect on constraining the operation of rule systems.

Rather than say a theory of the format of rules and their functioning?

We are perhaps being carried away with success. I imagine we will get back to theories of more structural rules sooner or later, but I think it is worth pursuing the extreme possibilities.

How does Subjacency fit in the recently developed Government-Binding framework?

Well, I have not had any really new ideas about it for some time. It seems to me that it is plausible to suggest that subjacency is in fact precisely a property of movement rules. In my view it is becoming clear that it is not a property of other rules. Again there are serious problems there. One of the problems is that extraction from NP does not correlate as smoothly as one would like with some of the other movement constraints. I do not know what the reason for that is, maybe it is a different phenomenon, maybe I was wrong in trying to generalize, maybe there are some other factors that have not been understood. And then of course there are other languages, Swedish-like languages, for example, as studied in Engdahl's recent work.[36] I do not understand what is happening there. I think that just has to be worked out.[37]

It could be argued, perhaps even plausibly so, that linguistic theory is quite unlike the natural sciences in that the total number of classical problems that linguists are working on is rather limited. Isn't it an uncomfortable shortcoming of the field that there are too few classical problems to work on?

Too few classical problems? I guess the answer to that would be yes if there was no more work to do on the existing classical problems, if research were somehow being impeded by the shortage of problems, if it were hard to find research topics in exciting areas. I do not feel that that is true. It seems to me that there is a range of problems where intriguing

---

36. Cf. Engdahl (1980).
37. For some recent contributions, see Taraldsen (1981), Engdahl (1981), Chomsky (forthcoming).

questions keep arising and sometimes get answered, and where the answers raise new questions and so on. Surely it would be better to have more, but I do not know what the right number is. It seems to me that the right number of problems is a number which suffices to keep active research going.

Would you not agree that for better or worse the present classical problems are those problems really that you have decided to think about?

I do not really think that is true. I do not feel that way. There are plenty of cases where other people have started major lines of research. Take, for example, the *wh*-island condition, which has inspired quite a lot of work and has led to all sorts of developments.[38]

But that is a bad example. The Wh-Island condition was first suggested in Current Issues. In Ross's dissertation it was only mentioned in passing in the context of his discussion of the A-over-A-principle, and then it was not until your Conditions-paper that it was taken up again.

Well, not really. As a general condition it was really formulated by Ross. Sure, people had thought about it before: there were some examples of limitations on *wh*-movement in *The Logical Structure of Linguistic Theory*, but they were just examples, they did not fall into a pattern. In a sense no one person ever discovered anything but I think that the discovery that there were a number of patterns to these phenomena was at least made explicit in Ross's dissertation in a way that it had not been done before. Or to take another example which has been tremendously fruitful, take Perlmutter's observations about missing subjects and the complementizer constraint.[39] That has become a classical problem. It didn't look like a classical problem at the time, in fact it just looked like an odd observation. But the point is, very often odd observations have a way of becoming classical problems when people begin to think about their impli-

---

38. An early mention is found in Chomsky (1964) and Chomsky (1968). The classical point of reference is Ross (1967). Some later highlights include: Kuno and Robinson (1972), Chomsky (1973), Chomsky (1977a), Rizzi (1978b), Van Riemsdijk (1978a,b). Many of the contributions to *Linguistic Inquiry* 9,4 deal with the issue, in particular Den Besten (1978), Kayne and Pollock (1978), Milner (1978b), Taraldsen (1978), all of them contributions to the 1977 GLOW conference in Amsterdam. For some recent discussions, cf. Sportiche (1981), Reinhart (1981).
39. See footnote 32, 33, 34. For more recent work, see in particular Jaeggli (1980, 1982), Borer (1981), Aoun (1981), Rizzi (1982), and Chomsky (1981).

cations. Or take Jeffrey Gruber's work on thematic relations[40] which did look like an odd offshoot at the time. I remember I wasn't particularly interested in the topic, but it has certainly led to important investigations. Or, take for example the work on Romance causatives and clitics that derives from Kayne's book. That has proved to be a very rich area of research with all kinds of implications.[41] That has become a classical problem. But should there be more classical problems in Romance? Well, maybe, but it would be nice to see that one put away.

The set of linguistic phenomena that have held your attention over the years has been very varied. Yet there is only a quite small set of truly recurrent themes: Wh-movement, NP-movement, bound anaphora, disjoint reference, Pro, and a few other. Other topics such as extraposition, the structure of AUX, Gapping, V-movement, or VP-deletion are conspicuously absent from this list of evergreens. Is there a rational explanation for this bias? Take Gapping, for example. Since Ross started the discussion there has been an ample literature on this topic.[42] Is it your belief that the analysis of these gapping phenomena does not hold equal promise for theoretical linguistics?

I simply don't know what the answer is. I work on some problems where I seem to have some ideas, and I don't have many ideas about gapping. Also, the periods in which I've been specifically working on grammar are scattered in my own work. For example, in the early fifties, I was working extensively on grammar, virtually nothing else. *The Logical Structure of Linguistic Theory* represents that. Plenty of people thought of other things later. For example I didn't even notice Raising. I do not think it was until Rosenbaum,[43] or anyway, years later, that it became obvious. That should have obviously been thought of, like other phenomena such as gapping. In the late fifties I really wasn't working much on these questions. I was doing mathematical linguistics and generative phonology, and apart from that I was trying to make sense of how all this fit into a broader range of questions about psychology and innate structures. I really wasn't doing much technical work in syntax at that time. In the early

---

40. See Gruber (1976); the work published there originated in the mid-sixties. Cf. also Jackendoff (1972, 1976), Bowers (1981), Marantz (1981), Williams (1981a).
41. A selection of the major contributions includes Bordelois (1974), Kayne (1975), Quicoli (1975), Burzio (1978), Rizzi (1978a), Rouveret and Vergnaud (1980). Quicoli (1980), Burzio (1981).
42. Cf. Ross (1970). A good overview of the relevant literature can be found in Neijt (1979).
43. Rosenbaum (1967). Cf. also Postal (1974).

sixties other people began to come in, Lees, Klima, and others.⁴⁴ I was involved in many different things. Actually, it's only been in the last ten years that I've been working intensively again on straight grammatical questions, as better explanatory theories have been developed with much broader scope and greater depth.

Recently, languages other than English have been forced on you so that Universal Grammar can no longer be twenty-five sentences of English. That must really be worrying you.

I think that is terrific. The reason that I don't work on other languages is that I don't know any very well, it's as simple as that. My earliest work on generative grammar was on Hebrew, because that's the kind of thing you do if you're a linguist. The way I was trained, you pick some languages. I even started with informant work. I went through the whole business. I started off as a linguist with the usual training and with phonemic analysis and the like. You were supposed to get informants. OK, so I got an informant and I worked. I probably still have somewhere all the notes I took from my work with the informant. And then it occurred to me at one point that it was idiotic. I mean I didn't know anything about phonetics, and I didn't care for it. Then I started to work on what I understood better, namely syntax and morphophonemics using the informant when I didn't know something, and then it occurred to me at some point that that was idiotic too, because why wasn't I working on English, where I knew everything, and why was I even bothering to work on this language that I knew only partially? I had to keep going back to the informant and I did not know what his reactions were based on and so on. And at that point I just stopped, and started working on English, which I've been doing ever since. It seems to me that those early moves were correct ones, but that doesn't indicate any feeling that one shouldn't work on other languages, it's just that I'm not going to work seriously on other languages. If you guys work on Dutch, it is fascinating, and if people work on Italian, terrific, and I want to pick up what comes from it.

---

44. Cf. the introduction of Chomsky (1975) and the discussion in Chomsky (1977c), as well as references cited there.

Nevertheless, for you, it seems, extended coverage of data has always been secondary to conceptual unification. Not only in terms of your own research strategy but also with respect to the way you present your work.

I'm not sure if I agree. I've consciously tried to extend the range of data, with whatever success, but I certainly feel that explanation is much more important than gross coverage of data. The reason is, very simply, that gross coverage of data is much too easily obtained, in too many different ways. There are a million ways in which you can give a kind of rough characterization of a lot of data, and therefore you don't learn anything about the principles at all. You might raise the same question about the natural sciences. I think that over the course of centuries, and we can learn something from this, they have focused very sharply on particular questions. In fact, it was argued in the 17th century that Galilean physics was much too narrow in restricting the data it considered. For example, take the concept of motion, obviously fundamental to 17th century physics. As compared to, say, Aristotelian or scholastic physics, Galileo restricted that concept very sharply. Aristotelian or scholastic physics included under motion things like the growth of plants and perception and what not. All that was motion. Then Galileo comes along and says: I'm not concerned with anything but mechanical systems. That was a very sharp restriction of phenomena, justified by the fact that it could give you explanatory depth, whereas if you wanted to cover all the other phenomena, you could just do it at a qualitative level. I think that all the natural sciences proceeded like that. It's not that we just want to mimic the natural sciences, but there were reasons, and the same reasons hold here. There are certain phenomena, like anaphora, which have just been extremely good probes; they've raised questions that have to be answered, and there are other things that also do, but I haven't seen many. Most phenomena simply do not make good probes. They are really just puzzles which are unexplained. It seems to me to make good sense to work intensively in those subareas where sharp questions seem to arise that can be answered in ways that have an explanatory character.

What is the relationship between conceptual improvement and extension of some domain of linguistic data?

It should turn out, and it sometimes has turned out, if the conceptual improvements are correct, that they bring in new domains of data. For example, as far as I know, much of the data on which the binding theory is based had never really been studied, prior to *Conditions*. Of course people knew the examples, but they hadn't been studied.

But there is no logical necessity that conceptual unification and broader coverage of facts go together.

No, there's no necessity. In fact you can certainly have conceptual unifications, and even right ones, that don't predict anything new. Often it's hard to know when new things are predicted. You only find out later.

Chapter 2
Issues in Formal Grammar

Since the introduction of trace-theory the role of thematic relations has become increasingly marginal. In the introductory chapter of your book, Essays on Form and Interpretation, and especially in On Binding,[1] the control-problem was dealt with in terms of grammatically relevant functions like subject or object, rather than thematic roles directly, if you like. In the Pisa-presentation of your Government and Binding theory thematic roles were totally absent. However, quite unexpectedly these concepts have now been resurrected in the form of the theta-criterion. Why?

This is fairly recent, of course. It is still somewhat amorphous in my mind, but I'll just tell you what I've been thinking about. One observation is that parts of the base structure seem to be explicable in terms of case theory. At least it seems to me possible to partly eliminate base ordering in terms of other considerations like case theory.[2] Of course, if that is possible that's a step forward. Then the next question that immediately arises is: what about the set of arguments described in a base rule? If the sequence part can be accounted for in terms of something else, what about the set part? Thus if the order of the complements of a verb can be reduced to some other consideration, then the next question is: can we reduce its set of complements to something else? And that immediately raises another question which has always been in the back of everybody's mind, namely that there's a redundancy between the lexicon and the base grammar. In part they say the same thing. Maybe the way to eliminate this redundancy is to say that the base rules are simply the expression of the redundancies in the lexicon.

That's a possible approach, but it is not an obvious one. It seems that there's an irreducible minimum that the grammar must contain, namely that in the lexicon each particular item will have to be associated with some set of complements. You have to say of *persuade* that it takes an object and a sentential complement. There doesn't seem to be any way to eliminate that. And the question is, does the categorial component of the

---
1. Chomsky (1977b) and Chomsky (1980b).
2. Cf. Chomsky (1981b) and Stowell (1981).

base itself have to say nothing. Maybe it just says generate anything you like, and all the redundancy of the lexicon has just to do with the properties intrinsic to the lexicon itself. In that case the categorial component doesn't have to express either sets or sequences, it just has to allow for the options. If you go that far, the question comes up: what are these properties of the lexicon? The one notion in descriptive semantics that seems to have been of any use at all, so far almost the only one, is the notion of thematic relation. Some people like Jackendoff have done some quite interesting work in developing this notion and its implications. I think it's at least a reasonable guess that thematic role is a fundamental notion in semantics, and maybe serves as a unifying notion. Apart from the areas of semantics that have to do with logical form (quantifiers etc.), thematic role seems to be the only notion so far that has any interesting characteristics, as far as I can see. So let's assume that it is a fundamental notion and that in fact the choice of complements to an element in the lexicon really has to do with thematic role. What we're now saying is that every lexical item carries along with it a certain set of thematic roles, theta-roles, which have to be filled. That is its lexical entry, and from that we can determine everything in the base structure except for what can be determined by case theory and except for some idiosyncrasies like SVO and SOV order, which just seems to be a parameter.

Pushing a little further, let's talk about the items that fill the theta-roles. Suppose we have a verb which takes an object and a sentential complement, and imagine that elements fill those theta-roles. An item will be inserted in a phrase marker where it fills a theta-role, at least in the complement system. Maybe it is true in general that an item is inserted if and only if it fulfills a theta-role. Then you immediately get a distinction between positions in phrase markers which have a theta-role and positions which don't. In fact there is an obvious difference, for example idiom chunks distinguish such cases. They will appear in positions which don't receive theta-roles. And noun phrases that are referential will appear in positions that do not receive a theta-role only if they're somehow linked to positions which do receive a theta-role. Roughly things seem to work that way if you think about how thematic roles are assigned. That suggests a stronger principle: items can be inserted where and only where they get a theta-role, either by their position or by the position of their trace. That of course immediately relates to other proposals that were around, like Freidin's Principle of Functional Uniqueness.[3] We can then

---

3. Freidin (1978).

ask a further question: could it be that every item has only one theta-role? Indeed, many principles of grammar seem to assign unique roles to elements, and though not necessary, it is at least plausible that every referential expression should in fact fill exactly one theta-role. Just as you wouldn't expect a particular noun phrase to be governed by two verbs, you wouldn't expect it to get its theta-role from two verbs or from two constructions. A not unreasonable though not necessary hypothesis is the theta-criterion which says that there is one and only one theta-role for every referential expression.

Thinking that far, we then come back to some insistent prodding from Jan Koster, who has been continuously asking me to explain why I distinguish PRO and trace. It seems to me that they differ strikingly with regard to the theta-criterion. That is, PRO typically occupies a theta-position, and trace typically occupies a non-theta-position, at least non-case-marked trace. What you get is three different things. You get PRO and operator-bound case-marked trace always filling a theta-position or else being linked to one by a trace. On the other hand you get non-case-marked trace, which is quite different: it transmits a theta-role, and doesn't have one. Those seem to be very significant differences. They relate to the fact that PRO cannot have, say, existential *there* as its antecedent, but that trace can. From an entirely different point of view I had already more or less decided that PRO unlike trace had some features.[4] And from this point of view that would make additional sense, because it would say that the thing that has the features in fact behaves quite differently in the thematic system. I think that there is indirect supporting evidence deriving from ECP, which indicates that the two items have a different syntactic function. So many things converge into making it look as if notions like theta-role and theta-criterion could be fundamental notions.

Yes, but it would seem that the inference works both ways. In particular, the Government-Binding theory predicts a number of things: the difference between the try *and* seem *cases, for example. Try takes only PRO, and* seem *takes only trace as its S-structure complement subject. You could derive these results from the theta-criterion to be sure, but they also follow immediately from the Binding theory. So this part of the theta-criterion at least is implied by the Government-Binding theory. What are the relevant*

---

4. In more recent work, however, Chomsky has abandoned the idea that there are intrinsic differences among empty categories. Cf. Chomsky (1981b: chapter 6) and Chomsky (forthcoming).

considerations regarding the directionality of the deductive link between these two subtheories?

At this point a question arises which I'm very confused about. Assuming the theta-criterion to be correct, the question is: do we want it to fall out as a consequence of other things, or is it something to which we make appeal in determining the character of the grammar? That's really the question that you are now asking. For example, if we can explain the differences between trace and PRO in terms of theta-role or in terms of the binding theory, then the theta-criterion need not be stipulated. On the other hand, there are some places where it seems to be useful, maybe necessary to stipulate it. For example take the question of why you can't have *John killed* from *killed John*. Why can't you have inversion? One possibility is that you don't have all the theta-roles filled, and that would be appealing to the theta-criterion. Another possibility would be that you get a case-marked trace, so it has to be a variable. But of course it would also be nice to have that fall out as a theorem.

In fact, I think that here the choice is not obvious. If we accept the theta-criterion we can deduce that case-marked trace, at least in this case, has to be a variable. If we accept that case-marked trace has to be a variable, we can deduce this case of the theta-criterion. There are many such interactions, and I just don't see how they fall out. I think one of the most interesting questions now is to see how they fall out. We have these various notions or principles, theta-roles and the theta-criterion and the binding theory, and if each is assumed as a primitive, that is redundant. We can deduce parts of each from parts of the others, and that means that it is an important kind of problem. We need a more unified theory which will extract the redundancy in the correct way. Right now these things overlap too much.

It's interesting that, although as you say the theta-role has been brought back in, one thing has not been brought back in, and that is the difference between the different thematic relations. Nothing has been said here about the difference between Goal and Source for example. Part of the reason is I don't understand this very well. I never know how people are able to pick out thematic relations with such security, I can't.

But given the problem of identifying thematic roles and assigning them to functional arguments, the natural thing to do seems to be to rely as minimally as possible on the theory of theta-roles, particularly since properties of this theory are reducible to purely structural notions of other systems of the grammar that are not easily reducible to the theta-criterion.

Maybe that is right, maybe it will turn out that all properties of the theta-criterion fall out. Another thing that led me to thinking in these terms was that if you look at the formulation of the binding theory in the form in which it was presented in the Pisa lectures, the three principles A, B, C, were each very complicated.[5] Jan Koster pointed out to me in a letter that they looked too complicated. That is a plausible criticism. If you are going to have three binding principles, it would make sense to require that each of the principles ought to hold of one of the types of expression, without any interaction among them. That wasn't true of the formulations in the Pisa theory. Each one said something like "if A or B then either C or D", and then the next one would say "if E then either A or non D", etc. There was an interaction between the three, whereas the simplest, the ideal form would be something like this: if you have such and such an expression, then you have such and such a binding property; if you have another type of expression, then you have a different type of binding property.

One could argue, though, that because of this interaction between the axioms of the Binding theory the system had a few interesting properties: it yielded the theorem that variables must be case-marked, and the theorem that PRO is necessarily ungoverned. In the present reformulation of the theory it has to be stipulated that variables are case-marked.

It had many properties, yes. For example you got the definition of variable as case-marked trace as a theorem, which I don't see how to get from the simpler formulation.[6] That's true, but you could argue that they

---

5. The original formulation of the binding theory was as follows (cf. Bennis and Groos [1980]):
   A. If alpha is an anaphor (reflexives, reciprocals, etc.), then (i) it is a variable, or (ii) it is bound in every governing category.
   B. If alpha is a case-marked NP, but not a pronoun, then (i) it is an anaphor, or (ii) it has to be free in every governing category.
   C. If alpha is pronominal (i.e. pronoun or PRO), it is free in every minimal governing category.
   In Chomsky (1981b), the binding theory appears in a considerably simplified version.
   A. An anaphor is bound in its governing category.
   B. A pronominal is free in its governing category.
   C. An R-expression (name, variable) is free.
6. Cf. footnote 5. See also Chomsky (1982). A partial derivation of the theorem is attempted in Chomsky (1981b: 3.2.2).

weren't real theorems anyway, because the theory was so complicated. Anyway, I am just telling you what I was thinking about it, which may or may not prove to be the right direction. It struck me that the principles weren't motivated in their complexity, and I wanted to find something more motivated. That requires thinking through more carefully what types of expressions there are. It seemed to me that there are basically three types of expressions: anaphors, referential expressions, and pronominals. Then you could say: each one has a particular binding property, and that seems to work out more or less. It's a little different from the other theory. It doesn't derive the theorem about case-marked trace directly the way the other one does. I don't know whether that's right or wrong. And then, of course, what makes these three types of expressions different? Well, the theta-role enters surely, so that looks like another way of thinking about it.

For some reason or other, throughout the history of the theory of grammar, there have always been semantic approaches to problems of language. Quite often they are popular too among linguists. The appeal of Montague Grammar, for example, appears to be partially due to the model-theoretic approach to semantics which is presupposed by it. Why does the model-theoretic approach not appeal to you?

Model theoretic semantics is a very important development. There is no question about that in logic. It was designed to provide an analysis of certain notions, like the notion of logical necessity and a family of notions related to it. And for some purposes I think it does that, although even with regard to notions like logical necessity, it raises a number of questions. But let's say that it is a good theory of logical necessity. The question is what it does beyond that. It has been very widely used as a technique of descriptive semantics. Yet, we have to ask how broadly it applies beyond the notion of logical necessity. I'm very skeptical for various reasons. Let's divide the expressions in a language that have to be dealt with by semantic theory into three types – just more or less thinking of the history of the subject – with regard to the kind of contexts in which referential expressions appear.

In the first place there are purely extensional contexts and structures like, say, coordination. For those contexts, as everybody knows, we don't need any possible world semantics. That is, a non-possible world semantics will suffice. The second class of expressions is the class that involves the logical modalities like necessity, and possible world semantics seems reasonable for that category. Then there's a third type of category, and in fact that is the core of the work in classical, at least Fregean semantics, and that is roughly the belief contexts, or propositional attitude contexts, and in those contexts, as everybody knows, possible world semantics fails. There isn't any imaginable way to make it work. If you believe that something is such and such, then it is just not the case that interchanges that maintain truth in all possible worlds, will maintain the set of beliefs. It doesn't even work for mathematical necessity, or for causal necessity, let alone the propositional attitude contexts. So the immediate, superficial observation is that possible world semantics is unnecessary for extensional contexts, fails for propositional attitude contexts, and works, if you like, for logical necessity. To the extent that that is true, possible world semantics is in fact the dictionary entry for 'logically necessary', and that is its role in semantic theory.

Of course that is only a first approximation. You can develop more complicated varieties of the theory. You can introduce relations of accessibility between worlds and you can talk about continuity and the way things might follow different paths in the future etc. You can undoubtedly try to do more complicated things with the theory than the first approximation would suggest, but I'm impressed by what seems to me the lack of insight that follows from most such approaches. My own feeling is that possible world semantics perhaps really is the dictionary entry for 'logically necessary', and that it just doesn't tell you anything about other areas. At this point one gets into other kinds of questions. Suppose we do try to approach the analysis of modalities like *might have been* in the linguistic sense, not in the logical sense. Then some very strange questions arise, basically Quine's questions[7], which I don't think have ever been satisfactorily answered. I doubt that they can be. These are basically questions of essentialism.

The problem arises when we want to understand the sentence "Nixon might not have been elected president in 1968". If we try to distinguish that from "Nixon might not have been human" in terms of possible world semantics, we're in a familiar way led to the assumption that we can pick out an individual, Nixon, in many possible worlds, in many possible circumstances, some existing and some non-existing. It is the same individual throughout. The only way we can do that is if we have some properties which carry through all possible worlds, that is properties which are invariant properties of him as an individual. That means that there must be

---

7. Cf. Quine (1953, 1960).

some essential properties of things, metaphysically necessary properties of things, as distinct from other properties which are accidental. I think that is an almost unintelligible notion, with perhaps one exception. You might argue that the property of being Nixon is an essential property of Nixon, but that really doesn't help much. I can't think of any other property that it makes sense to think of as an essential property of the thing, other than being what it is, being self-identical in other words. There are many arguments in the literature trying to make it plausible that other properties would fall into the two categories, accidental and essential. So, for example, people will say, as Kripke has argued for example,[8] that this distinction is not a philosopher's distinction, that it is the common man's distinction, that it is intuitively clear that it might have been that Nixon was not elected president, but not that it might have been that he wasn't human. I think that intuition is right. At least I certainly think that there could have been a world like this one, except in the respect that Nixon wasn't president. But there couldn't have been a world differing only in that Nixon wasn't human. I think that's right, but I think that the intuition has nothing to do with essentialism. It has to do with the fact that language doesn't have names in the logician's sense. A name in the logician's sense is just a symbol connected somehow to an object, and language doesn't work like that. Language only has names that fall into categories: the name "Nixon" is a personal name and the name "red" is a color name, and so on. And given that "Nixon" is a personal name (if we didn't know that it was a personal name, we would not know how to use it), the two sentences in question are (i) "the person Nixon might not have been elected", true, (ii) "the person Nixon might not have been human", false. Reason: persons are human. So in fact it's not that that thing over there, Nixon, has the essential property of humanness, but rather that we're putting him in the category human, and we refer to him as Nixon. And if we take him out of that category we can't refer to him in that way anymore. He is in the conceptual category 'person', and his name belongs to the associated linguistic category, so we do end up with a necessary truth, but not one that is based on any essential properties of things.

I think that as soon as we extricate ourselves from the conceptual and linguistic categories, if we really try to invent a name, say N, referring to Nixon, and we try to divest this name of any of its linguistic properties, and divest our thinking of any of our conceptual categories, then I have no intuitions left anymore about whether it is the same person if his hair

---

8. Kripke (1972). Cf. also Katz and Katz (1977).

is combed on the other side. It is different in some respect, and the intuitions have all faded away, because they're all connected with the interactions of conceptual categories and linguistic categories. I think that all the examples work like this, so it just seems to me that at various levels, there are very fundamental difficulties with these approaches and the areas where they work effectively are areas where you deal with such concepts as logical necessity, where these questions don't arise.

There are other questions that one could raise. If one believes that possible world semantics is the way in which some domain of semantics works, then he has one or two choices. He can say: this relates to cognitive psychology in a broad sense, that is, it is about the ways in which all this is represented in the mind. Or he could say: it has nothing to do with the way things are represented in mind, it is just a kind of mathematics. If he takes the first approach, there are serious problems, because it is not at all clear how possible worlds are mentally represented or how people can have access to calculations using possible worlds when they make their judgements. Maybe that can be worked out, but at least it isn't very obvious. I think many of the people in the field have taken the other option. They are working on a kind of mathematics, they are doing some type of semantics that is not psychological. I don't see any sense in that type of move myself.

One can also mention other problems. What is the status of the "objects" that populate the domains postulated in possible world semantics? Insofar as anything works out in using this device in the descriptive semantics of natural language, it seems to work about as well when we consider real objects (e.g., Nixon), non-existent objects (e.g. Pegasus), impossible objects (e.g., round squares), things that we do not think of as objects at all (e.g., the "objects" associated with certain idiom chunks, or the average man, or John's lack of interest in mathematics, etc.). This seems to me to suggest that what is called "possible world semantics," in its application to natural language, is not semantics at all, but rather another form of syntax, postulating a new level or new levels of mental representation – what David Lewis has called "mentalese".[9] The question of the relation of language to the world, of ontological commitment, remains outside this discussion. But these new syntactic levels have to be justified exactly as others do, at least if we adopt the "psychological" interpretation of this enterprise. That raises a whole variety of new questions, which I don't think have yet been properly considered.

---

9. Lewis (1972).

Although you started out with Morphophonemics of Modern Hebrew and introduced the theory of the lexicon with Aspects of the Theory of Syntax and Remarks on Nominalization, you have always kept clear of morphology and X-bar theory since then. Do you feel that there has been interesting progress in these areas beyond the original suggestions in Aspects, Remarks, and The Sound Pattern of English?[10]

I do not think there are many spectacular successes to point to in morphology or in the X-bar theory. Maybe there is a reason for the primitiveness of these systems. That is, as far as X-bar theory is concerned, maybe in fact you can get away with a rather restricted version of it, if you have both case theory and the theory of thematic roles, the theta-criterion theory. I would like to see to what extent introducing those two concepts might fill in the gaps in a very schematic X-bar theory. If it turns out that they do, that would account for why the X-bar theory does not get very deep. Maybe it is not. Of course this would leave open all the problems about specifiers, most of the things that Ray Jackendoff and Lisa Selkirk and other people dealt with.[11]

The question of the order of the complements with respect to their heads seems to be left open too. The theta-criterion cannot say anything about this and it is not so obvious how this aspect of the underlying order of constituents would follow from case theory.

I've suggested that some kind of adjacency condition on case assignment might play a role in determining constituent order. Maybe here some of the Greenberg universals[12] will be important. There have also been a few attempts at developing functional explanations for some of these problems, as in Kuno's work.[13]

Still, a restrictive version of X-bar theory is supposed to play a crucial role in the argument that the class of transformational grammars is finite. You yourself have laid out this argument on several recent occasions.[14] *Finite-*

---

10. The latter is Chomsky and Halle (1968).
11. See mainly the references given in footnote 2 of Part II, chapter 1. In addition, cf. Bowers (1975), Bresnan (1976), Selkirk (1977), Van Riemsdijk (1978b).
12. Cf. Greenberg (1963).
13. See in particular Kuno (1973, 1974).
14. In particular Chomsky (1981a, 1981b, forthcoming).

ness follows from a restrictive theory of the base and the "move alpha" theory of transformations.

The class of core grammars at least is finite; here the question of periphery crucially arises, because if we imagine, say, that you could, given enough evidence, add a transformation with an arbitrary structural description, then of course the class of grammars would be infinite.

One step in your argument that the class of core grammars is finite is that the lexicon must be finite. But on the other hand it has often been claimed that there are productive rules of morphology. That would lead to an infinite lexicon. Why should the non-finiteness of the lexicon be a priori less interesting than that of syntax?

Well, for example, if you could have an infinite number of, say, verbal structures, with more and more configurations of strict subcategorization relations, then it would be interesting, but that does not seem to be true. That is, the points at which the lexicon seems to be potentially infinite are basically names, you can always name a phenomenon.

But we were thinking, really, about properties of word-formation rules.

Well, of course a lot of languages must have a finite vocabulary, take for example Semitic, where there are heavy constraints on the structure of roots and rules of word formation. Of course, in modern Semitic languages these are not observed, you borrow words from other sources. But if you really kept to the Semitic principle of word formation, there would be a finite number of words, because there is no other way to make words. Where we have options to get an infinite vocabulary it appears to be through pretty trivial mechanisms usually.

So you are not impressed by the fact that a rule like 'attach affix' generates an infinite class of word structures. Doesn't that imply that morphological 'overgeneration' is to be filtered out through conditions on representations? More or less analogously to the way reflexive affixes are dealt with, as in Muyskens's work on Quechua,[15] perhaps a kind of upside down syntax: a mapping from words into Logical Form? Now, that may be interesting.

---

15. Cf. Muysken (1981).

That may be interesting. That could be. But apart from that, I think that most of the devices of word formation seem to be fairly trivial. Compounding, affixation, and maybe one or two other things. It is striking that you do not get new configurational structures. For example, you do not find words that make more and more complex causative structures without bound. I do not know; maybe something like that happens in Japanese. Maybe you get double causatives but not triple causatives.[16]

Just now you mentioned configurational structures. What precisely do you mean by your claim that word formation does not create new configurational structures?

The only recursive rules in morphology, to my knowledge, are a matter of layering. You have a unit, you add something to it, you get a new unit, you add something to it, you get a new unit, and so on. And that is a very primitive sort of recursiveness.

All the same, why is morphology limited in just this fashion? What prevents rules of morphology from introducing structure, be it configurational or lexical? Your position seems to imply that the grammar of synthetic languages is reduced to near-triviality. That just cannot be true. After all, if Japanese causatives are lexical, and you can get double causatives, why not triple ones?

Maybe it is true for some of the poly-synthetic languages. It could be that there really is a rich theory of morphology which is syntactic in character. Maybe it is a property of the kinds of languages we are thinking about that morphology is so limited. About other types of language, I really have nothing useful to say, I just haven't thought about them, and don't know of much work that seems relevant to the questions we are now discussing.

Phonology seems to be in much better shape. Just as in syntax, there are a limited number of areas where something interesting is happening. Recent work by Vergnaud, Halle, and others[17] shows spectacular progress in the

---

16. Cf. Farmer (1980).
17. Some major references are Halle and Vergnaud (forthcoming), Liberman and Prince (1977), and Vergnaud (1977). A good recent survey of results and references can be found in McCarthy (1982).

domain of suprasegmental phonology, for example, while new and substantial insights into local phenomena such as assimilation and deletion are lacking.

My feeling at least was that the way to work on those processes was through the linking theory at the end of *The Sound Pattern of English*, which, so far, only Mary-Louise Kean has worked on.[18] The main drift in phonology has gone off in a different direction, the study of syllable structure, what used to be called 'suprasegmental' phenomena, and so on. So I think the topics you mention remain to be dealt with.

In a sense, the average type of phonological rule that one finds in the literature now is comparable to an Aspects-type transformation in syntax. A step parallel to, say, 'move alpha' just has not been taken yet.

Again, I think that certain of the deep ideas in phonology may ultimately prove to be the linking rules and Kean's complement convention. Those are interesting ideas because they have very strange consequences. Maybe the consequences are still wrong, but you can think of ways of adjusting them. At least they have the right properties, again simple ideas which yield very strange consequences as you work them out. But that has not been a major topic in phonology for the last 10 years or so.[19]

It appears that there are only two people in the world who have any ideas about linking at all, Mary-Louise Kean and you. Mary-Louise Kean has decided to devote her linguistic career to the study of aphasia. That means there is only you to do the work. Why didn't you do it?

Well, my work on phonology was one of the very minor casualties of the Vietnam war. Also there are aspects of it that just do not appeal to me personally. I do not care much about phonetics, and I do not understand much about it. I do not know, maybe it is too close to the world or something.

In the work by Halle and Vergnaud and others that we mentioned before it is claimed that unbounded phenomena that were originally dealt with in terms of conditions on Q-variables[20] are in fact reducible to systems of lo-

---

18. Kean (1975, 1981).
19. For a noteworthy exception, see Kloeke (1981).
20. Cf. Halle (1975).

cality: the seemingly unbounded properties fall out from the inherent properties of the formalism which forces locality. That seems to be an interesting direction to follow. The locality principles in syntax are comparable to the conditions on Q-variables in phonology. Couldn't we come up with a local formalism in syntax too?

I don't really think you have non-local phenomena in phonology in the sense in which you do in syntax. I'm not sure how far the analogy can be pushed, I mean, what is there really outside of harmony?

Well, there is alternating stress, for example.

That is true, and I think there is an indication in Dorothy Siegel's work that there is also some kind of locality principle in morphology.[21] The question is whether there is more than just that they all involve bounded domains.

The thing about harmony and alternating stress is that the perpetuation of a very local notion suffices to account for them. Now, in a certain sense that is true of syntax with successive cyclic movement, but that is not a very local notion. It seems to be the case in syntax and semantics that there are really unbounded processes like for example PRO interpretation, in fact, anything that does not involve movement. I do not think there is anything like that in phonology, nothing that is not decomposable into a series of local steps. But even phenomena in syntax that are in some sense locally bounded, for example by subjacency, still involve interconnections that are very far from local. They are structurally bounded, but not bounded in extent. So I don't know how far that analogy can be pushed.

And then the question arises, is there anything real about the apparent analogy between movement and for example vowel harmony. It seems to me there is something inherently local about phonology and morphology. Of course you could imagine an unbounded phonology, say a phonology in which the beginning of a sentence and the end of a sentence would be related by phonological rule. But if we found such a phenomenon we would call it syntax.

But suppose one were to argue that one of the relevant domains in phonology is not the sentence, but the word. The inherent locality of phonology as

---

21. Siegel (1978). Cf. also Allen (1978), Lieber (1980), Williams (1981c).

you would have it is then a reflection of the finiteness of wordstrings. The question can now be reformulated as follows: what makes 'local properties' of wh-movement fundamentally different from 'local properties' of, say, vowel harmony?

Suppose we found mirror image properties in phonology, a language where the beginning of a word and the end of a word had to share a certain property. Then, I think, we would really redo phonology in a radical way, and then we would talk about the syntax of a word instead. But that does not seem to be the case.

In part the move that you describe, the Vergnaud & Halle approach, might be a successful alternative to an earlier bad guess. The earlier analyses of these phenomena as non-local could be reduced to a kind of locality principle because the first guess didn't make much sense. Maybe something like that can be done in syntax as well. Do you have some proposal in mind?

Not really, but to the extent that you take syntactic features seriously, the idea of projection in the sense of Vergnaud (1977) could play a role in syntax as well. If complementizers have some kind of categorial identity of their own they could be made locally adjacent in the feature projection. So given a COMP-projection and a rule of COMP-attraction this would yield successive cyclicity, to give just an example.[22]

It's not outlandish. Perhaps the special properties of complementizers might relate to the fact that maybe they're the head of S-bar, that they really have the properties of heads, as I assume is implicit in your suggestions. But that doesn't seem to have much of an analogue in phonology.

Well, Aoun[23] *argues that notions like head and governance apply in phonology too.*

Yes, that's true, he has, and in an interesting way.

Turning to a different though related topic, why have you never since, say, LSLT done any extensive work on the formalization of linguistic theory, the appendix of "On Binding" being a rare exception?

---

22. For an application of Vergnaud's (1977) theory of syntax, see Van Riemsdijk (1981).
23. Aoun (1979).

I have no principled reason. One engages in formalization when it seems to be worth doing. The Lasnik and Kupin article is a relevant case.[24]

But formalization might sometimes serve a heuristic function. The Lasnik and Kupin article is an example. Their formalism offers a new and elegant way of representing reanalysis, for example.[25]

Yes, it also raises some interesting questions about adjunction[26]. Another example is the Rouveret-Vergnaud paper[27] which is formalization at a different level. It has certainly been productive in leading people to think of how techniques of indexing could be used in syntax and phonology, for example. I thought the appendix of *On Binding* was worth doing because it was worth seeing what could come out of using those notions. But again, I do not see any point in formalizing for the sake of formalizing. You can always do that.

The Peters and Ritchie formalization of transformational grammar[28] *seems to have served quite a different role in the history of the field. Some linguists have interpreted their results as giving carte blanche to even more powerful devices than transformational rules.*

Peters and Ritchie were formalizing something which I guess is probably even richer than the framework of *The Logical Structure of Linguistic Theory*. Incidentally, people shouldn't be misled by that. There's a lot of confusion about their result. What is usually described – not by them – as their result is just sort of an observation. They point out that with an unconstrained theory of deletion you can generate all recursively enumerable sets. That result doesn't really derive from the richness of their transformational theory, but from the fact that you can delete designated elements. Anybody who's familiar with Turing machines will know that if you allow deletion of designated elements you can do almost anything. The interesting theorem that they proved is that if you have cyclic transformational rules, and they meet the survivor property,[29] then you can

---

24. Lasnik and Kupin (1977).
25. Cf. Chomsky (1980a,b). For detailed discussion of some consequences, see Huybregts (forthcoming).
26. Cf. also Van Riemsdijk (1978b: chapter 7).
27. Rouveret and Vergnaud (1980).
28. Peters and Ritchie (1973). Cf. also Peters and Ritchie (1971) and Ginsburg and Partee (1969).
29. Cf. Peters (1973).

only generate recursive sets. In contrast, if you have a certain type of phrase structure grammar, maybe even a context-free grammar with deletion, you could probably also generate nonrecursive sets. However, it's the principle of successive cyclicity that allowed the survivor property to be formulated in such a way as to restrict the generative capacity. That may be right or wrong, but that is another question. In that result, the vast richness of the transformational apparatus didn't play much of a role.

However, one might argue that maybe the system which they formalized does give you something like the outer range for possible rules in non-core grammar. It certainly seems vastly too rich for anything needed in core grammar. That is not a criticism of what they were doing, they were just formalizing informal practice.

Even though they are less known in the field for their cycling function theorem than for their 'result' that formalized versions of unrestricted transformational grammar have Turing power, their aim was quite different from what Lasnik and Kupin had in mind when they did their formalization of a transformational theory.

Lasnik and Kupin have a very different aim. They were really working on linguistic theory in much narrower sense, and they were not trying to prove any theorems really. I don't think there are any theorems to prove in that domain, at least nobody knows of any. They were simply trying to formalize a much more restrictive and much more realistic theory of universal grammar.

What do you mean by a much more 'realistic theory'?

Well, closer to reality.

Do you think that their version of reduced phrase markers which cannot always be represented in the form of trees is more promising than the LSLT version of reduced phrase markers which can?

I've thought about it some, and I think that they are right. I think they have a better theory. For one thing, one nice property of it is that it does restrict the possibilities. There are fewer reduced phrase markers than unreduced phrase markers, and that means that there are some statements that you can express within the framework of *The Logical Structure of Linguistic Theory* that you can't express with theirs. For example, if alpha uniquely dominates beta, that is different from beta uniquely dominating alpha in the LSLT theory, but not in their theory, and that is all to the good. I don't know of any evidence that you need the richer theory. I think that their theory is a very good one really. I think it works very nicely for idiom rules which in their formalism amounts to just adding another string to a phrase marker. I'd also like to see somebody work on things like coordination from their point of view. The idea of reduced phrase markers for things like coordination and some notion of set union may very well be right. There are also interesting implications for restructuring, as you mentioned earlier, which really ought to be pursued.

Focusing on constructions like coordination and gapping, Edwin Williams has recently proposed an alternative way of dealing with across-the-board phenomena.[30] *He introduced the notion of simultaneous factorization. Doesn't his ATB theory have a number of desirable properties?*

I think that's one of the problems to deal with, and his approach might be the right one. Or, you might try to deal with this problem by assuming that the across the board deletion really is a specific deletion of a repeated item.[31] That is one approach. You can imagine other approaches through a kind of set union theory of coordination.

Fundamentally there are two different ideas about coordination, only one of which has been intensively explored. One is that, say, *John saw Bill and Tom saw Mary* is base generated as a long phrase marker with two parts, one to the left of the other, with each being an S or something. That is the standard approach. Another approach would be to say that you really have three-dimensional phrase markers. That is that *John saw Bill and Tom saw Mary* have no order, each is just a phrase marker. If we think of phrase markers in the Lasnik and Kupin way, they're just in different dimensions, and then there's a rule that says: put them in the same dimension. That would be one of the properties of coordination. And that could be true for internal (phrasal) coordination too. It could be, for example, and occasionally this shows up in the literature, that you might have some parts of phrase markers in another dimension, such that certain constituents are unordered with respect to one another, rather in the manner of branching quantifiers.[32] In the Lasnik and Kupin approach

---

30. Williams (1977, 1978, 1981b).
31. Chomsky and Lasnik (1977: appendix 1.). Cf. also George (1980).
32. Cf. Hintikka (1974), Gabbay and Moravcsik (1974).

you might try formalizing this by saying that these three-dimensional trees are just sets which don't happen to be reducible to a single tree. It is not necessarily the case that every phrase marker in their sense has to be tree-represented, and you can imagine a union of two phrase markers, one for *John saw Bill* and the other for *Tom saw Mary*, which will have certain strings in common, like S in this case. And in that bigger set it might be quite possible to define all the grammatical relations. Then you can imagine maybe a phonological rule, which at some point gives them an order. That's just a rather different approach, not only to coordination, but to the whole mass of phenomena that go along with it, such as gapping. That I think would be really worth exploring.

You seem to have a preference for this option over the ATB-alternative. Why?

It is not so much an alternative to the ATB theory as another possible way of thinking about it. I think set union captures something that is missed in tree representations. For one thing the linearization of tree representations seems to me extrinsic to the structural properties of coordination. For example, tree representation loses the fact that in *John danced and sang*, John is the subject of *danced*. All it says is that John is the subject of danced and sang. Or take something like *John and Bill liked him*. *Him* is disjoint in reference from both *John* and *Bill*, but that does not follow in any obvious way from c-command. So in fact many structural and semantic properties of coordination seem to me to reflect this set union representation while they are obscured in the linear notation. That makes me wonder whether linearization is not like phonology in that it provides some way of taking the abstract representation which has the properties you would expect and turning it into something you can say.

Nevertheless we have a strong feeling that basically William's analysis used an order-free theory as well, the conjuncts being analyzed simultaneously. In fact, he even presented a linearization rule.

Well, that is true. It's done simultaneously, but that is a notion that does not make much sense in a linear theory. You could have an indefinite number of conjuncts and they are all analyzed simultaneously. Whatever the operation, it is not a linear operation. It is really the same operation applied to a set of things.

So coordination, apparently, is not a topic on which we can focus very easily. Would you be able to give us, say, ten thesis topics that you would like to have brilliant graduate students work on?

I find it very hard to know what to say. You can think of problems, but not really of topics. Topics are only topics for people with ideas about them. Otherwise they are just problems, and the things that people have ideas about are usually related to what they are working on. That is really your hardest question so far.

All right, but what we really mean, of course, is: what are some of the areas that you would most like someone to have some bright ideas about?

Well, take the issue we were talking about before, the heavy overlap between the various subsystems, each of which seems interesting. I am not sure it is a thesis topic, it may be too difficult. But this is a class of problems within which there are probably some thesis topics, like for example the question of the relation of the notion variable and the notion case-marked trace. That might suggest a thesis topic. It would be part of the more general question about how these various subdomains interact and what the proper unified theory is. That is probably more than a thesis topic, or maybe even less than one if somebody comes up with a really smart idea.

In a way, suppose we go back to the question of the ideal department.[33] If we could have an ideal department from the point of view that it really produces some good students, the almost perfect thesis topics would be work on other languages, trying to carry work on other languages to the level of depth that has so far only been achieved in three or four languages. By now universal grammar is no longer 25 sentences in English, it is also 25 sentences in Dutch, and 25 sentences in Italian, and so on. Far more than this, of course, but still a limited set. It would be very nice to have some comparable understanding of some other languages today. And that is really hard, it takes a very constructive mind because it is much too easy to take a look at another language and just conclude that everything goes wrong, as it usually does at first sight. It is much harder to come up with the kind of analysis that Luigi Rizzi came up with for Italian.[34] Or take Tarald Taraldsen's analysis of Norwegian relatives,[35]

---

33. Cf. Part I, chapter 3.
34. Rizzi (1978b).
35. Taraldsen (1981).

which again seem to violate every possible constraint, except that he found some ingenious way to show that they did not. I think many people are intelligent enough to do it, but they are not psychologically attuned to it. They are much more psychologically attuned to destructive work, it is much easier. Another advantage of that type of thesis topic is that it is getting quite hard to work on English, the Romance languages, Dutch, and so on, because a lot of the easy work has already been done. It is getting harder and harder.

But on the other hand, in the absence of any knowledge about the properties of some constructions and phenomena it is also extremely hard to work on what you call the easy stuff. You have to devise all your own constituency tests and so on.

What I mean is that the easy research topics have been exhausted. It is much harder to do a thesis now than it was 20 years ago, because then you could pick just about any topic and find something new to say about it. Of course, while work is harder in some dimensions, it is easier in other respects. For example, many obvious questions, now come to mind immediately that could not have been raised before, because the concepts were unavailable, and there were fewer partial successes and insights to rely on. For example, how does the binding theory, or the empty category principle, apply in some other language? Or does it?

Chapter 3
Core and Periphery

In your recent book, Rules and Representations,[1] *you have stressed that what is important is the notion grammar, which is fundamental, rather than language, which is epiphenomenal. You argued that language was the more abstract notion of the two. This must have shocked the rest of the world. What makes you think that language is more abstract than grammar?*

I do not know why I never realized that clearly before, but it seems obvious, when you think about it, that the notion language is a much more abstract notion than the notion of grammar. The reason is that grammars have to have a real existence, that is, there is something in your brain that corresponds to the grammar. That's got to be true. But there is nothing in the real world corresponding to language. In fact it could very well turn out that there is no intelligible notion of language. Even if there is, the notion will raise new problems and more difficult ones because it is at a higher level of abstraction from actual mechanisms. To take another example, the system of rules that you have in the brain tells you how to pair rhymes, therefore it generates the set of rhyming pairs. It also generates millions of other things, and one (or more) of these things we may decide to call "a language" for some reason. But there is no reason to believe that that decision is anything more than some accidental, historically conditioned decision. There is no obvious reason why any of the systems generated by this grammar should be regarded as more real or significant than any other.

In fact the notion language might turn out just to be a useless notion. For example, if we fix a certain level of acceptability then this internally represented system of grammar generates one set, and we say OK that is the language. If we fix the level a bit differently, the same grammar generates a different set, and we can say that is the language. There is no meaningful answer to the question: which is the real language? And, of course, as every linguist knows, the common sense notion of language is hopeless. Nobody even tries to make any sense out of that. So the question is, is there any sense of "language" that is worth saving? It is far from

---

1. Chomsky (1980a).

obvious that there is. This relates again to the question of weak versus strong generative capacity. It means that all studies on generative capacity were giving a very misleading picture. Maybe they are useful for some reason, but they cannot be relied on very much as telling you anything about the nature of the grammar because they are all conducted at a very high level of abstraction, namely at the level of language as compared with grammar. This is the point I discussed in *Rules and Representations* in a somewhat different context. It was mainly a debate with philosophers who feel that the notion of language is somehow clear and the notion of internally represented grammar is somehow suspect. It seems to me that it is actually the other way around. The notion of internally represented grammar is quite clear, obviously not clear in detail: we do not understand what it is, or what the mechanisms are and so on, but that there must be such an object and what it might be like is quite clear, I think. On the other hand, the concept of language is very obscure, and it is not obvious that there is any intelligible or significant notion. If you are talking about languages you are always talking about an epiphenomenon, you are talking about something at a further level of abstraction removed from actual physical mechanisms. I would like to say that it seems to me an obvious point, but I had never really realized it before.

Reading the literature, one cannot escape the conclusion that notions such as markedness and periphery are being used as euphemistic terms to refer to phenomena that are not understood or do not fit into the core.

The distinction is in part theory-internal, but that is unavoidable and quite reasonable. I am sure that the peripheries and the theory of markedness have structure, but I just do not have any good ideas about what it should be. I suggested something in the Pisa paper[2] which I do not think is correct, viz. relaxing some of the conditions of core grammar. Maybe that is somewhat the right idea, but I do not really feel that there is any evidence. I do not even think it is clear whether we should make a sharp distinction between core and periphery. Maybe these are more closely related notions of some sort. But whatever the answer to that is, it is obviously going to be the case that learning of exceptions is a highly structured matter, you cannot learn just any class of exceptions.

---

2. Chomsky (1951a).

The poverty of the stimulus argument applies equally well to the periphery as to the core.

Yes, there are subregularities. This surely is going to be a big topic in the study of morphology, if it ever gets anywhere. There, there seem to be all kinds of subregularities and it is not just random nonsense. I think this may have a lot to do with questions about abstractness in phonology too. For example there are a lot of general processes in phonology like the rules involved in getting forms like *sug-gest* and *suc-ceed* and so on, which are certainly not going to be productive. Or take the Vowel Shift; these are obviously not productive rules, but they are rules that might very well organize the memory. They impose strong patterns and give principled ways of organizing materials that are otherwise quite chaotic. I would imagine that if they turn out to be real, as I suppose they are, it is because they provide a kind of organization of non-core areas, where core-areas might be the productive rules. And these would have to do with ways of imposing a tight and interesting organization on systems.

What you suggest is that the study of the way subregularities relate to the core could produce a highly structured markedness theory. Is that what lay behind that last chapter of The Sound Pattern of English?

When we did Sound Pattern I thought the last chapter was the most interesting one, and again I was in a minority position. I think Marie-Louise Kean is about the only person who has worked on it since.[3] That was a big improvement, but it was not a particularly popular piece of work. Still I think that is the direction to go to make a really interesting theory of markedness.

Is there going to be a similar type of markedness theory in syntax? In your Pisa paper, "Markedness and Core Grammar", you seemed to have a different conception of markedness.

Well, what I suggested there was very heavily based on a factual assumption, that the picture noun phenomena are marked, which they may very well be. At any rate I assumed that they are not part of the core in that theory. Then the question is why they behave the way they do. Well, the specified subject condition is something like a theorem. So you might argue that the theorem holds in marked cases even though the general

---

3. Kean (1975), Kean (1981). Cf. also Kloeke (1981).

principles are relaxed. But I do not think it is a very good answer and the reason is that the specified subject condition is only one of many possible consequences of that theory. The question is why does that consequence hold, not some other consequence in this area where the general conditions are relaxed. I guess that that is why I started trying to work out the idea of accessible subject[4] which would still give you some kind of theory of markedness. That is, you might argue that the unmarked case is where no notion of accessible subject enters and the marked case is where the notion of accessible subject does, and in which case you have this odd constellation of properties. That seemed to me a more promising approach than the one that I suggested in Pisa.. For one thing I think it's a better theory of conditions than the one I gave at GLOW. But for another thing, I think it's a better theory of markedness, because now we can say something much more reasonable, namely that it is the concept of accessibility that is marked, as I mentioned earlier.

These picture noun cases really have a most remarkable history. They have been shifted back and forth between marked and unmarked. Was it bad conscience that made you readmit them into the core system?[5]

In the paper I took the most extreme view with regard to their being marked, at least in anything I've written. I've always assumed they're a little odd in their behavior, but they really just didn't fall into the theory I outlined there at all, so I just had to say they're totally marked. I gave a half-baked argument about that, and there was some bad conscience, I must concede. Maybe it had to do with trying to fit the paper into a program on markedness. But I was uneasy, and remain uneasy, about the fact that it isn't clear, if you assume them to be marked, why they have exactly the properties they have, as I've just mentioned.

Kean has argued that a theory of markedness should be rooted in substantive concepts.[6] *In phonology that makes a lot of sense, but in syntax it is not that perspicuous.*

---

4. Cf. Chomsky (1981b: 3.2.2.).
5. The phenomenon referred to is the fact that anaphors such as *each other* can take an antecedent outside the tensed clause that they are contained in examples like '*they* believe that pictures of *each other* were on sale'. These were treated as unmarked in Chomsky (1973), as marked in Chomsky (1981a), and then again as unmarked in Chomsky (1981b) – unless the reference to accessible subject is marked, as suggested in the text.
6. Kean (1981).

The question is how to do it. I think she is right. One of the problems is that in phonology there is so much wider a range of data available from different types of languages, whereas in syntax we are really working with such a narrow class of fairly well-studied languages.

Recently Kean claimed that the data problem is the same in phonology and syntax. It seems to us that in theory she is right, but that in practice large quantities of usuable raw data from different languages are more readily accessible in phonology than in syntax.

It is simply a fact that phonology is just a small finite system. A good fieldworker can maybe not learn everything, but can learn quite a lot of the phonology of a language in a comparatively short time. Syntax just is not like that at all. A language does not even enter into the domain of discussion unless very substantial work has been done. I think that the Greenberg universals for example are ultimately going to be fairly rich from this point of view. They have all the difficulties that people know, they are "surfacy", they are statistical, and so on and so forth, but nevertheless they are very suggestive.

Case theory might be precisely that domain in syntax that is most likely rooted in substantive concepts such as Location, Direction, or Proximity. Hence case theory might be the ideal starting point in syntax for developing a theory of markedness.

Yes that might be. Simple versions of Case theory work reasonably well in English in ordering the complements, for example. I suppose one can generalize that. It is a suggestive direction. I think it would be interesting to explore this idea in trying to deal with W* language phenomena not in terms of X-bar but with a relaxation of case theory. I would be interested in seeing how that might work. I think it would be very interesting now to start working on languages with richer overt case systems like Russian, Greek, Latin.[7]

---

7. An interesting suggestion is made in Horvath (1981) with respect to Hungarian. Horvath proposes that the adjacency condition on objective case, marking, as present in English (cf. Stowell (1981)),does not hold in languages with a rich case marking system and corresponding free word order, but that it may show up in other ways. So, in Hungarian it is focus assignment which is subject to the adjacency condition which thereby imposes ordering constraints of a slightly different nature.

In 1955 you argued that natural languages could not be adequately represented in terms of Phrase-Structure Grammar. Instead you founded Transformational Grammar. Then you started undermining the transformational stronghold. This paradox is only an apparent one in light of the projection problem. Now that we have only a finite class of core transformational components and hence of core grammars, given some assumptions on the base and the lexicon, one might say that the variation space of grammars accessible to the language learning child provides a strictly finite set of options, and that therefore the problem of language acquisition is solved or near-trivialized.

At least one version of it is solved, but there are other learnability problems. For example, there is the problem that Ken Wexler and Peter Culicover are interested in,[8] the depth, the complexity of the data that is required to uniquely determine the grammar. They show that depth-two data suffices in principle for the grammars that they had in mind, and that could turn out to be true or false independently of whether the number of grammars is finite or not. But it is true – it is hard to imagine many mathematical problems about the acquisition of systems of a finite class. The types of questions that a mathematical theory of learnability can deal with are probably somewhat limited if it is true that the number of core grammars is finite.

Could Wexler and Culicover's work also be relevant for psychologists who study child language and construct real time models of language acquisition.

Their work is an existence proof. It says that if grammars have certain types of properties then they will be able to be acquired by certain types of learning systems. You can imagine that having suggestive implications, or deriving either sustenance or refutation from experimental work. It has not happened yet, but still I think it is important work.

Take work on core grammar. Since we have been talking about parameters for some two or three years now, people have with increasing frequency been constructing scenarios saying suppose that this is a parameter, what kind of evidence could be used to argue for or against the plausibility of a given parameter. And sometimes these scenarios obtain a certain amount

---

8. Wexler and Culicover (1980).

of complexity and specificity which seem to constitute fertile grounds for studying language acquisition.

Yes, I think so, very much so in fact. It seems to me that the approach that you are outlining suggests a rich new area of investigation. Most language acquisition work has been rather boring in my opinion. It has dealt with superficial properties of language at a very early stage. But there are several places where there are active research programs dealing with more complex linguistic phenomena. An example is Tom Roeper's work.[9] It seems to me that the questions you mention could be very intriguing to investigate. For example if our theories are more or less right, it ought to turn out that if children get information that something is a reciprocal then they ought to put into play a whole range of constraints as to whether and how it can be interpreted and construed. And I think it is certainly worth trying to find out if it is true. Actually there is some work from Tom Roeper's group bearing on this. There is one thesis on reciprocals in which the conclusion is that the conditions do not hold for the use of reciprocals at early stages, but I think the data were misinterpreted.[10] At any rate, these are the right kind of questions.

Actually what strikes me as the most interesting work in child language acquisition – maybe because my wife did it[11] – was based directly on linguistic properties that were worth studying intrinsically, and I think that is the kind of work that we need to pursue. People who have worked on language acquisition studies have often tended to work on what is easy rather than on what is important.

Currently, conditions on rules are being replaced by conditions on representations. With the possible exception of subjacency, there is no syntactic condition on rule-applicability left between D-structure and S-structure. All we have is conditions and filters on Phonetic Representation and Logical Form. Some linguists might argue that the autonomy thesis of syntax is true in a trivial sense only, what remains of syntax is just the rule schema "Do anything anywhere anytime": What is the content of the autonomy thesis.

---

9. See, for example, Roeper (1981). Several of Roeper's students have done work along similar lines, especially Goodluck, Matthei, Phinney, Solan, Tavakolian. Much of these studies have been published in the University of Massachusetts Occasional Papers in Linguistics, Amherst.
10. Cf. Matthei (1979). For a recent study on subjacency, see Otsu (1981).
11. Chomsky, C. (1969).

The term syntax can be used in many ways. What we might mean by syntax is the system of rules and representations of the language faculty, including representations that many people call "semantic", also phonology, at least all of abstract phonology. In fact a better term for it might just be the computational component of the language faculty or something like that.

So let's put forth a thesis, which will ultimately be the thesis of autonomy of syntax. It says that there exists a faculty of the mind which corresponds to the computational aspects of language, meaning the system of rules that give certain representations and derivations. What would be the parts of that system? Presumably the base rules, the transformational rules, the rules that map S-structures onto phonological representation, and onto logical forms, all of that is syntax. In this sense,[12] for example, logical form rules or SI-1 as this area called in Reflections on Language would be syntax. Now, of course some of the syntax has a lot to do with sound, for example the markedness rules and the linking rules that we were talking about earlier are syntax from this point of view, but of course they are deeply involved with properties of sound. Ultimately, they have their form and their way of operating because of the way they're interpreted in the domain of sound. Nevertheless they have an internal autonomy, they have their own properties, and as they function they don't refer to elements of the physical world, they just refer to the representations that they construct. The same is true for the level of logical form. That is to say rules like, say, quantifier movement and the binding conditions and the like are completely formal rules. They just have to do with computational manipulations, but of course they have a direct, and immediate interpretation in the semantic domain, with respect to quantifiers, anaphora etc. Still, I want to include all that as syntax.

The question is: does syntax in that sense exist as an independent system? That might not be true. For example, it might be that the rule of quantifier movement only applies when it is raining outside. If that is true, then syntax does not exist as an autonomous, independent system. You might think of less crazy possibilities. Maybe the rule of quantifier movement only applies if some pragmatic conditions hold, if you're engaged in conversation for example. Then again, syntax would not exist. The thesis of autonomy of syntax would in fact say that this system is pretty well selfcontained. Undoubtedly, the system interacts with other systems, but the interaction is more or less at the periphery. Now, that by

---

12. Cf. Chomsky (1975: chapter 3).

no means has to be true, and maybe it is completely false, but it seems to me that this hypothesis has held up pretty well. I don't see any reason to question it right now.

Incidentally, I might say that there is an analogous question about the autonomy of the language acquisition device. This really has to do with the autonomy of syntactic theory or linguistic theory or universal grammar, and again there is a certain debate over the question. The question is: does it make sense to try to characterize the mapping from data, preanalyzed by some set of primitives, to grammar, without bringing in the interaction of other elements, such as human interaction or whatever? I'm sure that if you counted noses, people in developmental psychology would overwhelmingly doubt this autonomy thesis. I don't think that they have a coherent argument, or a coherent alternative, but I don't doubt that they'd vote against it if asked to vote. Here we are asking whether the way in which the development of the grammar takes place is, to a very high degree of approximation, independent of other kinds of social and even cognitive interactions. And these are questions we can't have *a priori*, dogmatic opinions about, but I think that that thesis of autonomy holds up pretty well too, as far as we know. In fact if it didn't hold up, it would be very surprising to find much uniformity among people in the knowledge of their language, because there obviously are vast differences in the conditions under which language is acquired.

This point has to do with what might be called external autonomy. Let us discuss now internal autonomy. In what sense are the subcomponents or subsystems of syntax autonomous with respect to one another.

That's again an interesting question. Some people like Ken Hale have argued that it is a desideratum, that it ought to be a working hypothesis that the components within syntax are also as autonomous as possible.[13] Take a concrete case, the rules mapping S-structure onto phonetic representation ought to be completely autonomous from the rules mapping S-structure onto logical form. I think he's right, it is a good working hypothesis. Of course it might be false, but it's a good hypothesis because it gives you a more restricted theory, and obviously that is always what one is looking for, a theory with more explanatory power. But again, it could be wrong. We might discover for example that quantifier movement depends on whether some filter, which for some other reason is on the pho-

---

13. Hale (1976). Cf. also Hale, Jeanne, and Platero (1977).

netic side, is operating. That could be, but again I think that this thesis of autonomy holds up pretty well too. There are plenty of outstanding problems which might indicate that it is wrong, but I think it's been a very productive hypothesis which, so far at least, isn't obviously wrong for the various components that people have thought about.

What are the crucial properties of the autonomous transformational component? The crucial properties seem to be subjacency, proper government of the trace (the Empty Category Principle) and the requirement that movement be to a non-theta-position.

Suppose the transformational part boils down to something like 'move alpha', in the core at least, maybe with a few parameters. I think that that possibility has led to a certain amount of confusion in the field. It has led to the quite erroneus belief that the transformational depth of derivations is reduced. Of course, that does not follow. In fact it could turn out that the set of transformations proposed in *The Logical Structure of Linguistic Theory* is still exactly the set proposed or used today, but that they happen to have been now all formulated in the form 'move alpha'. I think that that is not far from true actually. If I look over work of 25 years ago, there are some transformations that I now think exist, like subject raising for example, which just weren't discussed in the fifties as far as I can recall. And there are a few others that I now think shouldn't be there, like the nominalization transformation. My own feeling about it is that to a very large extent the class of operations that were thought of as transformations has held up reasonably well, that is that those are still the class that have the properties of movement rules, or however you want to name that class. The progress that has been made, which I think is misunderstood, is that there's been a continual reduction in the amount of apparatus postulated to express the operation of these transformations. In other words, certain general properties of the whole class have been factored out, conditions have been formulated making it unnecessary to stipulate special cases of those properties with regard to each particular transformation. The ultimate aim would be to try to get a theory in which you have no ordering and no obligatoriness and no structural descriptions, and that is a good ideal. If you get to it, however, it tells you nothing at all about the flattening of transformational derivations. On the contrary, it may leave them unchanged. Or if they change, it would be for other reasons. It might even deepen them, by postulating that there are more transformational operations.

Suppose we conceive of a model as composed of several subparts each with its own rules and representations. But it appears to be the case that some principles are operative in more than one component of the grammar.

I think some of the work in recent years suggests that the systems that are important are not necessarily coexistensive with these components of rule systems. For example, the locality system is one that might be found in various components. You might find that Chinese *Wh*-movement from S-structure to logical form has the same properties as overt *Wh*-movement in English.[14] If that is correct, then it means that subjacency could show up in various components. There are various other more or less autonomous systems of this kind: binding theory, case theory and control theory, and so on. It seems to me that some of the most productive new thinking has isolated systems of this kind, which have their own complex properties and their interactions with other systems.

When discussing the primitives of linguistic theory, you sometimes relate the conditions of epistemological priority which the set of primitives must satisfy to the projection problem. One conclusion you draw is that grammatical relations are very implausible primitives to build a theory on. Why are primary linguistic data not equally amenable to pretheoretical analysis in terms of grammatical relations?

The argument depends on a certain conception of what linguistic theory should be like. Suppose we think of linguistic theory, just like any theory, as a set of concepts and a set of theorems. Now, the set of concepts can be organized in all sorts of ways. The concepts have interconnections, and you want to express those interconnections as tightly as possible. The way to do that is through a constructional system in which you select a set of primitives, and a set of axioms which meet the condition that the concepts of the theory are definable in terms of the primitives and the theorems are derivable from the axioms. In principle you can pick your primitives any way you like, as long as they meet this condition. But in fact there are almost no theories which are at the point where one can even raise these questions very concretely. Nevertheless it's a direction in which one is moving.

The first requirement on a primitive basis is that it be sufficient, that everything ought to be definable in terms of it, and that the set of axioms

---

14. As argued in Huang (1982).

involving the primitives be sufficient to provide a basis for proving the theorems of the theory. That is what is required. But within that requirement there are a lot of ways to proceed. Now, if you think of linguistic theory within the framework of explanatory adequacy and language acquisition and so on, then there are other requirements. The set of primitives has to meet a condition of epistemological priority. If linguistic theory is supposed to be a model of how an idealized language acquisition system works, then the primitives have to have the property that they can be applied to the data pretheoretically. Of course that can really never be done, because there is no such thing as pretheoretical data, everything is somehow analyzed. But one has to try to find the set of primitives which have the empirical property that the child can more or less tell in the data itself whether they apply before it knows the grammar. And to the extent that we can reach that goal, we have a plausible linguistic theory which can face the task of offering an explanation for linguistic phenomena within a framework of explanation formulated in terms of language acquisition.

So what would be a reasonable primitive from this point of view? Something like "precede" would be a reasonable primitive, because presumably non-linguistic mechanisms or linguistic mechanisms independent of the particular grammar, could determine whether something precedes something else in speech. And phonetic features might be reasonable primitives if we think that there are peripheral analytic devices that can at least detect features. And mathematical notions might be reasonable devices if we think that they're just available to the language faculty from other capacities. There are many reasonable looking candidates for primitive notions. Maybe even notions like "word" are primitive, if we can assume that the data at least in part comes in such a way that word-like units are presented individually for example. Any such primitive that we put forward actually involves an empirical assumption about what is necessary for language acquisition. For example, if someone says that "word" is a primitive, he is saying in fact that if people were presented with language without any indication of words, they wouldn't be able to learn it. That certainly looks false, so that one might raise questions even about whether a notion like word is a primitive.

The claim we're making about primitive notions is that if data were presented in such a way that these primitives couldn't be applied to it directly, prelinguistically before you have a grammar, then language couldn't be learnt. Of course nobody knows how to get such a set of primitives, but that's the property it ought to have. And the more unrealistic it is to think of concepts as having those properties, the more unrealistic it is to regard them as primitives. So now, take grammatical relations, say the notion subject. The question is: is it plausible to believe that in the flow of speech, in the noises that are presented, before the grammatical rules are available, it is possible to pick out something of which one can say: here is the subject? That seems wildly implausible. Rather it seems that somehow you must be able to identify the subject on the basis of other things you've identified, maybe configurational notions which are somehow constructed out of accessible materials or maybe out of semantic notions, which are primitive for the language faculty. We have to assume that there are some prelinguistic notions which can pick out pieces of the world, say elements of this meaning and of this sound. Somehow something like that's got to go on, and whatever those notions are, you might say that in the case of the notion grammatical subject, there is some perhaps complex characterization in terms of these notions. But any such approach to the notion of subject makes it a nonprimitive notion.

Now, having said that, let me backtrack. There is another possibility. That is to assume that there's no primitive basis that serves to actually define the more abstract concepts such as subject, but rather that there is just a network of concepts, and that they sort of touch reality at various points, and that they're tightly enough interconnected so that the way of making them fit to the data presented is fairly restricted. In this case, there need not be any primitives. But from this point of view it also ought to follow that you should be able to construct different grammars with the same data. If you really believe that there's one grammar for a given set of data, or something very close to that, then you're pretty well bound to believing that there's a narrow type of constructional system with a set of epistemologically prior primitive notions in terms of which everything is literally defined. The weaker the constraints on the concepts, the more ways there are going to be to realize the system with fixed data. So, again, if in fact the situation in language acquisition is such that subjects and objects and so on are close to uniquely determined, that there isn't much of a range of possibilities about it, then you really would expect all of these notions to be defined notions, since it obviously makes no sense to say that these meet the condition of epistemological priority. So it's in that respect that I think one should be very sceptical about theories that take it as a point of principle that these notions are primitive.

The Generative Enterprise Revisited

Linguistics in the 21st Century

An Interview with Noam Chomsky
[Interviewed by Naoki Fukui and Mihoko Zushi,
November 22, 2002]

1. Linguistics: The Development of Linguistic Theory in the past 20 Years

How do you characterize the development of linguistic theory in the last 20 years? Has there been what might be called "the third conceptual shift" in the field since the original The Generative Enterprise interview took place some twenty years ago? What are the continuities and departures from earlier works in generative grammar?

I think the most dramatic change that's taken place in the past twenty years is not really in linguistic theory, but just in the scope and depth of linguistic work. There's been just an enormous explosion of work on the widest imaginable range of typologically variable languages of every conceivable type in very much greater depth than ever before. Also [there have been] explorations in new areas, like a lot more work on formal semantics and its various aspects, a lot of work on properties of prosodic systems and metrical systems and others that's new. The field's just exploded in scale, quite apart from theoretical changes. In fact you can see it very clearly here [at MIT]: Twenty years ago, any faculty member could be on any committee, any generals committee, any doctoral committee, but now it's very highly specialized. There are very few people who can feel confident looking at work of students over the range, and usually it's only a few who pay close attention. I don't know if that's permanent; my guess is that it's going to go the other way; if things are really understood, it'll sort of fall together. But at the moment at least, it's a period of extreme variation and enormous amounts of simply new material.

As far as linguistic theory is concerned, at the time of *The Generative Enterprise*, the principles-and-parameters approach was just about taking shape, and – I don't mean it's universally accepted – it was that framework, in my opinion, that led to the explosion of research. It simply allowed questions to be formulated in completely new ways without a lot of the constraints and demands of earlier approaches. The big achievement of the principles-and-parameters framework – I don't recall how clear it was at the time, but in retrospect it's quite clear – was that it gave at least a possible resolution to what had been a real paradox, namely the conflict between the effort to achieve descriptive adequacy – which led to more and more complicated, elaborate formulations within particular languages, for different constructions, and across languages – and explanatory adequacy. So on the one hand [we found] that pressure towards diversity and complexity, and on the other hand, the concern for explanatory adequacy, which demonstrated that the truth had to be just the opposite: That languages had to be basically cast in the same mold; there had to be at most slight differences among them or else the acquisition problem is unsolvable. So there was that tension, and the principles-and-parameters approach, which didn't just come about in a minute but had been developed through a lot of work during the preceding twenty years, attempted to extract from particular constructions underlying principles which would leave a residue which would be simpler; and the underlying principles could then be attributed to the universal grammar, to the initial state. If the values of parameters can be set on the basis of simple data, and the principles are fixed, that would resolve the tension. The task is huge, but at least a possible resolution of the paradox came into focus.

Now that work kind of coalesced around the late 1970s, in the principles-and-parameters approach which was, I think, the only real revolutionary departure in linguistics maybe in the last several thousand years, much more so than the original work in generative grammar. It effectively abandoned the notions of rules and constructions that had been at the core of all linguistic work for thousands of years. And it proposed that these [rules and constructions] are taxonomic artifacts like aquatic mammals or something: They're there all right, but they're just superficial reflections of something else. And what there really is are the fixed principles and the parametric variations, and the principles are cross-linguistic and have nothing special to do with constructions.

Now if that's correct, it's a completely new approach to language, and it does offer a way of resolving the tension. The variety of languages can now be finite, as a matter of fixing the parameters, and the principles are fixed, and their interaction should lead to one or another language more or less the way, well, I think the analogy I was using at the time, back in the late 1970s, was to regulatory mechanisms in biological development, as had been discovered some years earlier by François Jacob and Jacques

Monod.[1] Their classic work is that minor changes in regulatory mechanisms of otherwise fixed genetic systems could lead to great superficial differences – a butterfly and an elephant and so on – just by slightly modifying tiny regulatory mechanisms and so on. And that's the kind of model that intuitively suggested something like principles-and-parameters: Small changes in a fixed mechanism could lead to superficially different things, like Warlpiri and English, or Mohawk and English (Mark's work [Mark Baker]), and so on. And that work has been extremely effective. For example, Mark's recent book[2] tries to show, very interestingly, that Mohawk and English – which look about as far apart as you can be – are essentially identical if you make a few slight changes in parameters.

And that's the thrust of what seems to me the most significant work of the period, trying to show how it can be that languages superficially look different but are really basically identical. And it's been a tremendous research project. Whether it turns out to be right or wrong, it's been extremely successful, just inspiring research, not only within linguistics but in related fields. So psychology of language just got revivified; and the study of the acquisition of language, which had been kind of dormant, took on a new form and has also exploded. We were looking at the obvious questions: How are grammars acquired? Can you get some real evidence for the persistence of principles? And that has led to an enormous amount of new and exciting work. And the same has happened within processing, and sooner or later it will happen in the brain sciences, I think. So that's been extremely important.

On the other hand, there are other tendencies which happen to be of particular interest to me. As soon as the fundamental question (the tension between descriptive and explanatory adequacy) had a possible solution, so that we have at least a picture of what a genuine theory of language might be. Prior to that there was no picture because they all were haunted by the paradox, but here's a picture of what a theory of language might be. Then you can go back to some earlier questions that had been mentioned but left dangling; those are the questions that ultimately enter into the Minimalist Program. They had been noticed before and kind of mentioned in *The Generative Enterprise*; actually they're mentioned in *Aspects*[3] and things like that, but left to the side. And the point is pretty straightforward. We take the picture we put on

---

1. Cf. A quote from Jacob 1977.
2. Baker, M. 2001. See also Baker, M. 1996.
3. Chomsky, N. 1965.

the board in the first introductory linguistics class: experience, arrow, box, question mark, I-language.

Experience → ❓ → I-language

So how does the initial state map experience into the I-language? That's a problem basically of morphogenesis: How does an organ grow? And it's well understood that in the growth of an organ, there's more than just experience and the genetically-determined initial state. So for example neither experience nor the genetically-determined initial state determines how a protein is going to fold, because that comes from physics and chemistry. The genetic instructions may say, "Produce this protein," and experience may trigger something there. But that leaves open the question how the protein folds: Is it going to become a piece of the skeleton, or nervous tissue, or so on. And that's coming from the outside. It must be that an enormous amount of the development of an organism is coming from the outside, in that sense. It's not much studied in biology, and not because people don't know it's there, but because it's too hard. You study what you can study, not what you'd like to study. And these questions which are surely fundamental are to the side. And essentially the same questions arise in the theory of evolution. Everyone agrees that natural selection is very important, but it has to operate within constraints that are not going to allow many options, and they are coming from the outside.

Anyway, these questions were mentioned in earlier generative grammar, but dismissed. However, they did begin to come into visibility by the early 1980s, when I used to start every class of mine with: "Let's imagine that language is perfect; then what would it be like?" That was an effort to try to show that it was perfect, and it always went astray, became way too complicated. But that was the question: Could we show that there is some sense in which extra conditions or outside conditions are driving linguistic development – and in fact the form of the initial state as well – to be in some sense perfect, kind of like a snowflake is perfect? It just works that way because that's the way mathematics and physics would say. And it never worked; so it always led into one complication or another.

By the early 1990s that kind of work at least seemed to me to be reaching some success. To illustrate, around 1990 Howard Lasnik and I wrote this review[4] of the way syntax, in the broad sense, looked to us. It's reprinted as the first chapter of the book *The Minimalist Program*.[5] And when I look

---

4. Chomsky, N. and H. Lasnik. 1993.
5. Chomsky, N. 1995.

back to it, I see that almost nothing in it seems to be correct. That is, the project of the next ten years, at least for me, was to submit every assumption in that picture, and other assumptions, to a critique which asked: Can we really give a principled explanation for this, and if we can't, is there a way to get rid of it? Going back to the picture on the board, the study of the output, the I-language, is a theory which tries to reach descriptive adequacy. That's basically the answer to the question: What is the language? A look at the box, the mapping, is a different kind of question: How did the language get that way? The question we're now thinking about is the question "why?" Why these principles and not some other principles? These "why" questions, that's the Minimalist Program. We don't know how far we can go, but to the extent that you can answer the "why" question, you will have shown that there's a principled reason why things are the way they are. It's not just abstracting principles from the final state and putting them into the initial state, which is a major step forward, but actually extracting them from the language altogether and showing that they really belong somewhere else. They're just general principles of organic nature.

Since we're talking about computational systems, we should naturally look for computational principles, like computational efficiency principles and so on, and ask to what extent are they entering into the determination of the initial state, the principles that enter into the state that's attained. So going back to the thing that Howard and I wrote: At the time, we kind of took for granted, if you look at the sections, there's a section on d-structure, a section on s-structure, a section on transformations, and so on. And if you think what was really assumed there, it should have been possible to see that it couldn't possibly be right, because there were three ... four ... I guess five relatively independent generative systems, each of them essentially a cycle, all doing the same thing, but operating separately. There was one that formed d-structure by X-bar Theory, which is basically cyclic. There's the transformational cycle, which is mapping d-structure to s-structure. There's a covert transformational cycle, which is mapping s-structure to LF, with the same kinds of transformations and also cyclic. And there's something mapping LF over to the semantic interface, a compositional semantics of some kind and, again, cyclic. And there's something mapping s-structure to PF, which is also basically cyclic; and, whatever you think, phonology's at least partially compositional. All right, so we have five separate compositional operations, all doing about the same thing. Nature can't be that ugly.

The point that was particularly noticed was the overt and covert transformations. The question was constantly asked, why does the LF cycle reproduce the overt cycle? But in fact the question holds for all of them:

Why should there be five independent computational systems, all cyclic, all compositional, all basically operating on the same things? Well, looking at it now, I think the minimalist critique of the past 10 years has given substantial reasons to suppose that none of these things exists: d-structure, s-structure, and LF just don't exist. There's no X-bar Theory forming d-structure. Of all of those levels, the only ones that remain are PF and the semantic interface. The others, the strictly internal linguistic ones – LF, d-structure, and s-structure – probably don't exist.

But if that's true, we have only one cycle; there's one operation, Merge, a free operation that says, "Build bigger things out of smaller things." The essence of the recursive system comes free, and it's just used successively to build bigger and bigger things. At some point in the derivation, you've got a syntactic object, call it a "phase" by definition (whatever it turns out to be). That syntactic object is handed over to the interpretive systems; it's transferred to the phonology and the semantics. They do whatever they do to it, and then they're finished with it, and they forget about it. You can then proceed with the derivation, creating a bigger syntactic object which at the next phase does the same thing – it doesn't look back to the earlier product. And they essentially go on indefinitely. You can, because there's no limit to the complexity of the sentence. And at some point maybe you stop and apply the final Spell-Out, interpret the maximal syntactic object so far constructed, and you're done. But then there's one cycle, with no intermediate structures.

As far as the transformations are concerned, the difference between overt and covert, what looks to be now like a reasonable proposal is something like this: They both apply at the phase level, and the only difference between them is ordering. So there is a Transfer operation at the phase level which hands things over to phonology and semantics. On the phonology side it's called Spell-Out, but it's essentially just half of the Transfer operation. The operation of Displacement, which is really just internal Merge, applies either before or after Transfer; those are two options. If it applies before Transfer, it's going to be overt movement; if it applies after Transfer, it'll be covert movement. The approach is basically what Jon Nissenbaum developed in a recent MIT dissertation.[6] That raises lots of questions: How do you get the properties of covert movement? Why does it appear to violate islands? A huge mass of well-known empirical problems immediately fall on your head. But that looks like a plausible thing to do, in which case the overt and covert distinction disappears. X-bar Theory is

---

6. Nissenbaum, J. 2000.

gone, because you just have Merge. There are problems about how you identify labels; incidentally, Chris Collins[7] has argued maybe you don't have to, perhaps you can do it in a different way. I think that's an open question.

There was, I think, a mistake of mine – introducing traces – which was simply my own misunderstanding. If you look back at $LSLT^8$ in the 1950s, that picture was actually correct in retrospect. A transformation was basically just a copying operation: that is, you take something and you copy it somewhere else. And then I added a Delete operation, which was necessary because the picture in $LSLT$ was mapping from some underlying structure to the phonetics, and then you had to Delete along the way. So the actual transformations had an extra level of complexity, namely copy and erase. But when EST [Extended Standard Theory] sort of took shape that picture didn't work any more. You couldn't just copy and erase. That's where the trace came from, so you'd insert trace; it should have just been a copy. That was a mistake; it should have just been a copy, forgetting the Delete operation. The Delete operation presumably – at least, arguably – is coming from the outside. If you want to minimize computation, if you want to spell things out as little as possible, you will spell out only one of the two identical elements, either the new one introduced by the operation (the "higher one" in the configuration) or the one in the "base" position of initial Merge (the "lower one" in the configuration). The higher one cannot be deleted, or there will be no distinction between overt and covert Move. So therefore the lower one must be deleted. These considerations should derive from outside the language faculty, from general principles of minimal computation. If that can be worked out properly, nothing would have to be said about this within the theory of the language faculty itself.

If that's correct, it's one of a number of things that point in an interesting direction. That makes language itself more like a snowflake, meaning minimize computation; but it makes language use harder. The main problem in processing problems is how you find the gap that's associated with something that says there's going to be a gap. Well, if you never erase it, it would be trivial. The gap wouldn't be there; so you just see the thing that's missing. So for processing, it would be a lot easier if you didn't erase. But for minimization of computation, it's a lot easier if you do erase. So it looks as

---

7. Collins, C. 2001.
8. Chomsky, N. 1955. (See Introduction to the 1975 edition for an informative discussion about the status of different versions of $LSLT$.)

if, to put it metaphorically, language is kind of designed for ease of computation, but not for ease of use. I think there are quite a number of things that point in that direction. So it's as if you were sticking a liver into the body and you don't care how good it will be for the person, but you want it to fit very well into the surrounding systems. So it's that kind of criterion.

If this is correct, then you throw out traces; you've got copies. And you forget about reconstruction, because you don't have the downward movement rules to reconstruct. There are still many problems when you reconstruct and so on, but the materials are all there to approach them in what looks like an appropriate way. The idea that we assumed then – that there are two different kinds of operations, one which forms phrase structures and one which carries out movement – is probably incorrect. If this is correct, there's only one operation, Merge. Unless you stipulate that it can't happen, Merge is either going to be external or internal. If some configuration X has been constructed, the next step of computation can extend it by Merging Y to it, and Y can either be something outside of X (external Merge) or within X (internal Merge). External Merge plays the role of the former phrase structure rules; internal Merge, leaving a copy, plays the role of transformational rules. Presumably, you don't stipulate that internal Merge is disallowed, so internal Merge is allowed, leaving a copy, one that needn't be spelled out. So you end up with a kind of a picture like that. But just comparing it very roughly to the picture, say, that I had ten years ago, if I were to start a class ten years ago, it would have been the first section of that review [Chomsky and Lasnik 1993]. If I were to start it now, it's this, which has almost nothing left in it from the basic conceptual apparatus of that review – though a good deal remains under various modifications; and then we'd see where we'd go from there.

So at least the part of linguistic theory that's of particular interest to me is that part. That's a personal judgment; other people would say different things.

Economy and Minimalism

(i) Two kinds of minimalism:

Let us ask a few questions regarding some of the general issues that seem to be raised by the Minimalist Program in a particularly illuminating way. First of all, there seem to be two related but distinct kinds of minimalism. One is what we might call "methodological minimalism," a methodologically-driven effort to improve scientific theories. The other is what might be called "substantive minimalism," which claims that the object of our inquiry itself (the human language faculty) has a certain optimal character.[9] *Can you elaborate on these?*

That's a confusing problem, and I don't think many people are convinced [of the need for the distinction]. (My friend Norbert Hornstein isn't at all convinced.) It's a subtle, but I think, real distinction. So let's think again of the snowflake and think of something towards the opposite end of perfection – take the vertebrate spine. (I learned a little about this about ten years ago when I was in the hospital for a couple of months with spine problems and was reading about it and talking to neurosurgeons, and so on. So I'm a minor expert on the spine, from the inside out.) Apparently, the spine is extremely badly designed for vertebrates. Not just humans; it doesn't have anything to do with correct posture. Cows have back pains too, but they don't know how to complain about it. And it just seems to be badly done. It looks as though if you asked some smart engineer in the Mechanical Engineering Department to make one of these things, he could do it a lot better. Nature just did it out of what was around, and it sort of works, but everybody has back pains, and sometimes serious ones.

Furthermore, if you think a little further, there are things that Nature just doesn't use. Take metals, for instance. Metals are terrific for construction; that's why you can use them for everything. And they're all over the place; they're extremely abundant in the earth's surface. But they're just not used in organisms. About the only way in which they're used, I think, is as magnets for navigation. But they're not used as construction materials. So these are just ways that Nature didn't find to make things that really work. In fact, it's being replaced, so nowadays people are ending up with artificial hips and all sorts of things, which may well work better than the originals.

OK, let's take a snowflake on the one extreme and say the spine on the other. And let's say you want to make a theory of both of them. Well, in each case you want the theory to be as good as possible. So, in the case of the snowflake – that's what excited Kepler and everybody else, because it's so obviously perfect – and then you wanted to explain it and you finally nowadays can produce a pretty good theory about snowflakes. And it explains why they are perfect. The best theory of snowflakes will be the one that explains why they are perfect and couldn't be improved, given the na-

---

9. Cf. An Interview on Minimalism, chapter 4 of Chomsky, N. 2002. See also Martin, R. and J. Uriagereka. 2000.

ture of the world. Now let's take the spine. We also want the best theory of the spine, so that the neurosurgeon who's going to operate on your spine we'd like him to have the best theory of this rotten mess. That's the methodological minimalism. You want the best theory of whatever object you're looking at whether it's a snowflake or a spine or something jerry-rigged to sort of work.

The other kind of minimalism is interested in the difference between a snowflake and a spine. So is a snowflake the optimal way it can be, given the conditions of Nature? The answer is apparently "yes." Is the spine the best way it could be, given the options allowed by Nature? Probably not. It may be the best way it is from another point of view: history. Maybe if you take the long millions of years through which this thing gradually evolved, OK, that's the best thing Nature could come up with, on the various paths it's taken. But if you started over and you just ask: "What's the best possible way to construct an object which will have the functions of the spine?," it's alleged that you could do it much better. So it's not perfect; it's very imperfect. You still want the best theory of it, but it's not perfect. Well, those are just two different questions.

The question about language is, "To what extent is it like a snowflake and to what extent is it like a spine?" If you would have asked traditional linguists, it's the spine, or worse, just a hopeless mess. And if you asked in say the 1950s, Martin Joos' famous statement was just standard belief, and Sapir [Edward Sapir] said the same thing, and others: Languages can just differ in arbitrary ways.[10] So it could be anything. That's what Whitney [William Dwight Whitney] believed and others and if there's anything fixed, it's what the structuralists were proposing, that there's a fixed array of phonological features, let's say as Jakobson [Roman Jakobson] proposed.[11] But that's minimal, very minimal constraints on variety. Other things, it's just whatever there is. And in fact as soon as we move beyond sound structure and morphology, there almost is nothing very systematic in traditional scientific grammar. It was often assumed that you form sentences by the laws of thought, with some language-specific guidelines that could vary very widely, even arbitrarily, some claimed. There's words and their internal structure and you kind of put them together and beyond that the linguistic system itself does not have much of a determinate structure. Saussure [Ferdinand de Saussure] had no place for sentences in his system. It's somewhere between parole and langue,

---

10. Joos, M. ed. 1957.
11. Cf. Jakobson, R, C. G. M. Fant, and M. Halle. 1952.

but neither. It's not langue because it doesn't have a structure and it isn't a social product. And it can't just be parole, an act of will, but it's kind of hanging around there somewhere.

But once you begin to look at it carefully, insisting on fixed generative rule systems, you find that the apparent variety and complexity is extraordinary. And now we're back to the paradox again. And the question is whether you can show that you can not only resolve the paradox and the "what" and "how" questions in some serious way, but maybe you can even go beyond and show that there's something about that that approaches perfection, that really arises from the way things like principles of efficient computation operate on a system like this. If we look a step further, if you take the final state, the I-language – notice there's really no difference between looking at the initial and at the final state, the difference between explanatory and descriptive adequacy is just terminology. You're just looking at states of the language faculty, and you look at all of them the same way. Some of them are more articulated than others. But of course there's plenty in between.

Now if you ask yourself about the properties of the state – any state you pick – parts of it may have a principled explanation. To have a principled explanation, you can now see clearly what this means: It means in part it comes from external principles – say efficient computation. To the extent that that's true, it has a principled explanation. Another part is that it comes from conditions imposed by the interface. So whatever the language is, it's at least got to interact with other systems of the body. And first guess is there's two of them, the traditional assumption from Aristotle, in essence: sensory-motor and some conceptual-intentional interface. So it has to interface with those two systems. In traditional terms, an expression of a language has sound and meaning. Well, these systems have their own properties. They are properties independent of language. So the ear is what it is, independent of language; maybe there's some interaction but not an overwhelming thing. So the first reasonable approximation is the external systems are just there and the language is inserted into them. Just like the first approximation would be the body's there and the liver is inserted into it and has to interact with the other systems. If it produces something other than bile – let's say some chemical that the rest of the system can't deal with – then it might as well not be there. So presumably an organ that's in the body – unless it's totally vestigial – is interacting with other systems of the body. The language organ is going to be interacting with these other two systems: They impose their own requirements – that's the interface conditions. And if you can show that some property of the internal state of the language faculty satisfies those conditions, you also have a principled explanation.

So there's going to be two sources of principled explanation: (1) interface conditions; and (2) language external – in fact organism external – conditions, just general principles of organisms. Everything else is unprincipled. It means there's no current explanation, and there may never be an interesting explanation. It might be the result of evolutionary accident, or it might be the way that brains work for some reason that nobody understands and probably never will. Anyhow, it's unprincipled at this level of explanation. Actually you can ask similar questions about any organism, but it's rarely done because the questions are too hard; but you could always ask them. In this case, we have a principled explanation coming from interface conditions and computational considerations, and unprincipled descriptions.

The Minimalist Program is really just the effort to make as many things principled as possible and see how far you can go. The point can be illustrated by the comparison which we just discussed between the EST and what I think now may be correct: a single cycle, cutting out levels and other entities that had no principled basis. How far can you go with that? We don't know. But the farther you go, the more you're approaching the second kind of minimalism, substantive minimalism. That's independent of methodological minimalism, which you're going to try to achieve for the unprincipled part. You'll also want the best theory of that, even though it doesn't satisfy substantive minimalism. So I think one can make the distinction. And the reason why it's tricky to make is because you seem to be doing the same things, when you're following one path and when you're following the other. So you're often following pretty much the same path when you do one or the other, but with a sharply different conception in mind.

(ii) The "evaluation measure" and minimalism

From the very outset of the history of contemporary generative grammar, you have been talking about the evaluation procedure, particularly the "simplicity measure." For example, in The Logical Structure of Linguistic Theory (Chapter IV, p. 119), you say "Note that when we speak of the simplicity of linguistic theory, we are using 'simplicity' in the still vague sense in which simplicity is an ideal for any science, whereas when we speak of the simplicity of grammars, we are using it in a sense which we hope to make as precise as the definition of 'phoneme' or 'morpheme.' The simplicity of linguistic theory is a notion to be analyzed in the general study of philosophy of science; the simplicity of grammars is a notion defined within linguistic theory." Thus, both kinds of minimalism (methodological and substantive) seem to have been present, at least in a preliminary form, from the earliest work of contemporary generative grammar. It is just that the object of these criteria has been elevated, as a result of empirical investigations over the years, from particular grammars to universal grammar, roughly corresponding to the level at which we can realistically address the problem of "explanatory adequacy." What is your view on the development of these kinds of minimalism in generative grammar, particularly as they relate to the levels of adequacy?

One of these [questions] is the same, the first quote here [from *LSLT*], the simplicity of linguistic theory. And that's just getting the best theory. So that's common to everything, including the spine, the snowflake, whatever it is. You want the best theory you can. And there is some notion of simplicity involved in that. I was borrowing part of this from Nelson Goodman (I was his student at that time).[12] That's the kind of simplicity he was interested in, just general simplicity for systems altogether. My own feeling is that those are just the guiding intuitions of scientists.

So scientists are looking for things like symmetry, and they're happy if they find it. Hermann Weyl wrote a book on symmetry,[13] because everybody thought that's what we ought to find. But there's kind of a standard joke in physics that the only numbers are 1, 2, 3, and infinity; 7 is not a possible number. If you can explain things in terms of numbers like 1, 2, 3, and infinity, you've got something right. If you've got something like 7 or 83, you probably don't know what you're talking about. In fact a lot of chemistry was considered, for most of its history, not really science. One of the reasons was it had numbers like 83 and it didn't have simple principles. So whatever that notion is, it's some kind of driving intuition of the sciences. You don't know how to formulate it. You sort of learn it, and you learn it the way you learn how to be a shoemaker. You work with a master craftsman, and either you pick it up or you don't pick it up. If you pick it up, you're a good shoemaker. So I suspect not much is going to be learned about that.

---

12. Cf. Goodman, N. 1943.
13. Weyl, H. 1952.

The other kind, the simplicity inside linguistic theory, that's the evaluation measure. I don't think that has a counterpart in minimalist simplicity, because it was assumed at that time that language was like the spine. It was extremely ugly, and we had all kinds of complexity. And the simplicity measure (internal) had to do with the problem, essentially, that later came to be called language acquisition, the LAD [Language Acquisition Device] story. So how does a child go from the data to a particular grammar? (See the diagram introduced at the beginning of this interview.) In structuralist linguistics, the idea was you did it procedurally. That plainly didn't work. You get the phones and the phonemes and the morphemes; and it just gets nowhere.

So an alternative seemed to me to pick up an idea which – I didn't know it at the time – but it essentially comes out of Peirce [Charles Sanders Peirce]. It's attributed, incorrectly, to Popper [Karl Popper], who was famous for it, but it really comes from Charles Sanders Peirce, who had a much more sophisticated version of it.[14] Popper's idea was that a scientist just shoots out hypotheses at random. And then [s/he] checks them for confirmation. Peirce had a more sophisticated point. He argued that the mind has to have an essentially genetically-determined class of admissible hypotheses. So the mind is just structured so that certain hypotheses are admissible. Other possible ones are not part of our cognitive capacity and are not theories that are intelligible to us. So there are admissible hypotheses. The method of selecting them is what he called "abduction" and there's nothing to say about it apart from exploring the nature of our cognitive capacities; I am giving a possible interpretation of Peirce, perhaps not what he had in mind. But there is a method of testing them. Once you've hit on some admissible hypotheses, you can put them to empirical tests. And then you can pick one or the other. How do you test them? And what's the analog in the case of language?

In the case of language, the analog would be that linguistic theory – that is, the theory of the initial state, or universal grammar as it's later called – creates a class of admissible hypotheses. It says this is the format for grammars, for I-languages. This is the format, they look like this. Then the child has to pick one. Well, we have to have a technique of abduction; we can't just leave it where Peirce did because the child in fact picks one. So how could he pick one? There is an approach which works in principle; it's a finitary approach, but astronomical. So it can't be right.

---

14. Cf. Peirce, C. S. 1957.

But at least it's a finitary approach, so that's giving some coherence to the topic. And that's where the evaluation measure comes in.

Suppose we have a measure so that for any two instances of the admissible languages, we can say "Count the number of symbols," and it'll be whatever it is. And you can measure the two as more or as less. And you throw out the one that's more, and you stick with the one that's less. And you keep doing that until you get to the minimum. Well, that does give a procedure, a kind of ridiculous procedure. When you start, you have the data. You start with the I-language as one symbol and you see that that doesn't work. You go to 2 symbols and that doesn't work. You finally get to 50,000 symbols – and that does work. And that's the first one you got to, so that's your language. So that actually is a discovery procedure. It's just one that's totally unfeasible, so it can't be the right one – but at least it is a discovery procedure. So the evaluation procedure does yield a discovery procedure, in that sense. In some sense, it provides the conceivability of an answer, but not an actual answer. How did it work? If you look at the details, these are basically efforts to capture what looks like a linguistically-significant generalization. So if two things happen in the same environment, you want to be able to collapse the rules so that the formulation of them is shorter than if two things happen in different environments. On the other hand, there are plenty of things you don't capture, like cyclicity of the form: "ABC turns to CBA" (ABC → CBA) – you don't want to capture that. That is the basic meaning of the brackets and "X arrow Y in context A—B" (X → Y /A—B) and all that kind of business. Those are all notations designed to try to capture linguistic generalizations by mapping a straight system of rules – which are just going to be things of the form "α → β," something changes to something else – into some other form by a notational transformation where the number of symbols in the output will be the evaluation of the original, by capturing the concept of linguistically-significant generalization.

That's what the evaluation measure was supposed to be. The only place where it was really tried in any detail was in my undergraduate thesis, *The Morphophonemics of Modern Hebrew*,[15] which in excruciating detail applied this to show that a particular grammar for the language in question was at least a local maximum; that is, if you interchanged any two rules, it got worse. It's a hopeless task, of course. And sooner or later these things were given up because they don't make any sense. But that was the idea; that's the evaluation measure. And in fact up until princi-

---

15. Chomsky, N. 1949.

ples-and-parameters approaches came along, there was no alternative. That's the way it was up until principles-and-parameters. That was the only acquisition procedure, discovery procedure available. And it did require an evaluation measure. So you look at *The Sound Pattern of English*,[16] and there's a lot of symbol counting, counting features and so forth. And maybe there's something right about all that. But the principles-and-parameters approach just kind of cut it to shreds, because you don't need an evaluation measure. You just set the parameters.

So substantive minimalism emerged only after the principles-and-parameters approach was introduced?

It had been recognized as a problem – if you look at *Aspects* there's two sentences on it, and they're just throwaways. Because it didn't seem you could do anything with it. Actually, it's somewhat similar in general biology; it's almost never discussed. And people like, say, D'Arcy Thompson[17] and Turing[18] [Alan Turing], there's some genuflection toward them, but it's basically regarded as a failed research program, or maybe premature.

(iii) The "domain-specificity" of the language faculty under minimalism:

It is generally held in generative grammar that the faculty of language is a kind of a mental organ with its specific properties not reducible to other cognitive capacities. If you look at earlier versions of universal grammar (UG), that is certainly true. For example, phrase structure rules and grammatical transformations in standard theory have their own formal properties not deducible from other formal operations outside of language. That is also true for earlier theories of UG in the principles-and-parameters framework; for instance, X-bar theory is highly specific to language and its characteristics do not seem to be reducible to external factors. Properties of UG are something that we have to discover by looking at language alone, basically. However, in the theory of UG within the current minimalist framework, this strong "domain-specificity" of the faculty of language may no longer hold. Thus, the operation Merge, the basic recursive procedure for structure-building, can be regarded as an instance of a general

---

16. Chomsky, N. and M. Halle. 1968.
17. Thompson, D. W. 1942.
18. Turing, A. M. 1952.

combining (or concatenating, if linear order is defined) operation not subject to associative law, yielding "hierarchical structures" (i. e., [A # B] # C ≠ A # [B # C], where # represents Merge). And we can find similar operations outside of language, e. g., logical implication. In fact, if the "strong minimalist thesis" is to be maintained, nothing in the faculty of language is supposed to be, strictly speaking, "domain-specific." This is not to say, however, that the faculty of language cannot exist as an autonomous system; it can. I think we can think of the concept of "speech organ" as a point of reference. That is, no component of "speech organ," the lungs, the air pipe, the tongue, the teeth, and so on, is designed for speech per se. They have developed for other purposes, breathing, eating, etc. Nevertheless, we can think of "speech organ" as a system specifically dedicated to speech. The language faculty may be interpreted in a similar way. What is your opinion about the domain-specificity of the faculty of language under the minimalist conceptions?

I think you're exactly right. When language looks like a hopeless mess, it looks very domain-specific, for exactly the reasons you say. On the other hand, to the extent that you can make some progress in the minimalist program, domain-specificity of language is reduced to some special arrangement of elements that are not language-specific. To illustrate, suppose (almost unimaginably) that the strongest minimalist thesis turns out to be correct: Language is an optimal solution to the interface conditions (in some reasonable sense of optimal), and those conditions are part of general primate biology. Then domain-specificity of language – the sole "innovation" in the evolution of language – would be the recursive linkage of the interface systems. And any partial achievement in the minimalist program would yield a similar (though more limited) conclusion about domain-specificity. OK, so the sensory-motor system is just like some basically primate system, well maybe a little different, like a monkey's different from a chimpanzee, but not fundamentally different. And the thought systems are identical – again, with minor variations. It's very unlikely to be true, but that would be an extreme claim. And then what's unique to humans is just that there is the recursive system interconnecting them. If there is a recursive system interconnecting them, it should be like a snowflake. So it should just be the way which Nature instantly finds of connecting these things when it decides to interconnect them. That would be the ultimate perfection.

If that were true, the only thing that would be domain-specific would be the existence of the interconnection. And of course that's not going to be true. So there are going to be special things about, at least, the conceptual system and probably the sensory-motor system and there's a lot more. At least as far as we know, there's no hope of just reducing the whole internal system to just: Here's the one and only way to do it. So there are a number of things that look as if they're going to be domain-specific. For example, what particular form of computational complexity we use, and there are a lot we could think of. And then plenty of other things.

However, it could turn out – and I take it that's what the drift of your question is – that every component of the faculty of language is doing something else. And that what's domain-specific is the organization of these various components. That wouldn't be so unlikely, because if you look at, say, organs of the body it's kind of what they're like. Any particular cell might be involved in all sorts of things. And in fact that's why it doesn't make any sense really to talk about the function of any organ of the body, except for varied interest-relative purposes. So let's take again the skeleton. It has lots of different functions, depending on what you're thinking of. It's part of the immune system, it's part of the circulatory system, it helps you keep up so you don't fall on the floor, it does all sorts of things. But what's unique to it is just some interaction of various things, including the proteins that are part of it and so on and so forth. And something like that could turn out for the faculty of language. If so, it wouldn't be very surprising.

(iv) On displacement/dislocation and interpretable/uninterpretable features:

Let us now ask a couple of questions regarding the inner workings of UG as it is currently conceived. Why does this apparent "imperfection" exist? You have offered a suggestion which goes as follows, if we understood correctly. Language has to provide two kinds of information, as required by the "thought system" with which it interacts, namely, (i) locally-related thematic relations (Theme, Patient, etc.), and (ii) edge-related information (such as new/old information, topic, focus, specificity, etc.), which are traditionally called the "deep" and "surface" properties, respectively. And displacement is just an optimal way of satisfying this external requirement imposed by the "thought system ," and furthermore, uninterpretable features are needed as an optimal way of implementing dislocation. If this is the reason for the existence of displacement, isn't there any room for parametrizing it? Thus, the second type of information (new/old information, topic, etc.) need not be signaled by being located at the edge. Rather, a language may be equipped with some other device provided by its lexicon, e. g., overt particles, to provide the second type of information. In this case, a phrase can be assigned both kinds of information in the same place, rendering displacement (and hence relevant uninterpretable features) unnecessary. Japanese seems to be a case in point. Do you think displacement is not only a universally available property of human language but also a universally manifested (either overtly or covertly) property? Or is it indeed parametrized? If it is parametrized, why is it so? (This is of course part of the more general problem: Why are there parameters?)

This is kind of speculation, but the suggestion is that the external system – the conceptual system – has a kind of duality of semantics. It's been sort of hanging around for a long time – deep and surface interpretations. So it looks as if there's a real difference between, on the one hand, argument structure and, on the other hand, essentially everything else including information-related, discourse-related, scopal, and so on and so forth. We don't know very much about the language-external conceptual-intentional systems. Part of the problem is it's almost impossible to study them except through language. So you don't get independent information about them. In principle, it's a possible subject; maybe there will be ways to study these outside systems not through language, like with other primates. Anyhow a plausible speculation, I think, is that the duality that's always been noticed is real. And that's an interface condition, that the language faculty has to provide that duality. Now we get to internal and external Merge. One way to do it is straight and seems to work, essentially without exception. And that is that argument structure is given by external Merge. So that's Theta Theory, broadly speaking. That part seems pretty stable. Almost everybody's theory says that in one way or another. So let's say that's right. That allows a number of other ways to give the duality. One of them is internal Merge, which would suggest that these should typically be edge phenomena. And to a significant extent, they are. But you're quite right; there could be other ways – in fact there are. Like other kinds of particle Merge could do some of these things. Or maybe things like *wh*-in-situ. So all we can say, I think, is that internal Merge comes free. So it's a way of expressing the duality that doesn't cost anything. But language could pick other things that do cost something – like having a special preposition. Maybe there are language-internal reasons why that doesn't cost anything. Maybe the language is so constructed with pre- and post-nominal constructions that adding another one for, say, focus, isn't any cost. But I think that does raise exactly the questions you are raising. I don't have any thought about them, just seems to me like an optimization question that's unanswered for alternatives that are around.

All languages ought to be equally costly, in this sense?
Yes, they ought to be. And you raise the question: Why are there parameters? And that raises the further question, should all languages be equally costly in some sense? I think Mark [Baker] raises this at the end of his book [Baker 2001], but leaves it kind of hanging. I don't know how you answer it. The only possible answer I can think of – and it's a remote possibility – relates to a kind of a mini-max problem involved with parameters. The more parameters a language has, that the linguistic system has, the harder it's going to be to acquire a language. If everything was Japanese, it'd be a cinch. On the other hand, it would be a greater burden on the genetic component, which has to provide more information – not just something equivalent to what the parameters are, but also what their values are. So maybe there's some point at which you have to try to attain an optimal number for two conflicting things: (1) not too much burden on the genetic component; (2) not too much burden on the task of acquiring language. Maybe that gives you the parameters. Maybe in some future, somebody will be able to demonstrate something like that. That's a possible question. It's the same kind of possible question that arises about, say, phonology. One question that's hanging around is why phonology's such a mess. If you look at the mapping from syntactic structures to phonetic form, every possible computational principle you could think of is violated. Inclusiveness is wildly violated, the input is probably 100% different from the output, so you can't have any Faithfulness or anything like that.

So what kind of "optimality" is OT [Optimality Theory] looking for?
Well, I think that's a play on words actually. What is called "optimality" in this context is something different; it may be completely correct, but it's not optimality in the sense of the preceding discussion.

On the other hand, there is a fundamental problem about OT, which I've never understood. I've asked a couple of times but don't see the answer to it. And that is, if you have a Gen-Eval system, then prima facie every input is going to come out with the same output: namely whatever is the highest value. So every sentence in the language will come out /ta/ or something like that, whatever the optimal syllable is. In order to get around that, there's a Faithfulness requirement. But Faithfulness is not going to work because the input to the phonology in a broad sense is phonological features. And the output, namely phonetic features, are completely different. In fact they probably are 100% different. It's a different vocabulary. So Faithfulness will always be zero. And the only way you can get around this is by not talking about the input and the output, but about some intermediate point, where you've already pikked the features that are going to be in the output. So then you can talk about Faithfulness. In fact if you look at the actual work, I think that's what is done. It doesn't look at lexical items. It looks at relatively shallow structures, things like prosodic structures or places where you've already got the more or less narrow phonetics. And then you can do it. Who knows if it's right?

That's an empirical question to be settled by research, but it's not optimality in the sense of the previous discussion. If the principles of language turn out to be OT-style constraints, and the parameters turn out to be ranking of these constraints, then we could, if we liked, raise the questions of the minimalist program and ask to what extent the postulated structures are "principled" in the sense we've discussed. But I think it's just a play on words. That's not a criticism, just using the word differently.

(v) Parametrized Merge?

Continuing to address a problem of parametrization, do you think the binary nature of phrase structure is strictly universal? Our question is this. In the approach based on Attract, including the probe-goal system, Merge is required to be binary due to considerations of optimal computations of downward search (Cf. Chomsky, N. 2001. Beyond Explanatory Adequacy, p. 14). On the other hand, n-ary Merge seems mathematically more general, if not simpler, and you have argued (Miller and Chomsky 1963, pp. 480–481) that the structural complexity as measured by the "node-to-terminal-node ratio ($N(Q)$)" (in the P-marker Q of the terminal string $t(Q)$) grows as the amount of branching per node decreases, suggesting that multiple-branching is "more economical" than binary branching, and that the role of transformations is to decrease the structural complexity by converting mostly binary underlying P-markers to derived P-markers with multiple branching structures (Miller, G. and N. Chomsky. 1963. Finitary Models of Language Users. In Luce, R., R. Bush, and E. Galanter, eds., Handbook of Mathematical Psychology II, chap. 13, pp. 419–492. Wiley.).

One possible way of (partially) accommodating these apparently conflicting claims might be to analyze Merge as generally an n-ary operation which is required to be binary when Attract/Agree applies, leaving room for "truly non-configurational" languages. What is your current view on binary and multiple-branching structures?

Well, that [the possibility of parameterizing Merge] is an interesting suggestion. The thing with George Miller that you mentioned [Miller and Chomsky 1963] had, I think, a different question in mind. It's hard to see how you could even formulate it in current theories. We were assuming then that a theory of transformations actually did change structure. If transformations are just internal Merge, they're not going to change structures.

On the other hand, there is something right about it, but I think it probably has to do with operations in the phonological component, because there is a lot going on in the phonological component that moves things around: heaviness constraints, all sorts of things to meet prosodic conditions, a lot of the stuff that David [Pesetsky] was talking about as "cascades."[19] All of that stuff rearranges in all kinds of ways. And it does seem to give very flat structures; that's why you don't get the expected hierarchies for c-command and so on. So maybe there's something happening down in the phonological component. In fact, if you really look at these, they yield what we think of as impossible structures. You can move things around – extrapose something from here and it goes out there. And you end up with structures that you can't even put together in hierarchic form. And that's OK in the phonological component. It's not being semantically interpreted, so it doesn't make any difference. So maybe things like that happen, and that could look like this. On the other hand, there do seem to me problems. The point you make is correct: If you have a probe-goal system, it's sort of driving it toward binary Merge, just for search reasons. But suppose you had multiple Merge, and you applied it. If you find a goal along one path, how do you know if it is the "closest goal"? It becomes a rather intricate problem.

It's kind of a look-ahead problem.

Yeah, it's kind of a look-ahead problem. So if the system works in terms of feature-matching and active elements with unvalued features, it ought

---

19. Cf. Pesetsky, D. 1995.

to be binary. However, there could be things that just don't have valued features, and they could have different properties. Unpleasant if true, but we can't change the facts.

So there's no room for truly non-configurational languages, as far as the narrow syntax is concerned?

Not in this system.

Strict binarity of Merge in the narrow syntax and then in the phonological component, there are operations which flatten the structures...

Unless there is something like what Ken [Hale] was talking about years ago, a non-configurational grammar.[20] Well, that's sort of what he was thinking, back twenty years ago. On the other hand, the languages that that was proposed for have, as far as I understand, turned out to be a lot more configurational – like Japanese. Japanese was the model of a non-configurational language. And the same apparently with Warlpiri, so I gather. But, like all of these things, they're so open, I don't know what to think.

Actually, one point I might make is that I had assumed all along that transformational grammar was just one of a number of options, like LFG [Lexical Functional Grammar], HPSG [Head-Driven Phrase Structure Grammar], and others. And I'd kind of guessed that they'd probably turn out to be the same thing under some proper interpretation. But if what we've been discussing turns out to be correct, then transformational grammar is the only option – to be more accurate, it would be the null hypothesis.

The reason is that internal Merge is free, and everything else is costly. So every other approach to expressing non-argument structure is introducing something, and usually pretty complicated things. Whereas the edge interpretation is adding nothing. You have to stipulate to stop it. So it looks as if – if I'm understanding it correctly – that the original proposals, in something like their original form, were sort of on the right track – for the wrong reasons. It just has to be this kind of system. And there's a heavy burden of proof to meet for any proposed alternative.

---

20. See, among others, Hale. K. 1983. See also Chomsky, N. 1981. (Particularly, section 2.8.)

Linguistics and other Sciences

(i) The Galilean/Newtonian style in linguistics

First of all, could you explain your views on the so-called "Galilean/Newtonian style" in the sciences, and the role such a research style has played in the history of linguistics, particularly in generative grammar?

It hasn't had any role in linguistics until very recently, or for that matter in most other domains either. In biology, it's almost denied; it's considered totally wrong. So the standard approach in biology is François Jacob's famous phrase: "Nature is a tinkerer."[21] It just puts together things as they come along. There are many eminent biologists who say that to talk about something perfect in organic nature is ridiculous. Everything is wildly imperfect; it's just the result of evolutionary history and evolutionary accident and so on and so forth.

Turing and D'Arcy Thompson were, I would say, well, they're not unique, surely; there were others, but they're very unusual, in that they were serious scientists who also believed in something like the Galilean style. Turing himself took a very strong view; his view was that ultimately biology will be physics and chemistry and the rest will be in the history department. Evolution will just go up to the history department – the history of the earth and stuff like that. But it's not even regarded as serious science; not a lot of biologists would agree with it.

In the physical sciences, it [the Galilean style] was highly successful in one domain, but not in others. So for Galileo, he thought it was going to be universal; his vision was that Nature is perfect, whether it's the motion of the tides or the flight of birds or whatever you look at. And it's the task of scientists to prove it. And if we don't prove it, we fail. However, by the end of his life, he had gotten quite disconsolate about it. Remember he had a notion of "perfect." "Perfect" means "We can build a perfect machine that will duplicate it [Nature]." Now, on account of Newton's theory, we can't do that – but Galileo didn't know it. He did know, however, that every attempt he made to show that some aspect of Nature was perfect failed. At the end, he sort of thought, "Well, we'll just never understand it." But that is the Galilean style, and it got reinterpreted with

---

21. Cf. Jacob, F. 1977.

Newton, in a way that was quite significant. It bothered him [Newton], but I don't think its significance has always been quite realized.

Up until Newton, it had been assumed – in the scientific revolution and Newton himself assumed – that perfection in Nature means you can construct a perfect machine to explain it. And "machine" meant machine, in the intuitive sense, including parts and gears and things bumping into each other and so on. Newton proved it's never going to be possible. That was the "absurdity," as he called it, that troubled him all his life. And it led people right away – Locke and later Hume and others – to recognize that Nature is just incomprehensible to us. The way Locke put it, motion has effects which we cannot conceive motion to possess, like action at a distance.[22] And that was considered the really hard problem in philosophy, philosophy of mechanical science.

And there were a lot of attempts in subsequent years to do something about it. All the great scientists – Euler and Gauss and others – tried to get over this, and finally it was just abandoned. It was never solved. Scientists got used to, got into the habit of saying, "OK, we'll call this a machine." But what it really meant is just what Hume said: Nature is not intelligible to us, and we have to lower our sights.[23] We lower our sights to intelligible theories, not to grasping the secrets of Nature. We'll never do that; we can't, because it doesn't make any sense. But we can look for intelligible theories.

And then you get a new version of the Galilean style: Let's try to get theories which assign a lower level of perfection, an object that's as perfect as it can be, even though we can't quite comprehend its nature. And that's modern science. And then it does break into these two branches: (1) the best theory branch – the methodological minimalism – and that everybody sort of understands, although we don't know what's going on; and (2) this other notion of trying to see if the objects themselves are perfect – the substantive minimalism, to see if we can interpret to what extent they are the results of other principles, like chemical or biological principles or interface principles or computational complexity and so on. In some ways, we have a clear grasp of the substantive minimalism, but not of the methodological minimalism. So, say, Turing is studying some language and wants to know why it has stridents. The substantive minimalist question is very clear: Can he show that it has stridents because

---

22. Locke, J. 1690/1975.
23. Hume, D. 1841.

that's the way the laws of physics and chemistry work? That's a clear question. And the same with Merge, with search procedures and probe-goal theories. If you can show they simply follow from computational complexity issues, you've reached the goal of substantive minimalism. On the other hand, the methodological minimalism is very obscure; it's just "What does it mean to make a good theory?" What makes a theory a good theory – no one really understands that. You kind of know it when you see one, but you don't know how to characterize it.

But that's where mathematics started to come into play. That's sort of moving into the next question and the role of mathematics in the Galilean/Newtonian style ...

(ii) Mathematics: Intrinsic and Extrinsic connections with Linguistics

The role that mathematics has played in the development of the Galilean/ Newtonian style seems to have been enormous, perhaps even crucial. Sometimes, the mathematical results are too beautiful to be untrue, so that it seems justifiable to stick to the theory, while setting aside problematic or even conflicting data. In linguistics, we have not yet had full-blown mathematization of the field. There has been some mathematical work in earlier phases of generative grammar (such as your own work on formal languages and automata), but since then, virtually no serious mathematical work has ever been introduced into linguistics. Is this because the nature of human language, i. e., that it is a finite discrete system, inherently resists extensive application of mathematics? Or is it just that not enough empirical work has been accumulated that calls for true mathematization? Do you think mathematics will ever play an important role in linguistics as it did in the core natural sciences?

Well, that has to do with beautiful theories. If a theory has beautiful mathematics, you're happy. And in fact, as you say, you might throw out the facts because the theory's too beautiful not to be true. Nobody really knows what that means. But it's true; it's what people do. And in fact, they don't even care; they even use mathematics that they don't understand often – just as long as it seems to yield beautiful results.

But there's something there.

Oh, there's obviously something there. This is the kind of question that's always being asked in the sciences: How come Nature satisfies laws of mathematics? And it's a very obscure question. There could be a kind of Kantian answer. The answer is that our minds work by the principles of mathematics, and in so far as some aspect of Nature accommodates to our minds, we comprehend it. So it's not that Nature satisfies the principles of mathematics, but that that's the aspect of Nature that we can comprehend. There may be all kinds of other aspects that some Martian could comprehend.

So doesn't that suggest a kind of an intuitionistic approach to mathematics? Mathematics reflects a part of the cognitive capacities of human being ...

A particular kind of mathematics is part of it. If Nature accommodates to it, to some extent, we think we understand it. But there may be other things in Nature that don't, and we don't understand them. In fact, if you think about the kinds of questions that aren't asked, it's not very surprising. Most of the questions that were the basic questions for people like, say, Newton or Descartes or Galileo, nobody really even asks any more. They're not answered; they're just not asked. So how can there be action at a distance, for example. It wasn't asked, and finally the whole framework of looking at the issues changed radically, when relativistic conceptions introduced what Galileo and Newton would probably have regarded as further "absurdities." Or the kinds of questions that troubled people in the 18th century. For example, suppose a red ball is rolling along, and it hits a blue ball. It transfers its motion from the red ball to the blue ball, but it doesn't transfer its color. Its color is a property, and its motion is a property. And there are ways of looking at that. But it's not clear that they answer the question in the sense in which it was found troubling. Or how can motion be spontaneous? How can it just start from nothing? Well it does, it's all over the biological world; motion just starts. How is that possible? If you look at the most careful work on, say, insects, like Randy Gallistel's work on the organization of motion,[24] it's a very complicated story. Take the question, how a cockroach walks. It turns out to involve rather intricate mechanisms. But nobody even dreams of asking the question: What does the cockroach do, like why does it turn left?

---

24. Cf. Gallistel, C. R. 1980.

It's not even a question. But those are the kinds of questions that bothered Newton and Descartes and Galileo and so on. They're just off the agenda. You only look at a narrow class of questions, questions having to do with either mechanisms or mathematical models of mechanisms.

Then why does mathematics not seem to work so extensively for human language?

Well, it doesn't work for anything. There's no mathematics in biology. Not even in chemistry. Mathematics is of course used, but not in the sense we are talking about here, at least as far as I know.

How about physics?

It works in physics, but physics deals with very simple things. Remember physics has an advantage that no other field has: If something gets too complicated, physics hands it over to somebody else. Other fields have to deal with whatever level of complexity they're looking at. So if, say, helium turns out to be too complicated, you give it to the chemists.

So mathematics only works for the simplest things in the world? And that's physics.

Oh, there are other places where mathematics works; like, game theory works. So there are some kinds of systems for which game-theoretic or other mathematical approaches are apparently appropriate and useful. But you know mathematics is basically the study of very simple things. Mathematics does not study complex objects, either. It studies simple objects. As long as you keep yourself to the simple objects, you can do mathematics. Somewhere you mentioned the early stuff on formal linguistics. But remember that was extremely simple things. The topic studied there was weak generative capacity. It's part of the reason why I, at least, lost interest in it. It became a branch of mathematics – a small branch of mathematics. I lost interest myself around the early 1960s. And the reason was because weak generative capacity just doesn't relate to language. The entities that are studied – say, well-formed formulas – don't exist. So you get some interesting results, but it's not clear what they mean.

In fact, in all of this work of the late 50s and early 60s there was only one result that I know of that had any linguistic significance. And it's one you don't even find in mathematical linguistics textbooks. That's the fact that there's a constructive procedure to map context-free grammars into a strongly equivalent – crucially – non-deterministic push-down storage automaton. OK, that's just kind of a boring constructional thing. I did something;[25] Terry Langendoen fixed it up for his thesis.[26] It's not interesting mathematics. It's just a constructive procedure. But it's the one thing that has any linguistic significance. In fact, it's what underlies every parser. That's why every parser is a non-deterministic push-down storage automaton. It doesn't contribute much, but it explains why that's what every parser is. In so far as language is more or less context-free, you can parse it that way. But apart from that, I don't know of any results that are interesting. I mean, some results are amusing, but not linguistically significant.

Are all the results on weak generation simply irrelevant for linguistics? Can you think of any consequences?

Well, what I can think of is actually a study of strong generative capacity. For example, Kuroda has proposed a topological approach,[27] under which strongly-equivalent grammars are characterized in terms of homeomorphism, rather than identity ...

Strongly equivalent? See, that's interesting, because it's strong equivalence. As soon as you get strong equivalence, it has some possible linguistic meaning. But the trouble is at that point, you don't study it because the mathematics is too hard. I think that's the way mathematics works generally. As soon as you get the structures that are too hard, you can't study them. So there is essentially no mathematical linguistics on strong generation; it's just too complicated. In fact, the only ways in which it's studied – and they don't make any sense – is to take the structured expression and treat it as a linear string. Now you're back to weak generation, but you kind of lost all the linguistic motivation and significance.

So it's going to be a study of strong generative capacity where mathematics could play a role in linguistics?

There might be other things, like maybe if the study of efficient computation reaches sufficient clarity, depth of understanding, and empirical in-

---

25. Chomsky, N. 1959a.
26. Langendoen, T. 1961.
27. Kuroda, S.-Y. 1976.

sights, there may be things there. There could be. You just have to keep an open mind.

What about formal learning theory? It seems to be based on weak generation.

Yeah, that's why it doesn't do any good. In fact, Gold's theorem[28] and Dan Osherson's work[29] do not seem to have empirical relevance for linguistics, at least that I can see. It's interesting, especially Dan Osherson's stuff is very interesting. I just don't see any possible application. The only possible place in which it had any implication that I could see was kind of a hint. At one point in what they were doing they pointed out that, in their model, you could only get convergence if you had a finite number of outputs, a finite number of possible languages. I guess there's some suggestive connection, in that it sounds in the same realm as saying that acquisition of language is only possible with a finite number of parameters. It sort of has the same ring to it. But it's not a logical connection. Basically, their approach is kind of irrelevant to the questions we are asking about language, it seems.

Mathematics also seems to have an inherent connection with linguistics. You have suggested that the faculty of language and the "number faculty" (the ability to "count," the concept of natural numbers) may have the same "roots" in human evolution, sharing the same (or isomorphic) recursive procedure. If so, why can UG not become like number theory? Or why has number theory not become like UG? What are the crucial differences between the language faculty and the "number faculty"?

Well, you know that's the kind of question that may get some answers from imaging studies. For example, it would be interesting to discover whether the same parts of the brain are involved. That doesn't give a definite answer, but it might be suggestive. There is a plausible idea: The number faculty and the language faculty seem to be both uniquely human, and they have a property in common – namely recursive enumerability, digital infinity. So you could imagine that the number faculty is just what you get when you take the language faculty and you abstract away from it and drop all of its special properties and you keep only the property of recursive enumeration. That essentially gives you the number fac-

---

28. Gold, E. M. 1967.
29. Cf. Osherson, D. N., M. Stob, and S. Weinstein. 1985.

ulty. So a guess is, this weird organism has got a language faculty and it has a capacity of abstraction of some kind. So that abstraction threw away all the language-specific stuff and looked at the principle of enumeration itself, that's essentially arithmetic. Then comes the standard intuition that's the story about how God created the natural numbers; man created everything else.

Kronecker's famous words.

Yeah. On the other hand, if it turns out, see I mean like, some of the aphasia work and things like that do seem to shed some doubt on that, because it does seem that you get specialized deficiencies. So people can lose language and keep number, or conversely. If it was really an abstraction from the same thing, it's hard to see how that could happen.

The theory of natural numbers in mathematics seems to look quite different from linguistic theory.

Yeah, the theory's totally different. But it still could be it's just our minds at work on something which is available to us as an abstraction from the language faculty. I think Ken Hale had interesting ideas about this. He only wrote it up a little, and it's more anthropological work. When he was working on kinship systems, he didn't believe the standard theory of Lévi-Strauss [Claude Lévi-Strauss] and others that kinship systems are only functional. His work seemed to indicate that they may go beyond that, and furthermore that they're like science. Anthropologists tend to go into a village and get an informant and get some results. But Ken worked much more intensively. What he seemed to be finding everywhere, he said, is that if you went into a tribe no matter how primitive, there are going to be experts. They are the ones who know things. Other people sort of have a partial knowledge. But if you really want to know how these, say, kinship systems work, you're going to have to find the expert and they'll tell you things. And then his actual idea is that this is just like mathematics. These are what people play with with their intellects, on complicated systems. So it's kind of like the arts or like mathematics. It's just the mind – the same mind – working on different forms. You could write poems, you could do number theory, or you could develop kinship systems. But they're basically mathematical constructions, which have no function at all. In fact most people don't even know them. At least that is the way I understood him.

These ideas seem to be related to André Weil's article on the algebraic structure of kinship systems.[30] *He actually wrote it, at Lévi-Strauss's request, as an appendix to Lévi-Strauss' book on the structure of kinship.*

That's interesting!

(iii) Evolutionary Theory

What is your view on evolutionary theory and its relevance for linguistics? Is it a science, or could it become a science in principle? Also, in the original The Generative Enterprise *interview twenty years ago, you already mentioned the importance of D'Arcy Thompson's work on biophysics and Turing's work on morphogenesis, and you have recently reiterated their potential importance for the study of language. Can we realistically expect that work of this kind will eventually explain the nature and properties of economy/optimality in human language?*

Well, there isn't much in the way of evolutionary theory. There's a theory of natural selection; everyone assumes it's basically correct. There's a lot of work in molecular biology – see how things work in cells and stuff. It's obviously all connected to evolution. But how you actually get an organism, nobody really knows. You can't solve the problems of evolutionary theory until you know how a genome gets to an organism. That's a crucial part, because selection is on organisms. A big part of the explanation is missing if you don't fill that gap. It's basically not understood. That's why knowing the human genome tells you almost nothing about humans. You've got to know how the manufacturing plant works. When it gets the instruction, what does it do with it? And then you get into protein folding and other complexities and so on.

When you look at something that's really more or less understood, there seems to be ... like the evolution of the eyes. There's now extensive work on it, which I don't have a judgment about, but people who do have judgment take it seriously. For example, Walter Gehring's work on the evolution of the eyes.[31] If you actually look at it, it's pretty interesting, even without understanding much biology. He argues for monophyletic origins for all photo-sensitive things, probably even plants. That is, a single origin, contrary to prevailing ideas, which have been that the eye developed about a hundred times separately because it's so easy and so on. He claims

---

30. Weil, A. 1969.
31. Gehring, W. J. 1998.

there's one development. It begins with just a random process. There has to be one molecule around – or one class of molecules, called rhodopsin molecules, which have the property that they convert light into chemical energy. Somehow some of these things got into cells, just kind of randomly. That gives you the beginnings of a possible eye, something that will convert light to chemical energy. Then comes a long, complicated process which involves all kinds of principles of how genes get intercalated into sequences of genes in very special ways, but not in other ways. All kinds of physical constraints come along. Out of this comes a number of possible eyes, insect eyes, human eyes, photo-sensitive receptors, and so on.

Then you look around the organisms of the world, and it turns out they're all mixed up. There are some that have both the insect compound eye and the mammalian lens eye, just in different parts of the body. And things go up and back, and they all just seem to be developments from the same source along a very narrow channel of possibilities, given by the ways in which strings of genes can be put together. Well, that's not a general theory; it's just a highly specific account of how this particular development took place. If you look at the next organ, you don't know. So there's not much there in the way of evolutionary theory.

It's kind of striking that there's – you know Lyle Jenkins; he's a good biologist – out of curiosity, I asked him to do a data base search for me in insect biology, bee science, just to see how much work there had been done on the evolution of bee communication. It seems like virtually nothing [has been done]. The reason is everyone regards this as so complicated you couldn't possibly study it. On the other hand, if you look at the literature on the evolution of human language, [you find] stacks and stacks of studies. And it's incomparably more complicated. Bees are a perfect object for investigation: The bee brain is the size of a grass seed; it's got 800,000 neurons. It also has a very short gestation period. You do an experiment and you can cut them apart, anything you please. There's no problem about invasive experimentation. And there are hundreds of different species. They're all a little bit different, so you can do comparative work. There's every advantage over humans. But it doesn't seem to be studied very much. On the other hand, everybody's got to have a story about language evolution for humans. It's totally senseless.

Actually, this may surprise you, but I managed to get my name on an article on the evolution of language. It's coming out this week in *Science*.[32] It will surprise a lot of people. It's a joint article with Marc Hauser

---

32. Hauser, M. D., N. Chomsky, and W. T. Fitch. 2002.

and Tecumseh Fitch, over at Harvard; the three of us did an article which originally was more interesting than what they cut it down to. Marc works on primates mainly and Tecumseh Fitch is an experimenter and mathematical biologist – but both of them believe something along the lines, roughly, of some speculations in *Reflections on Language*[33]– that maybe the interfaces are not human-specific, but that what's specific is the linking. At that time [mid 1970s], it was pre-minimalism, so all the complications that were assumed didn't make much sense in this framework. Now if you rephrase that, you might say, well OK, maybe the interfaces are more or less – at least the interfaces you can study comparatively. So you can study the auditory system of a tamarin and other organisms. And you can do comparative work on the interface systems – to some extent even the conceptual ones like "Do apes have a theory of mind?" – that kind of thing. So you may be able to study those things at least from a feasible perspective, of evolutionary theory.

Now if the minimalist theory is anywhere near right, there's nothing much to explain about the evolution of the linking, except it's there. To the extent that you can show it's principled, there's no problem to explain it. It's just there. So what you have to explain is the evolution of the unprincipled part, which is much reduced. So that breaks up the problem into something which has parts, at least. So you can look at the parts. It doesn't give you an answer. The way the article turned out, which was interesting, there's a dense wall about the interfaces. I had written the part about the minimalist stuff; it was very elementary, the kind of thing I talk to high school students about. The reviewers said they couldn't understand it, including the linguists – good linguists. They said it's going to be too complicated and to cut that segment. So we took that page or two out. Which really surprised all of us, because it seemed pretty simple. So what's left is just the general picture and discussion of the interface systems.

And then comes D'Arcy Thompson and Turing, and the question is: How far can it go? My own guess is that ultimately Turing's probably right, that it will be the heart of biology. There is some work on it. There's a paper in the *Quarterly Review of Biology* by Maynard Smith and a couple of other guys about twenty years ago which tries to find properties of organisms that you could account for on Turing-like grounds.[34] And they found a lot of interesting things, like symmetries and stuff like that. But

---

33. Chomsky, N. 1975.
34. Smith, M., R. Burian, S. Kauffman, P. Alberch, J. Campbell, B. Goodwin, R. Lande, D. Raup, and L. Wolpert. 1985.

it's apparently a really hard topic. One thing that's sort of suggestive – I think I mentioned it in a footnote[35] – is this stuff of Cherniak's on the best of all brains.[36] Remember Corey Washington? He got me on to that. He's drifted around in the world and is now working on mathematical biology. He mentioned that to me; it's kind of interesting.

So could it work? Do you think the Thompson/Turing-type approach could eventually explain why language has what it has?

It could. Actually it could be that – if computational efficiency (this goes back to your earlier question on domain-specificity) is really a property of linguistic computation, there could be homologous elements elsewhere in the organic world, in fact in insects. The thing that immediately comes to mind is insect navigation, which is pretty interesting, and a lot is known about it. Insect navigation seems to involve things that mammals can't do. So insects apparently do path integration. An insect will kind of wander around and get to a point, and when it wants to go home, it goes directly home, which I don't think any mammal can do. So they are apparently somehow integrating over their paths, storing the variable, and are able to determine the shortest distance from where they started. Which suggests some computational efficiency arguments and – who knows – maybe the same thing might show up in language. But that would break down domain-specificity even more.

(iv) The Brain Sciences

The usefulness of non-invasive imaging techniques for the study of language seems undeniable, but it is actually very hard to have fruitful communications between linguistics and the brain sciences. Why? Which "field" should undergo major changes so that real "unification" of linguistics and the brain sciences becomes possible? Given what happened to chemistry and physics when they were "unified," one might guess that it's the brain sciences, not linguistics, that ought to undergo major changes ...

There is some stuff coming along; have you seen Andrea Moro's work? He's working with a couple of neuroscientists in Italy on matters related

---
35. Chomsky, N. 2001.
36. Cherniak, C. 1995.

to syntax and semantics, and the work does look intriguing.[37] Well, they're not finding out what's going on, obviously. They're just finding areas. But they are finding different areas for things like semantic processing, with deviant sentences and stuff like that.

Semantics and syntax are in different parts of the brain?

More complicated than that, but something along those lines. But it's like brain localization altogether: It doesn't tell you what's going on.

It is sometimes claimed that the "real evidence" comes from the brain sciences, not from within linguistics. This is somewhat reminiscent of earlier charges against generative grammar with respect to its "psychological reality." How would you respond to such claims?

It's just meaningless. It's the kind of criticism that was leveled against chemistry throughout its whole history. Chemistry throughout its whole history, up until the time I was a kid, was often considered not a real science, like physics, but rather just a mode of calculation. Even the Bohr model of the atom. When it came along, some prominent scientists regarded it as a mode of calculation only. You can't assign any reality to it because there's no physical basis for it. By the 1930s, it was recognized that all this was total nonsense. Chemistry was real, because it is the best theory we've got. But that insight has not penetrated beyond core physical sciences. Philosophers of mind still worry about – in fact I think they're just reiterating – all the known mistakes of scientists about chemistry. In fact, as recently as the 1920s – it just turned out that chemistry was right and physics was wrong. Unification took place, after radical changes in physics. There is no way of knowing how it's all going to turn out until the answers are known.

So what's going to happen, do you imagine, to linguistics and the brain sciences?

The brain sciences are fascinating and sure to be extremely important, but for the moment, there is not much in the way of general theoretical content, as far as I am aware. They are much more rudimentary than physics was in the 1920s. Who knows if they're even looking at the right

---

37. See among others Moro, A., M. Tettamanti, D. Perani, C. Donati, S. F. Cappa, and F. Fazio. 2001.

things? There's all kinds of junk going on in the brain; nobody knows what's in it. So you just keep pursuing it and see what happens.

This was kind of understood by the better cognitive neuroscientists. Forty years ago, Hans-Lukas Teuber was head of what became later the brain sciences and cognitive science programs here at MIT. He was an important cognitive neuroscientist who sort of started off the programs here; he got here around 1960. He wrote an important review, which was influential for me and other people, of perception and the neurosciences, around 1960; it was for some encyclopedia.[38]

He started off by saying something to the effect that "It may seem strange to begin a review paper on perception and the neurosciences by saying 'We don't know what perception is' and to end the paper by saying 'We don't know what the brain is' – but that's the way it is." So what's the point of studying it? He said the point of studying it is to provide guidelines for an eventual science of the brain and for an eventual better science of perception. That's all you can do. You study what you can study, and you hope it will provide some guidelines for others who are wandering in the dark.

There is no such thing as "real evidence." "Real evidence" is whatever contributes to theoretical understanding. Other stuff isn't "real evidence."

(v) Economics

Before finishing up this conversation, let us ask you a question about a slightly different topic, namely, the nature of modern economics (the "queen of the social sciences"). You occasionally argue that modern economics, no matter how fancy it has become due to the mathematics it uses, has a fundamental flaw, i. e., it is based on the wrong assumption that labor is highly mobile and capital is relatively immobile. (cf. Chomsky, N. 2002. "Intellectuals and Social Change," chap. 7, Understanding Power (The Indispensable Chomsky). Edited by P. R. Mitchell and J. Schoeffel. The New Press.) What is economics, then? Do you think it is a science, or if not, can it become a science? What's the real content of all those very fancy mathematical works in modern economics?

It's a very brief point, actually. You know the famous phrase "invisible hand"? That appears in *Wealth of Nations*[39] exactly once, in an argument

---

38. Teuber, H. L. 1960.
39. Smith, A. 1776.

against capital movement. That's the only place it appears. Adam Smith points out that if investors can invest wherever they want, then they're going to destroy their own countries, because they'll just invest where it's more profitable. He's talking about England. And then he says "Well, we don't have to worry about it, because investors in England – people with capital – are going to want to invest in England for various reasons – security, they like their neighbors, and so on and so forth. So, therefore, as if by an 'invisible hand,' the capital won't move." That's the argument; that's the one use of the phrase in the book: an argument against what has become the basic principle of neoliberalism, that capital should move freely. Adam Smith also took for granted that the free movement of labor is critical for free trade. And in fact, otherwise, the principles don't work, at least as he intended them. David Ricardo was the same.[40] Ricardo recognized that the theory of comparative advantage is going to collapse if, say, investors in England can make more profit producing both wine and textiles in Portugal, his model. But then he also gave some funny argument to say they're going to stay in England. But the theory doesn't work, at least in its classic formulation, unless capital is immobile and labor is mobile.

If you take a look at today, capital is highly mobile; labor is immobile. And in fact it's dramatic how it works. When NAFTA[41] was extended in 1994, it did free capital movement across the Mexican-US border. But that same year, Clinton [then US President Bill Clinton] militarized the border, for the first time ever. It's an artificial border; people were going up and back all the time, in both directions. It was militarized in 1994 to prevent Mexicans from moving to the United States, because they expected that NAFTA was going to devastate poor Mexicans and they'll be fleeing. So the point of NAFTA was to free capital movement and to block movement of people. It's not that economics is wrong. It's just that certain aspects of it have little to do with the real world.

If you want an answer to the question about how lowering the interest rate by one-quarter [per cent] is going to change the amount that consumers will be willing to spend or something, you probably want to go to your favorite economist. They have models that give answers to questions like that. But if you want to know anything about developing an

---

40. Ricardo, D. 1821.
41. The North American Free Trade Agreement. For relevant discussion on the nature of NAFTA, see, among others, Chomsky, N. 1999. See also Scott, R., C. Salas and B. Campbell. 2001.

economy, you certainly don't [want to go to your favorite economist]. There are some things that are so dramatic that you really can't miss them. The model for developing an economy is supposed to be free trade; that's the great model. It's what you impose on the world. Just take a look at the countries that have developed. Every single one of them – from England through the United States, France, Germany, Japan, Korea, Taiwan – every single one, without exception, developed crucially by violation of these principles. If the US had kept to these principles in the 1820s, we'd be exporting fish [today]. Exporting fish, fur, agricultural products – that was the comparative advantage of the US in its early days. It developed a textile industry, later steel and other industries, by following the earlier British model: heavy protectionism, and increasingly, direct state initiative in research and development. There isn't one single case on record of a country that's developed following the principles that are declared to be the optimal mode of development. By and large, many economists don't seem to care. The model says this is the way it will work. It doesn't matter if all history is against it.

Even take the idea that the US has a free enterprise economy. Take MIT; everybody at MIT knows perfectly well that the economy is based on the state sector. It's what pays our salaries every month. The whole new economy – computers, telecommunications, the whole business – comes out of the state sector to a substantial extent, mostly under the pretext of defense. So where does that leave free enterprise? It's not a matter of too many agricultural subsidies – yeah, that's an interference – but what about the whole state sector of the economy, which is huge? The whole new economy comes out of it; biotechnology comes out of it. Why is Kendall Square [a high-tech square near MIT] now shifting from electronics companies to biotech companies? One could say the cutting edge of the next stage of the economy is going to be biology-based. So that's where all the federal funding is coming from. And it's being funneled, as usual, through universities. So, therefore, around the periphery of universities will appear, instead of little electronics firms, you're getting little bio-tech firms. And, yeah, sooner or later you'll get something marketable, and you'll give it to private companies to market. But these crucial facts about the economy just aren't part of economic theory.

Why?

They give the wrong answers. Now we're off into the domain of ideology.

3. Prospects for the Future

We'd like to end the interview by asking about your views on the future of our field. What is your view on the future of linguistics in the 21st century? One likely scenario seems to be that a large portion of what's been done in traditional linguistics will continue to go on, perhaps not in the pre-generative manner but at the level of the first phase of the principles-and-parameters framework, and the very core of theoretical linguistics as currently being investigated within minimalism will sooner or later be unified with and "dissolved" into a part of the core natural sciences. What do you think?

Well, every speculation I would have made in the past would have been wrong. But my current speculation would be that probably the field is going to be very descriptive in the future, especially in the semantic and phonetic areas. There's just a huge amount of work to be done, and it's very complicated. People are just digging away at it. There doesn't seem to be much in the way of theoretical explanation, as far as I can see. Just getting things to work. And there's a huge amount of work to be done.

A good way to judge how a field is going to develop is to ask, "What's a feasible Ph.D. thesis topic?" And that's the way the field is going to develop, because people have to pick a feasible topic and then, likely, that's what they're going to work on. If I had a student come in and ask, "Should I work on a minimalist topic?," I'd say "No; they're way too hard. If you want a feasible topic, something you're pretty sure is going to be finished in four years, and that will be respectable, the best thing is a topic that's more descriptive. And then you've got some hope. If you want to try something more ambitious, OK – but not for a thesis." That tends to have the directive force for a field.

"Descriptive" at the level of the principles-and-parameters framework?

Something like that, although if you look at, for example, formal semantics where an awful lot of work is done, there's no principles-and-parameters. It's assumed to be uniform and invariant. Maybe it isn't, but it's assumed to be invariant. So it's just like a straight, one-to-one, instantaneous mapping from syntactic structures to some kind of interpretation. And then comes the question: What are the details of the mapping? If you look at it, it's kind of like phonology; it violates every imaginable computational principle. It's just not a question for people; it's not the kind of question they care about. They want to get it descriptively correct, get the scope relations correct, that sort of thing. I don't want to exaggerate. There are some deep and very suggestive ideas. But I think it is fair to say that the main problems, and they are huge and challenging, tend to be descriptive at this stage of understanding.

So you speculate that the field is going to remain largely descriptive?

Most fields do. Even physics. The famous people you've heard of do descriptive work. If you look through the American Physical Society, almost everybody does descriptive work. Other things are just too hard.

Including minimalism? Where is it going? What's going to happen to it?

I don't know. I would not have guessed ten years ago where we have gotten today. And right now it's very hard to see how you can deal with other things. Maybe there will be some good ideas; maybe not. You never know.

Until the next revolutionary idea ...

Until the next good idea comes along.

One last question. Our field has been traditionally placed in the humanities and social sciences, where we don't quite enjoy the feeling of fitting in. On the other hand, the natural sciences schools, at least in the current institutional structures, have flatly closed the door to linguistics. How could our enterprise, the generative enterprise, ever proceed in this century? What should we do now or in the next ten years, for example?

Language can and should be studied from many different points of view, hence in many different disciplinary contexts. The disciplinary lines are fairly artificial at best, mostly for convenience, and over time they should dissolve and surely not be regarded as straitjackets for inquiry and educational programs. The parts of the study of language that we've been talking about seem to me to fall, in principle, into human biology. If there is sufficient progress, I think there is a fair chance that institutional arrangements will evolve in that direction. But to predict the course of thought, ideas, discoveries – that is even more vain than predicting human affairs generally.

OK, thanks!

Bibliography

Allen, M. R. (1978): *Morphological Investigations.* Ph. D. Dissertation, University of Connecticut, Storrs.
Anderson, S. R. and D. W. Lightfoot (2002): *The language organ: linguistics as cognitive physiology.* Cambridge: Cambridge University Press.
Aoun, Y. (1979): Some considerations concerning the metrical representation of the syllable, unpublished, MIT.
Aoun, Y. (1981): *The Formal Nature of Anaphoric Relations.* Ph. D. Dissertation, MIT.
Austin, J. L. (1962): *How to Do Things with Words.* London: Oxford University Press.
Bailey, C. J. (1981): Theory, description and differences among linguists (or what keeps linguistics from becoming a science), *Language and Communication* 1,1. 69.
Baker, M. (1996): *The polysynthesis parameter.* Oxford: Oxford University Press.
Baker, M. (2001): *The atoms of language: the mind's hidden rules of grammar.* New York: Basic Books.
Belletti, A., L. Brandi and L. Rizzi (eds.) (1981): *Theory of Markedness in Generative Grammar. Proceedings of the 1979 GLOW conference.* Scuola Normale Superiore, Pisa.
Bennis, H. and A. Groos (1980): The government-binding theory: an overview, *GLOW Newsletter* No. 5., 7–31.
Besten, H. den (1978): On the presence and absence of *wh*-elements in Dutch comparatives, *Linguistic Inquiry* 9,4, 641–671.
Bloomfield, L. (1926): A set of postulates for the science of language. *Language* 2: 153–164. Reprinted in *Readings in linguistics* I, ed. M. Joos, 1957, pp. 26–31. Washington: American Council of Learned Societies.
Bordelois, I. (1974): *The Grammar of Spanish Causative Complements.* Ph. D. Dissertation, MIT.
Borer, H. (1981): *Parametric Variation in Clitic Constructions.* Ph. D. Dissertation, MIT. To appear with Foris Publications, Dordrecht.
Bowers, J. (1975): Adjectives and adverbs in English, *Foundations of Language* 13, 529–562.
Bowers, J. (1981): *The Theory of Grammatical Relations.* Ithaca: Cornell University Press.
Brame, M. K. (1978): *Base Generated Syntax.* Seattle: Noit Amrofer.
Brame, M. K. (1979): *Essays towards Realistic Syntax.* Seattle: Noit Amrofer.
Bresnan, J. W. (1976): On the form and functioning of transformations, *Linguistic Inquiry* 7,1.
Bresnan, J. (1978): A realistic transformational grammar, in: M. Halle, J. Bresnan and G. Miller (eds.) *Linguistic Theory and Psychological Reality.* Cambridge, Massachusetts: MIT Press, 1–59.
Brouwer, L. E. J. (1913): Intuitionism and formalism, *Bulletin of the American Mathematical Society*, vol. 20, 81–96. Reprinted with other writings by Brouwer in P. Benaceraff and H. Putnam (eds.) *Philosophy of Mathematics: Selected Readings.* Englewood Cliffs, N. J.
Burzio, L. (1978): Italian causative constructions, *Journal of Italian Linguistics* 3,2, 1–71.
Burzio, L. (1981): *Intransitive Verbs and Italian Auxiliaries.* Ph. D. Dissertation, MIT.
Cherniak, C. (1995): Neural component placement. *Trends in Neuroscience* 18, 522–527.
Chomsky, C. (1969): *The Acquisition of Syntax in Children from 5 to 10.* Cambridge, Massachusetts: MIT Press.

Chomsky, N. (1949): *The morphophonemics of modern Hebrew*. Undergraduate thesis. The University of Pennsylvania, Philadelphia. (A revised version was completed as a master's thesis in 1951. Revised version published in 1979. New York: Garland.)
Chomsky, N. (1955): *The Logical Structure of Linguistic Theory*. Harvard mimeographed. Published under the same title in 1975, New York: Plenum Press.
Chomsky, N. (1956): Three Models for the description of language. In the *IRE Transactions on information theory*, IT-2, 113–124. (Reprinted with corrections in 1963. In *Readings in mathematical psychology* II, ed. D. Luce, et al.; pp. 105–124. New York: John Wiley & Sons.)
Chomsky, N. (1957): *Syntactic Structures*. The Hague: Mouton. Reprinted 2002. Berlin/New York: Mouton de Gruyter.
Chomsky, N. (1959a): On certain formal properties of grammars. *Information and Control* 2, 137–167.
Chomsky, N. (1959b): A note on phrase structure grammars, *Information and Control* 2, 393–395.
Chomsky, N. (1962): Context-free grammars and pushdown storage, *Quarterly Progress Report* no. 65, MIT Research Laboratory of Electronics, 187–194.
Chomsky, N. (1963a): Three models for the description of language, in: R. Luce, R. Bush and E. Galanter (eds.) *Handbook of Mathematical Psychology* vol. II. New York: Wiley and Sons. (Reprinted as revised version of 1956 paper).
Chomsky, N. (1963b): Formal properties of grammars, in: R. Luce, R. Bush and E. Galanter (eds.) *Handbook of Mathematical Psychology* vol. II. NewYork: Wiley and Sons.
Chomsky, N. (1964): *Current Issues in Linguistic Theory*. The Hague: Mouton.
Chomsky, N. (1965): *Aspects of the theory of syntax*. Cambridge, Mass.: MIT Press.
Chomsky, N. (1966): *Cartesian Linguistics*. New York: Harper and Row.
Chomsky, N. (1968): *Language and Mind*. New York: Harcourt Brace Jovanovich.
Chomsky, N. (1970): Remarks on nominalization, in: R. Jacobs and P. Rosenbaum (eds.) *Readings in English Transformational Grammar*. Waltham, Massachusetts: Ginn and Co. 184–221 (Also reprinted in Chomsky (1972), 11–61).
Chomsky, N. (1972): *Studies on Semantics in Generative Grammar*. The Hague: Mouton.
Chomsky, N. (1973): Conditions on transformations, in: S. R. Anderson and P. Kiparsky (eds.) *A Festschrift for Morris Halle*. New York: Holt, Rinehart and Winston. 232–286 (Reprinted in Chomsky (1977b), 81–160).
Chomsky, N. (1975): *Reflections on Language*. New York: Pantheon.
Chomsky, N. (1976): Conditions on rules of grammar, *Linguistic Analysis* 2,4. (Reprinted in Chomsky (1977b), 163–210).
Chomsky, N. (1977a): On *wh*-movement, in: P. Culicover, T. Wasow, and A. Akmajian (eds.) *Formal Syntax*. New York: Academic Press, 71–132.
Chomsky, N. (1977b): *Essays on Form and Interpretation*. New York: North Holland.
Chomsky, N. (1977c): *Language and Responsibility*. New York: Pantheon.
Chomsky, N. (1980a): *Rules and Representations*. New York: Columbia University Press.
Chomsky, N. (1980b): On binding, *Linguistic Inquiry* 11,1, 1–46.
Chomsky, N. (1981a): Markedness and core grammar, in: *Theory of markedness in generative grammar*: Proceedings of the 1979 GLOW conference, ed. A. Belletti, L. Brandi and L. Rizzi, pp. 123–146. Pisa: Scuola Normale Superiore.
Chomsky, N. (1981b): *Lectures on Government and Binding*. Dordrecht: Foris. (Reprinted in 1993, Berlin: Mouton de Gruyter.)
Chomsky, N. (1982): *Noam Chomsky on the generative enterprise: a discussion with Riny Huybregts and Henk van Riemsdijk*. Dordrecht: Foris.
Chomsky, N. (forthcoming): *Some Concepts and Consequences of the Theory of Government and Binding*. Cambridge, Massachusetts: MIT Press. (Published under the same title in 1982.)
Chomsky, N. (1986): *Knowledge of language: its nature, origins, and use*. New York: Praeger.

Chomsky, N. (1988): *Language and problems of knowledge: the Managua lectures.* Cambridge, MA.: MIT Press.
Chomsky, N. (1995): *The minimalist program.* Cambridge, Mass.: MIT Press.
Chomsky, N. (1999): *Profit over people: neoliberalism and world order.* New York: Seven Stories Press.
Chomsky, N. (2000): *New horizons in the study of language and mind.* Cambridge: Cambridge University Press.
Chomsky, N. (2001): Beyond explanatory adequacy. *MIT Occasional Papers in Linguistics* 20, Department of Linguistics and Philosophy, MIT, Cambridge, Mass.
Chomsky, N. (2001): Beyond explanatory adequacy. *MIT Occasional Papers in Linguistics.* 20. MIT, Cambridge, Mass.
Chomsky, N. (2002): *On nature and language.* Cambridge: Cambridge University Press.
Chomsky, N. (2002a): Intellectuals and social change. In *Understanding Power (The indispensable Chomsky)*, ed. Mitchell, P. R., and J. Schoeffel. New York: The New Press.
Chomsky, N. (2002b): *On nature and language.* Cambridge: Cambridge University Press.
Chomsky, N. and G. A. Miller (1958): Finite State Languages, *Information and Control* 1, 91–112.
Chomsky, N. and H. Lasnik (1977): Filters and control, *Linguistic Inquiry* 8.3, 425–504.
Chomsky, N. and H. Lasnik (1993): The theory of principles and parameters. In *Syntax: an international handbook of contemporary research*, ed. J. Jacob, A. von Stechow, W. Sternefeld, and T. Vennemann, pp. 506–569. Berlin: Walter de Gruyter.
Chomsky, N. and M. P. Schützenberger (1963): The algebraic theory of context-free languages, in: P. Braffort and D. Hirschberg (eds.) *Computer Programming and Formal Systems.* Amsterdam: North Holland, 118–161.
Chomsky, N. and M. Halle (1968): *The Sound Pattern of English.* New York: Harper and Row. (A paperback edition published in 1991. Cambridge, Mass.: MIT Press.)
Cinque, G. (1980): On extraction from NP in Italian, *Journal of Italian Linguistics* 5,1/2, 47–99.
Collins, C. (2001): Eliminating labels. *MIT Occational Papers in Linguistics* 20. Department of Linguistics and Philosophy. MIT, Cambridge, Mass.
D'Arcy Wentworth Thompson (1961): *On Growth and Form*, edited and abridged by J. T. Bonner, Cambridge University Press (original publication 1917).
Dennis, M. and H. A. Whitaker (1976): Language acquisition following hemidecortication: linguistic superiority of the left over the right hemisphere, *Brain and Language* 3, 404–433.
Dougherty, R. C. (1973): A survey of linguistic arguments and methods, *Foundations of Language* 10, 423–490.
Dummett, M. (1917): *Elements of Intuitionism.* Oxford: Clarendon.
Emonds, J. E. (1976): *A Transformational Approach to English Syntax: Root, Structure Preserving, and Local Transformations.* New York: Academic Press.
Engdahl, E. (1980): Wh-constructions in Swedish and the relevance of subjacency, in: J. T. Jensen (ed.) *Cahiers Linguistiques d'Ottawa*, Proceedings of NELS X, 98–108.
Engdahl, E. (1981): Multiple gaps in English and Swedish, in: Fretheim and Hellan (eds.) *Proceedings of the Sixth Scandinavian Conference of Linguistics* (forthcoming).
Epstein, R., R. P. Lanza, and B. F. Skinner (1980): Symbolic communication between two pigeons, *Science* vol. 207, 543–545.
Farmer, A. (1980): *On the Interaction of Morphology and Syntax.* Ph. D. Dissertation, MIT.
Fillmore, C. J. (1963): The position of embedding transformations in a grammar, *Word* 19, 208–231.
Freidin, R. (1978): Cyclicity and the theory of grammar, *Linguistic Inquiry* 9,4.
Fukui, N. (1996): On the nature of economy in language. *Cognitive Studies* 3 (1): 51–71.
Fukui, N. (2001): *Shizen kagaku to shite no gengogaku—seisei bunpoo towa nanika.* [Linguistics as a natural science-what is generative grammar?] Tokyo: Taishukan.

Fukui, N. (forthcoming): *Henkan seisei bunpoo*. [Transformational-generative grammar] (Tentative title).
Fukui, N. and M. Saito (1993): Noam Chomsky's Impact on Linguistics in Japan, in: Otero, C. ed. *Noam Chomsky: Critical assignments*, pp. 735–739. London: Routledge.
Gabbay, D. M. and J. M. E. Moravesik (1974): Branching quantifiers, English, and Montague grammar, *Theoretical Linguistics* 1 (1/2), 139–157.
Gallistel, C. R. (1980): *The organization of action: a new synthesis*. Hilldsdale, N. J.: Lawrence and Erlbaum Associates.
Gazdar, G. (1979): *Pragmatics: Implicature, Presupposition, and Logical Form*. New York: Academic Press, 155–186.
Gazdar, G. (1981): Unbounded dependencies and coordinate structure, *Linguistic Inquiry* 12,2, 155–184.
Gazdar, G. (forthcoming): Phrase structure grammar, in: P. Jacobsen and G. Pullum (eds.) *The Nature of Syntactic Representation*. Boston: Reidel. (Published in 1982, 131–186.)
Gehring, W. J. (1998): *Master control genes in developmental evolution: the homeobox story*. New Haven: Yale University Press.
George, L. M. (1980): *Analogical Generalizations of Natural Language Syntax*. Ph. D. Dissertation, MIT.
Ginsburg, S. and B. Hall Partee (1969): A mathematical model of transformational grammar, *Information and Control* 15, 297–334.
GLOW Manifesto (1978): *GLOW NEWSLETTER* no. 1 (written by J. Koster, H. C. van Riemsdijk and J.-R. Vergnaud), 2–5.
Gold, E. M. (1967): Language identification in the limit. *Information and Control* 10, 447–474.
Goodman, N. (1943): On the simplicity of ideas. *Journal of Symbolic Logic* 8, 107–121.
Greenberg, J. (1963): Some universals of grammar, with particular reference to the order of meaningful elements, in: J. Greenberg (ed.) *Universals of Language*. Cambridge, Massachusetts: MIT Press, 58–90.
Gruber, G. (1976): *Lexical Structure in Syntax and Semantics*. Amsterdam: North-Holland.
Hagiwara, H. (1998): *Noo ni idomu gengogaku* [Linguistics that challenges the brain]. Tokyo: Iwanami Shoten.
Haider, H., M. Prinzhorn and H. van Riemsdijk (1987): Syntaxreport – generative Grammatik in Europa. Report on Generative Grammar in Europe, *Folia Linguistica* XXI/2–4.
Hale, K. (1976): Linguistic autonomy and the linguistics of Carl Voegelin, *Anthropological Linguistics*, March 1976, 120–128.
Hale, K. 1983. Warlpiri and the grammar of nonconfigurational languages. *Natural Language and Linguistic Theory* 1, 5–49.
Hale, K., L. M. Jeanne and P. Platero (1977): Three cases of overgeneration, in: P. Culicover, T. Wasow and A. Akmadjian (eds.) *Formal Syntax*. New York: Academic Press, 379–416.
Halle, M. (1975): Confessio grammatici, *Language* 51,3, 525–535.
Halle, M. and J.-R. Vergnaud (forthcoming) *Three-dimensional Phonology*. Published in1980. Journal of Research 1, 83–105.
Harman, G. (1963): Generative grammars without transformational rules: a defense of phrase structure, *Language* 39, 597–616.
Hauser, M. D., N. Chomsky, and W. T. Fitch (2002): The faculty of language: what is it, who has it, and how did it evolve? *Science* 298 (5598), 1569–1579.
Heyting, A. (1956): *Intuitionism: An Introduction*. Amsterdam: North-Holland.
Hintikka, J. (1974): Quantifiers vs. quantification theory, *Linguistic lnquiry* 5,2, 153–177.
Horváth, J. (1981): *Aspects of Hungarian Syntax and the Theory of Grammar*. Ph. D. Dissertation, UCLA.
Huang, J. C.-T. (1982): Move *wh* in a language without *wh*-movement, *The Linguistic Review* 1,4, 369–416.
Hubel, D. H. (1978): Vision and the brain, *Bulletin of the American Academy of Arts and Sciences* 31 (7): 28.

Hubel, D. H. and T. N. Wiesel (1962): Receptive fields, binocular interaction and functional architecture in the cat's visual cortex, *Journal of Physiology* 160, 106–154.
Hume, D. (1841): *The history of England: from the invasion of Julius Caesar to the revolution in 1688*. London: T. Cadell. (Reprint of original 1778 edition by Liberty Fund, Indianapolis, 1983.)
Huybregts, M. A. C. (not completed): *A formal Theory of Binding and Bounding*.
Jackendoff, R. S. (1972): Semantic Interpretation in Generative Grammar. Cambridge, Massachusetts: MIT Press.
Jackendoff, R. S. (1976): Toward an explanatory semantic representation, *Linguistic Inquiry* 7, 89–150.
Jackendoff, R. S. (1977): *X̄-Syntax: A study of Phrase Structure*. Linguistic Inquiry Monograph No. 2, Cambridge, Massachusetts: MIT Press.
Jacob, F. (1973): *The Logic of Life*. New York: Pantheon.
Jacob, F. (1977a): Darwinism reconsidered. *Le Monde* (September 6–8, 1977); translated in *Atlas* (January, 1978).
Jacob, F. (1977b): Evolution and tinkering. *Science* 196 (4295), 1161–1166.
Jaeggli, O. (1980): *On some Phonologically-Null Elements in Syntax*. Ph. D. Dissertation, MIT. To appear as Jaeggli (1982).
Jaeggli, O. (1982): *Topics in Romance Syntax*. Dordrecht: Foris Publications.
Jakobson, R., C. G. M. Fant, and M. Halle (1952): *Preliminaries to speech analysis: the distinctive features and their correlates*. Acoustic Laboratory Technical Report 13, MIT. (Reprinted in 1963, Cambridge, Mass.: MIT Press.)
Jenkins, L. (2000)): *Biolinguistics: Exploring the biology of language*. Cambridge: Cambridge University Press.
Joos, M. ed. (1957): *Readings in linguistics* I. American Council of Learned Societies.
Kaplan, R. (1972): Augmented transition networks as psychological models of sentence comprehension, *Artificial Intelligence* 3, 77–100.
Kaplan, R. (1975): *Transient Processing Load in Sentence Comprehension*. Ph. D. Dissertation, Harvard University.
Katz, J. J. and T. G. Bever (1976): The fall and rise of empiricism, in: T. G. Bever, J. J. Katz and D. T. Langendoen (eds.) *An Integrated Theory of Linguistic Ability*. New York: Thomas Y. Crowell Company, 11–64.
Katz, J. J. and J. A. Fodor (1963): The structure of a semantic theory, *Language* 39, 170–210. (Reprinted in 1964 in *The structure of language: readings in the philosophy of language*, ed. J. A. Fodor and J. J. Katz, pp. 479–518. Englewood Cliffs, NJ: Prentice-Hall).
Katz, F. and J. J. Katz (1977): Is necessity the mother of intension?, *The Philosophical Review* 86, 70–96.
Katz, J. J. and P. M. Postal (1964): *An Integrated Theory of Linguistic Descriptions*. Cambridge, Mass.: MIT Press.
Kayne, R. S. (1975): *French Syntax: the Transformational Cycle*. Cambridge, Massachusetts: MIT Press.
Kayne, R. S. (1981a): Two notes on the NIC, in: Belletti et al. (eds.) (1981), 317–346.
Kayne, R. S. (1981b): ECP-extensions, *Linguistic Inquiry* 12,1. (Reprinted in Kayne 1984, *Connectedness and binary branching*, pp. 47–86. Dordrecht: Foris.)
Kayne, R. S. and J.-Y. Pollock (1978): Stylistic inversion, successive cyclicity, and move NP in French, *Linguistic Inquiry* 9,4, 595–621.
Kean, M.-L. (1974): The strict cycle in phonology, *Linguistic Inquiry* 5,2, 179–203.
Kean, M.-L. (1975): *Theory of Markedness in Generative Grammar*. Ph. D. Dissertation, MIT. Distributed by the Indiana University Linguistics Club.
Kean, M.-L. (1981): On a theory of markedness: some general considerations and a case in point, in: Belletti et al. (eds.), 559–604.
Kingsolver, J. G. and M. A. Koehl (1985): Aerodynamics, thermoregulation, and the evolution of insect wings: differential scaling and evolutionary change. *Evolution* 39: 48–504.

Kloeke, W. U. S. van Lessen (1981): How strident is the raspberry? Likely, unlikely and impossible feature combinations in phonology, in: Belletti et al. (eds.), 363–486.
Kondo, S. and R. Asai (1995): A reaction-diffusion wave on the skin of the marine angelfish *Pomacanthus*. *Nature* 376 (6543), 765–768.
Koster, J. (1978): *Locality Principles in Syntax*. Dordrecht: Foris Publications.
Koster, J. and R. May (1982): On the constituency of Infinitives, *Language* 58, 116–143.
Krauwer, S. and L. des Tombes (1981): Transducers and grammars as theories of language, *Theoretical Linguistics* 8 (1/3): 173–202.
Kripke, S. (1972): Naming and necessity, in: D. Davidson and G. Harman (eds.) *Semantics of Natural Language*. New York: Humanities Press, 253–355.
Kuhn, Th. (1962): *The Structure of Scientific Revolutions*. Chicago: Chicago University Press.
Kuno, S. (1973): Constraints on internal clauses and sentential subjects, *Linguistic Inquiry* 4, 363–386.
Kuno, S. (1974): The position of relative clauses and conjunctions, *Linguistic Inquiry* 5, 117–136.
Kuno, S. and J. J. Robinson (1972): Multiple *wh*-questions, *Linguistic Inquiry* 3, 463–487.
Kuroda, S.-Y. (1999): Bunpoo riron to tetsugaku teki shizen shugi. [Grammatical theory and philosophical naturalism]. In *Gengo to Shikoo* [Language and thought] by N. Chomsky and S.-Y. Kuroda (Japanese Translation: Masao Oishi), pp. 93–134. Tokyo: Shoohaku Sha.
Kuroda, S.-Y. 1976. A topological study of phrase structure languages. *Information and Control* 30, 307–379.
Lakoff, G. (1970): Global rules, *Language* 46: 627–640.
Lakoff, G. (1971): On generative semantics, in: D. D. Steinberg and L. A. Jakobovits (eds.) *Semantics: an Interdisciplinary Reader in Philosophy, Linguistics, and Psychology*. New York: Cambridge University Press, 232–396.
Langendoen, D. T. (1975): Finite state parsing of phrase structure languages and the status of readjustment rules in grammar, *Linguistic Inquiry* 6,4, 533–554.
Langendoen, D. T. (1979): On the assignment of constituent structures to the sentences generated by a transformational grammar, *CUNY Forum* 7–8, 1–32.
Langendoen, T. (1961): *Structural descriptions for sentences generated by non-self-embedding constituent grammars*. Undergraduate honors thesis, MIT, Cambridge, Mass.
Lashley, K. S. (1951): The problem of serial order in behavior, in: L. A. Jeffress (ed.) *Cerebral Mechanisms in Behavior*. New York: Wiley and Sons, 112–136.
Lasnik, H. and J. Kupin (1977): A restrictive theory of transformational grammar, *Theoretical Linguistics* 4,3, 173–196.
Lewis, D. (1972): General semantics, in: D. Davidson and G. Harman (eds.) *Semantics of Natural Language*. Dordrecht: Reidel, 169–218.
Liberman, M. and A. Prince (1977): On stress and linguistic rhythm, *Linguistic Inquiry* 8, 249–336.
Lieber, R. (1980): *On the Organization of the Lexicon*. Ph. D. Dissertation, MIT.
Locke, J. (1690): *An essay concerning human understanding*. (Reprinted in 1975, edited with a foreword by P. Nidditch. Oxford: Clarendon Press.)
Luria, S. E. (1973): *Life: the Unfinished Experiment*. New York: Scribners.
Lyons, J. (1970): *Chomsky*. London: Fontana and Collins.
Mandelbrot, B. B. (1977): *Fractals: Form, Change, and Dimension*. San Francisco: Freeman.
Marantz, A. (1981): *On the Nature of Grammatical Relations*. Ph. D. Dissertation, MIT.
Marantz, A., Y. Miyashita, and W. O'Neil (2000): *Image, language, brain*. Cambridge, MA.: MIT Press.
Marcus, M. Ph. (1980): *A Theory of Syntactic Recognition for Natural Language*. Cambridge, Massachusetts: MIT Press.
Marr, D. and H. K. Nisihara (1978): Visual information processing: artificial intelligence and the sensorium of sight, *Technology Review* (MIT), vol. 81 (1).

Martin, R. and J. Uriagereka (2000): Introduction: some possible foundations of the minimalist program, in: *Step by step: essays in minimalist syntax in honor of Howard Lasnik,* ed. R. Martin, D. Michaels, and J. Uriagereka, pp. 1–29. Cambridge, Mass.: MIT Press.
Mascaró, J. (1976): *Catalan Phonology and the Strict Cycle.* Ph. D. Dissertation, MIT.
Matthei, E. H. (1979): Children's interpretation of sentences containing reciprocals, in: H. Goodluck and L. Solan (eds.) *Papers in the Structure and Development of Child Language.* University of Massachusetts Occasional Papers in Linguistics, Amherst.
Maynard Smith, J. (1986): *The Problems of biology.* Oxford: Oxford University Press.
Maynard Smith, J., R. Burian, S. Kauffman, P. Alberch, J. Campbell, B. Goodwin, R. Lande, D. Raup, and L. Wolpert (1985): Developmental constraints in evolution. *Quarterly Review of Biology* 60: 3, 265–287.
Maynard Smith, J., R. Burian, S. Kauffman, P. Alberch, J. Campbell, G. Goodwin, R. Lande, D. Raup, and L. Wolpert (1985): Developmental constraints and evolution. *The quarterly review of biology.* 60 (3): 265–287.
McCarthy, J. (1982): Non-linear phonology: an overview, *GLOW NEWSLETTER* no. 8, 63–77.
Miller, G. A. (1951): *Language and Communication.* New York: McGraw Hill.
Miller, G. A. and N. Chomsky (1963): Finitary models of language users. In *Handbook of Mathematical Psychology* vol. II, ed. D. R. Luce, R. R. Bush and E. Galanter, pp. 419–491. New York: John Wiley & Sons.
Miller, G. A. and S. Isard (1964): Free recall of self-embedded English sentences, *Information and Control* 7, 292–303.
Miller, G. and N. Chomsky. (1963): Finitary models of language users. In *Handbook of mathematical psychology* II, ed., R. Luce, R. Bush, and E. Galanter, pp. 419–492. New York: John Wiley & Sons.
Milner, J.-Cl. (1978a): Reply to the GLOW Manifesto concerning the object of inquiry, *GLOW Newsletter* no. 1, 5–9.
Milner, J.-Cl. (1978b): Cyclicité successive, comparatives, et cross-over en français, *Linguistic Inquiry* 9,4.
Monod, J. (1970): *Le Hasard et la Nécessite.* Paris: Editions du Seuil.
Montague, R. (1974): *Formal Philosophy: Selected Papers of Richard Montague,* edited by Richmond Thomason. New Haven: Yale University Press.
Moro, A., M. Tettamanti, D. Perani, D. Donati, S. F. Cappa, and F. Fazio (2001): Syntax and the brain: disentangling grammar by selective anomalies. *NeuroImage* 13, 110–118.
Muysken, P. (1981): Quechua causatives and logical form: a case study in markedness, in: Belletti et al. (eds.), 445–473.
Neijt, A. (1979): *Gapping: A Contribution to Sentence Grammar.* Dordrecht: Foris Publications.
Newmeyer, F. (1980): *Linguistic Theory in America.* New York: Academic Press.
Nissenbaum, J. (2000): *Investigations of covert phrase movement.* Doctoral dissertation, MIT, Cambridge, Mass.
Osherson, D. N., M. Stob, and S. Weinstein (1985): *Systems that learn.* Cambridge, Mass.: MIT Press.
Otsu, Y. (1981): *Universal Grammar and Syntactic Development in Children: Toward a Theory of Syntactic Development.* Ph. D. Dissertation, MIT.
Peirce, C. S. (1957): The logic of abduction. In *Peirce's essays in the philosophy of science,* ed., V. Thomas. New York: Liberal Arts Press.
Perlmutter, D. (1971): *Deep and Surface Structure Constraints in Syntax.* New York: Holt, Rinehart and Winston.
Pesetsky, D. (1982): Complementizer-trace phenomena and the nominative island constraint, *The Linguistic Review* 1,3, 297–343.
Pesetsky, D. (1995): *Zero syntax: experiencers and cascades.* Cambridge, Mass.: MIT Press.

Peters, P. S. (1973): On restricting deletion transformations, in: M. Gross, M. Halle and M. P. Schützenberger (eds.) *The Formal Analysis of Natural Language*. The Hague: Mouton.
Peters, P. S. and R. W. Ritchie (1971): On restricting the base component of transformational grammars, *Information and Control* 18, 483–501.
Peters, P. S. and R. W. Ritchie (1973): On the generative power of transformational grammars, *Information Sciences* 6, 49–83.
Phillips, C. (1996): *Order and structure*. Ph. D. dissertation, MIT.
Postal, P. M. (1972): The best theory, in: S. Peters (ed.) *Goals of Linguistic Theory*. Englewood Cliffs, New Jersey: Prentice Hall.
Postal, P. M. (1974): *On Raising*. Cambridge Massachusetts: MIT Press.
Premack, D. (1976): *Intelligence in Ape and Man*. Hillsdale, N. J.: Lawrence Erlbaum Associates.
Quicoli, C. (1975): Conditions on quantifier movement in French, *Linguistic Inquiry* 7,4, 583–607.
Quicoli, C. (1980): Clitic movement in French causatives, *Linguistic Analysis* 6, 131–185.
Quine, W. V. O. (1953): *From a Logical Point of View*. Cambridge, Massachusetts: Harvard University Press.
Quine, W. V. O. (1960): *Word and Object*. Cambridge, Massachusetts: MIT Press.
Quine, W. V. (1992): Structure and nature. *Journal of Philosophy* 89: 5–9.
Reinhart, T. (1981): A second COMP position, in: Belletti et al. (eds.), 517–557.
Ricardo, D. (1821): *On Principles of political economy and taxation*. 3rd edition.
Riemsdijk, H. C. van (1978a): On the diagnosis of *wh*-movement, in: S. J. Keyser (ed.) *Recent Transformational Studies in European Languages*. Linguistic Inquiry Monographs No. 3. Cambridge, Massachusetts: MIT Press, 189–206.
Riemsdijk, H. C. van (1978b): *A case Study in Syntactic Markedness: the Binding Nature of Prepositional Phrases*. Dordrecht: Foris Publications.
Riemsdijk, H. C. van (1981): On adjacency in phonology and syntax, in: Burke and Pustejovsky (eds.) *NELS XI*. University of Massachusetts, Amherst. Expanded and revised version to appear in D.-W. Yang (ed.) *Linguistics in the Morning Calm*, Seoul under the title Locality principles in syntax and phonology, 693–708.
Rizzi, L. (1978a): A restructuring rule in Italian syntax, in: S. J. Keyser (ed.) *Recent Transformational Studies in European Languages*. Linguistic Inquiry Monograph No. 3. Cambridge, Massachusetts: MIT Press (Reprinted in Rizzi (1982), 113–158).
Rizzi, L. (1978b): Violations of the *wh*-island constraint in Italian and the subjacency condition, in: C. Dubuisson, D. Lightfoot and Y. C. Morin (eds.) *Montreal Working Papers in Linguistics* no. 11, 155–190. (Reprinted in Rizzi (1982)).
Rizzi, L. (1982): *Issues in Italian Syntax*. Dordrecht: Foris Publications.
Roberts, P. (1967): *The Roberts English Series: Complete Course*. New York: Harcourt, Brace and World.
Roeper, T. (1981): A deductive approach to the acquisition of productive morphology, in: C. L. Baker and J. McCarthy (eds.) *The Logical Problem of Language Acquisition*. Cambridge, Massachusetts: MIT Press, 129–150.
Rosenbaum, P. S. (1967): *The Grammar of English Predicate Complement Constructions*. Cambridge, Massachusetts: MIT Press.
Ross, J. R. (1967): *Constraints on Variables in Syntax*. Ph. D. Dissertation, MIT.
Ross, J. R. (1970): Gapping and the order constituents, in: M. Bierwisch and K. E. Heidolph (eds.) *Progress in Linguistics*. The Hague: Mouton, 249–259.
Rouveret, A. and J.-R. Vergnaud (1980): Specifying reference to the subject: French causatives and conditions on representations, *Linguistic Inquiry* 11,1, 97–202.
Rubinstein, A. (2000): *Economics and language*. Cambridge: Cambridge University Press.
Sakai, K. (2002): *Gengo no nookagaku – noo wa donoyooni kotoba o umidasuka –*. [The brain science of language – how the brain creates language–] Tokyo: Chuuoo Kooron Shinsha.

Sakurai, A. and K. Sakai (2000): Gengo kakutoku no moderu [A model of language acquisition]. *Suuri Kagaku* [Mathematical sciences]. No. 444: 45–51.
Sapir, E. (1921): *Language*. New York: Harcourt Brace Jovanovich.
Schank, R. and R. P. Abelson (1977): *Scripts, Plans, Goals, and Understanding*. Hillsdale, New Jersey: Lawrence Erlbaum.
Scott, R., C. Salas, B. Campbell (2001): *NAFTA at seven: Its impact on workers in all three nations*. Economic Policy Institute.
Searle, J. R. (1969): *Speech Acts*. London: Cambridge University Press.
Searle, J. R. (1972): Chomsky's revolution in linguistics, *New York Review of Books*, June 29.
Searle, J. R. (1980): Minds, brains, and programs, *The Behavioral and Brain Sciences* 3,3, 417–457.
Selkirk, L. (1977): Some remarks on noun phrase structure, in: P. Culicover, T. Wasow and A. Akmajian (eds.) *Formal Syntax*. New York: Academic Press, 285–316.
Shannon, C. E. and W. Weaver (1949): *The Mathematical Theory of Communication*. Urbana: University of Illinois Press.
Siegel, D. (1978): The adjacency constraint and the theory of morphology in: M. Stein (ed.) *Proceedings of the 8th Annual Meeting of the North Eastern Linguistic Society*. University of Massachusetts, Amherst, 189–197.
Smith, A. (1776): *An inquiry into the natural causes of the wealth of nations*.
Smith, M., J. R. Burian, S. Kauffman, P. Alberch, J. Campbell, B. Goodwin, R. Lande, D. Raup, and L. Wolpert (1985): Developmental Constraints in Evolution, *Quarterly Review of Biology* 60.3, 265–287.
Sperber, D. and D. Wilson (1986/1995): *Relevance: communication and cognition*. Oxford: Blackwell.
Sportiche, D. (1981): On bounding nodes in French, *The Linguistic Review* 1,2, 219–246.
Stent, G. (1978): *Paradoxes of Progress*. San Francisco: Freeman and Co.
Stewart, I. and M. Golubitsky (1992): *Fearful symmetry*. Oxford: Blackwell.
Stich, St. P. (1972): Grammar, psychology, and indeterminacy, *Journal of Philosophy* 69, 799–818.
Stich, St. P. (1978): Empiricism, innateness, and linguistic universals, *Philosophical Studies* 33, 273–286.
Stich, St. P. (ed.) (1975): *Innate Ideas*. Berkeley: University of California Press.
Stowell, T. (1981): *Origins of Phrase Structure*. Ph. D. Dissertation, MIT.
Suppes, P. (1969): Stimulus-response theory of finite automata, *Journal of Mathematical Psychology* 6, 327–355.
Taraldsen, K. T. (1978): The scope of *wh*-movement in Norwegian, *Linguistic Inquiry* 9,4, 623–640.
Taraldsen, K. T. (1980): On the nominative island condition, vacuous application, and the *that*-trace filter, distributed by the Indiana University Linguistics Club.
Taraldsen, K. T. (1981): The theoretical interpretation of a class of "marked" extractions, in: Belletti et al. (eds.), 475–516.
Terrace, H. S. (1979): *Nim*. New York: Knopf.
Teuber, H. L. (1960): Perception. In *The handbook of physiology-neurophysiology* III, ed. Field, J., H. W. Magoun, V. E. Hall. Washington, D. C.: American Physiological Society.
Thompson, D. A. W. (1942): *On growth and form*. 2nd edition. Cambridge: Cambridge University Press.
Turing, A. M. (1952): The chemical basis of morphogenesis. *Philosophical Transactions of the Royal Society of London B* 237: 37–72.
Uriagereka, J. (1998): *Rhyme and reason*. Cambridge, Mass: MIT Press.
Vendler, Z. (1967): *Linguistics in Philosophy*. Ithaca, New York: Cornell.
Vergnaud, J.-R. (1977): Formal properties of phonological rules, in: R. E. Butts and J. Hintikka (eds.) *Basic Problems in Methodology and Linguistics*. Dordrecht: Reidel, 299–318.

Vergnaud, J.-R. (1985): *Dépendance et niveaux de représentation en syntaxe*, Amsterdam: Benjamins
Wanner, E. and M. Maratsos (1978): An ATN approach to comprehension, in: M. Halle, J. Bresnan, and G. Miller (eds.) *Linguistic Theory and Psychological Reality.* Cambridge, Massachusetts: MIT Press, 119–161.
Weil, A. (1969): On the algebraic study of certain types of marriage laws (Murngin system). In Lévi-Strauss, C. 1969. *The elementary structure of kinship*, pp. 221–229. Beacon Press. (Original version published as Sur l'etude algébrique de certains types de lois de marriage (Systèm Murngin). In: C. Lévi-Strauss. 1947. *Les structures elementaires de la parente.* Paris: Mouton.)
Wexler, K. and P. W. Culicover (1980): *Formal Principles of Language Acquisition.* Cambridge, Massachusetts: MIT Press.
Weyl, H. (1952): *Symmetry.* Princeton: Princeton University Press.
Williams, E. (1977): Across-the-board application of rules, *Linguistic Inquiry* 8,2, 419–423.
Williams, E. (1978): Across-the-board rule application, *Linguistic Inquiry* 9,1, 31–43.
Williams, E. (1981a): Argument structure and morphology, *The Linguistic Review* 1,1, 81–114.
Williams, E. (1981b): Transformationless grammar, *Linguistic Inquiry* 12,4, 645–653.
Williams, E. (1981c): On the notions lexically related and head of a word, *Linguistic Inquiry* 12,2, 245–274.
Wilson, E. O. (1975): *Sociobiology: the New Synthesis*, Cambridge: Belknap Press of Harvard University Press.
Woods, W. (1973): An experimental parsing system for transition network grammars, in: R. Rustin (ed.) *Natural Language Processing.* Englewood Cliffs, New Jersey: Prentice Hall.
Woods, W. (1978): Transition network grammars for natural language analysis, *Communications of the ACM* 13, 591–606.

Index

A/A (A-over-A) Condition (Principle), 88, 105
Aboriginal people, 48
Abstract,
  concept, 143
  entity, 58, 96–97
  idea, 80
  model, 19, 20–21
  notion, 131
  phonology, 138
  principles, 11, 40
  properties, 38, 58
  representation, 4, 128
  system, 79, 96
  theories, 70, 94
Abstraction, 40, 42, 60, 95, 97, 131–132, 177
Abstractness, 19, 133
Accessibility, 53–54, 116, 134
Accessibility between worlds, 116
Accessible grammars, 91, 98–99, 136
Accessible Subject, 134, 134 fn 5
Across-the-board (ATB) phenomena, 127–128
Adjacency Condition, 119, 135 fn 7
Adjunction, 125
Affixation, 121
Agree 168
Algebra, 178
  Boolean -, 79
Algorithm, 38, 40, 43
Ambiguity, 55
Analytic device, ix, 5
  peripheral -, 142
Anaphor, 92, 103 fn 34, 106, 18, 114 fn 5, 115, 134, 138
Anaphoric interpretation, 93–94, 99
Antecedent, 96, 103 fn 34, 112, 134 fn 5
Anthropology, 77
Anti-intellectualism, 96
Ape, 46, 48, 80
Ape language, 80
Aphasia, 122, 177
Arithmetic, 143, 58, 177
Artificial intelligence, 37–39
Assimilation, 122
ATN, *see* Augmented Transitional Network

Atom, 97, 182
Attach Affix Rule, 120
Attract 167–168
Augmented Transitional Network, 93
Automata, 22, 41–42, 89–91, 172,
Autonomous systems, 5, 8, 13, 138–141, 163
Autonomy Thesis, 9–11, 13, 137–140
AUX, 106
Auxiliary, 69, 90
Axiom, 14, 114, 141

Base,
  form, 55, 98–99, 111, 120, 137
  grammar, 87, 110
  ordering, 110
  rules, 110, 138
  structure, 88, 93, 110–111
Behavior, 19–20, 39, 48
  human -, 38
Behavioral psychology, 45
Behaviorism, 2, 40, 44–45
Behaviorist
  heritage, 45
  method, 19–20
  psychology, 2, 44
  theory, 90
Beliefs, 116
Big Bang, 50
Binding xv, 29, 87, 115, 124–125
  principles, 101, 114, 138
  theory, 100–102, 104, 108, 110, 112–114, 130, 141
Biochemistry, 38, 56
Biological
  capacity, 5, 10, 46
  changes, 46, 148
  communication systems, 49
  systems, x, 56, 171
  world, 49, 173
Biology, ix, xii, 13, 18–19, 33, 35–36, 49, 52, 68, 82, 95, 150, 162–163, 170, 174, 178–181, 185, 187
Black box 19
Body, ix, xi, 5, 60–61, 154, 157, 164, 179
Bound, 112, 114 fn 5, 121
Bounded domains, 123

Bounding, 100, 101
Brain, ix-x, 1–3, 5, 10, 13–15, 19–21, 36, 41, 46–47, 49–51, 56, 58–61, 131, 176, 179, 182–183
Brain sciences 10, 18–21, 25, 149, 181–183
Branching 127, 167–168

Calculus, 39, 83
Cartesians, 58
Capital 183–184
Case
　assignment, 102, 119
　objective -, 135 fn 7
　systems, 135
　theory, 103, 110–111, 119, 135, 141
Case-marked, 112–115, 129, 135 fn 7
Categorial Component, 88, 110–111
Causative, 106, 121
Cause and effect, 33
C-command, 128, 168
Chemistry, 21, 38, 56, 79, 150, 159, 170, 172, 174, 181–182
Chicago Linguistic Society, 74
Child Language, 55, 136–137
Chinese, 40, 141
Circulatory System, ix, 5, 55–56, 164
Class
　of core grammars, 120
　of grammars, 91, 98
　of transformational grammars, 136
　of word structures, 120
Classical problems, 104–106
Clitics, 106
Cognition, 12, 14, 33, 41
Cognitive
　domains, 5, 8–10, 12–15, 24, 46
　interaction, 139
　psychology, 44–45, 75
　sciences, 22, 33, 36, 43, 75, 183
Communication, xii, 8
　animal -, 45, 49, 179
　language and -, 8, 18, 41, 55
　symbolic -, 44
　theory of, 9, 41
Communicative intention, 55
COMP-attraction, 124
COMP-projection, 124
COMP-to-COMP, 99
Competence, 1–2, 89, 92, 95
Competence-Performance Dichotomy, 92
Complement, 87 fn 2, 112
　convention, 122
　sentential -, 110–111
　system, 111

Complements
　choice of -, 111
　order of -, 110, 119, 135
　set of -, 110
Complementizer, 124
　constraint, 105
　lexical -, 103 fn 34
　structure, 103
Compounding, 121
Computation, xii, 38–39, 43, 153–154, 157, 175, 181
Computational
　analysis, 44
　aspects of language, 46, 138
　capacity, 47–48
　component, 138
　description, 44
　facilities, 48
　models, 20, 38
　systems, 17, 37, 151–152
Computer, 24, 36–38, 41, 48, 58–60, 185
Concepts, xi, 12, 60, 89, 94, 110, 118–119, 130, 141–143
　abstract -, 143
　network of -, 143
　set of -, 141
　substantive -, 134–135
Conceptual, 59, 92
　capacities, 47
　category, 117–118
　change, 66–68, 83, 147
　system, 13, 17, 47–49, 164–165, 180
　unification, 56, 100, 108–109
Conditions
　binding -, 138
　boundary -, 53
　Island -, 99, 103, 105
　on anaphora, 93
　on core grammars, 132
　on form and function, 87
　on output, 104
　on Q-variables, 122–123
　on representation, 120, 137–138
　on rules, 88, 97, 99, 137
　pragmatic -, 138
　theory of -, 100, 134
Configurational
　notions, 143
　structures, 121
Conjuncts, 128
Constituency tests, 130
Constituent
　order, 119

structure, 66
Constraints 100, 104, 120, 135, 137, 143, 148, 150, 156, 167–168
Constructional system, 141, 143
Constructions
  mathematical -, 43, 177
  mental -, 43
Context-free Grammar, 43–43, 89–91, 98, 126, 175
Context-free Languages, 91
Contexts
  belief -, 116
  extensional -, 115–116
  propositional attitude -, 116
Continuity, 49, 116
Control, 69, 90, 92, 102, 110, 141
Coordination, 115, 127–129
Core, 131–134, 136
Core Grammar, 92, 120, 126, 132–133, 136, 140
Counterexamples, 71
Cycle, xii, 88, 151–152, 158
  strict -, 88, 99
Cyclic transformational rules, 125
Cycling Function Theorem, 126

Data,
  arrangement, 40
  coverage of -, 108
  depth-two -, 136
  linguistic -, 108
  pretheoretical -, 142
  primary linguistic -, x, 3–7, 9, 44, 141
  restricted -, 54
D-structure (*see* also Deep Structure), 137, 151
Deductive Depth, 100
Deductive Structure, 40, 100–101
Deep Structure, 35, 88
Deletion,
  across-the-board -, 127
  specific -, 127
Denmark, 52
Derivation xii, 114 fn 6, 138, 140, 152
Description,
  levels of -, 42
Descriptive Device, 66, 68
Descriptive work, 66, 68, 94, 187
Descriptivism, 40, 83
Designated elements, 125
Development
  uniformity of, 51
Developmental

  biology, 52
  psychology, 139
Dictionary Entry, 116
Direction, 135
Diode, 38, 58
Discrete infinity, 14–15, 49–50
Disjoint Reference, 93, 106
Displacement 152, 164–165
Domain-specificity 10, 162–163, 181
Dualism, 60
Dutch, 107, 129–130

E-language 3
Economics 183–184
Economy 12, 24, 154, 178, 185
ECP, *see* Empty Category Principle
Electrons, 97
Elegance, 56
Embedded
  clauses, 90
  structures, 69, 88, 90
Embedding
  center -, 92–93
  levels of -, 42
  multiple center -, 92
Empiricism, 70, 95
Empty Category, 93–94
Empty Category Principle (ECP), 101–102, 112, 130, 140
Empty elements, 93
Endocentric structure
  of phrasal categories, 87
Engineering, 36, 155
English, ix, xvi, 2–5, 23, 33, 40, 80, 99, 107, 119, 122, 129, 130, 133, 135, 141, 149, 162
Enrichment, 91, 98
Epiphenomenon, 132
Epistemological priority, 141–143
Epistemology, 34
Essentialism, 116–117
EST, *see* Extended Standard Theory
Europe, xv, 69, 71, 73–75
Evaluation, 48, 158, 160–162
Evolution, xii, 8, 55, 150, 170, 178–180
  differential -, 47
  human-, x, 15, 18, 47–48, 176
  of amino acids, 50
  of language, 1, 9, 13, 15–16, 18, 163
  of organisms, 49
Evolutionary
  leap, 49
  theory, 25, 50, 178–180
Exceptions, 132

Existential *there*, 112
Explanation,
  evolutionary -, 55
  formal -, 55
  functional -, 55, 119
Explanatory
  adequacy, x-xi, 7–8, 11, 16, 22–23, 53–54, 98–99, 142, 148–149, 159
  depth, 108
  power, 139
  principles, 72
  theory, 16–17, 53, 68–69, 79, 94
Extended Standard Theory (EST), 75, 98, 153, 158
Extraction, 103
  from noun phrases, 101, 104
Extraposition, 106

Factorization
  simultaneous -, 127
Faculté du langage, 89
Faithfulness 166–167
Features, 112, 124, 142, 156, 162, 164–165, 167–169
Feature framework,
  for categories, 87
Filter (*see* also NP-to-VP Filter, That-trace Filter), 55, 102, 137, 139
Finite, ix, 49, 99, 119–120, 148
  bound, 92
  discrete source, 89
  state device, 92–93
  state parsers, 92
  state transducers, 41, 92–93
  systems, 41, 135
Finiteness, 99, 118–120, 124
Focus, 129, 135, 164, 166
Focus assignment, 135
Formal instruction, 40
Formal proof, 43
Formalism, 123, 125, 127
Formalization, 124–126
Fractals, 50
Free, 114 fn 5
Functional
  arguments, 113
  structure, 93
  uniqueness, 111

Gapping, 106, 127–128
Gaps, 90, 93, 96, 119, 153
Generalization
  descriptive -, 70

Generalized
  base marker, 99
  transformation, 88
Generative Capacity, 126, 132
  strong -, 54, 91, 132, 175
  weak -, 49, 54, 89, 91, 98, 174
Generative Grammar, v, ix, xv–xvi, 1–3, 7–12, 15–23, 25, 29–30, 33, 35, 50, 57, 63, 65–66, 69, 71–72, 73 fn 11, 74–75, 77, 81–82, 107, 147–148, 150, 158–159, 162, 170, 172, 180
Generative Linguistics, 51, 80
Generative Phonology, 106
Generative Semantics, 30, 69–72, 74, 88 fn 6
Genes, 20, 57, 61, 179
Genetic drift
  random -, 49
Genetics, 21, 50, 57
German, 65, 185
Global Rules, 72
GLOW (Generative Linguists in the Old World), xv, 29, 57, 73–74, 105 fn 38
Goal, 113
Governance, 124
Governing Category, 114 fn 5
  minimal -, 114 fn 5
Government
  proper -, 102, 140
  theory, 101, 112
Government-Binding Theory, xv, 29, 87, 104, 110, 112
Grammar, (*see* also Accessible Grammars, Class of Grammars, Context-free Grammar, Core Grammar, Generative Grammar, Head-Driven Phrase Structure Grammar, Human Grammar, Lexical Functional Grammar, Medieval Grammar, Montague Grammar, Phrase Structure Grammar, Port-Royal Grammar, Relational Grammar, Renaissance Grammar, Strcturalist grammar, Transformational Grammar, Universal Grammar), x, 3, 6–8, 11, 22–23, 44–45, 53–58, 87, 91–92, 97–99, 106, 100, 112–115, 120–121, 131–133, 136, 139, 141–143, 149, 156, 158–160, 175
  theory of -, 29, 98, 115
Grammatical Relations, 128, 141, 143
Grammatical Sentences, 93
Greek, 135
Greenberg Universals, 119, 135

Head, 5, 87 fn 2, 119, 124
Head-Driven Phrase Structure Grammar 169

Hebrew, 91, 107, 119, 161
Helium, 43, 50, 174
Hemisphere, 51
Hemispherectomy, 51
Hereditary traits, 51
Hierarchy
  natural -, 98
  of formal languages, 54
  of preferability of grammars, 91
  of weak generative capacity of grammars, 91
History, ix, 77, 156, 170, 185
  human -, 14, 18, 46–47
  Intellectual -, 64, 94
  natural -, 66, 68
  of Ideas, 63–65, 82
  of linguistics, 22, 25, 64, 87, 96, 115, 125, 158, 170
  of mathematics, 48, 79
  of science, 60, 65
  of the universe, 49
Holland, 52, 74, 80
HPSG, *see* Head-Driven Phrase Structure Grammar
Human,
  body, 61
  evolution, x, 15, 18, 47–48, 176
  grammar, 45
  history, 14, 47
  intelligence, 61
  life, 47
  race, 62
  species, 5–6, 10, 14–15, 55
Humanities, 10, 40, 187
Humanness, 117
Hungarian, 135 fn 7
Hydrogen, 50, 58

I-language x–xii, 3, 5–8, 11, 16, 150–151, 157, 160–161
Idiom
  chunks, 111, 118
  rules, 127
Inclusiveness 166
Indexing
  techniques of -, 125
Indices, 91
Individual, 116
Individuation, 46
Inequality, 62
Infinitival relatives, 55, 103
Infinitivals, 99
Informant work, 107, 177

Information theory, 41
Innate
  ability, 62
  capacity, 61
  ideas, 61, 63
  physical properties, 62
  structures, 61, 106
Innovation, 50, 95, 163
Integers, 49
Intelligence, 5, 37–39, 61
Intelligence Test, 61
Intent, 47
Interaction, xi, 8–9, 11, 21, 33, 69, 102, 113–114, 138, 141, 148, 157, 64
  cognitive -, 118, 139
  human -, xii, 95, 139
  social -, 139
Interface, xii, 17, 151–152, 157–158, 163, 165, 171, 180
Interpretive rule, 96–98
Interrogatives, ix, 90
Introspective judgment, 59
Intuitions, 48, 79–80, 97, 117–118, 159
Invariance
  genotypical -, 50
Inversion, 113
Island-conditions, 71, 99, 103, 105
Italian, 71, 101, 107, 129
Italy, 74, 181

Japanese, xvi, 2, 5, 121, 165–166, 169
Judgments, 59

K-order system, 89
Katz-Postal Hypothesis, 88
Kinship systems 177–178
Knowledge, 2, 34, 39
  a priori -, 34
  human -, 34, 48, 177
  nature of -, 34
  of language, x, 1, 3–7, 10, 92, 139
  systems of -, 75, 92, 93, 95

LAD, *see* Language Acquisition Device
Language, ix
  biology of -, x, xii, 36
  chimp -, 45, 163
  finite -, ix, 49, 92, 99, 119–120, 136, 142, 176
  formal -, 22, 52, 172
  human -, 2, 9–13, 15, 17–18, 22–24, 46, 48, 155, 165, 172, 178–179
  knowlegde of x, 1, 3–7, 10, 92, 139

natural -, 34, 54, 87, 91, 118, 136
notion of, 131–132
ordinary -, 33
Platonistic view of -, 43
polysynthetic -, 121
properties of -, ix, 8, 42–43, 137
psychology of -, 95, 149
schizophrenic -, 51–52
study of -, ix, x, 2, 9, 34, 43, 59, 89–90, 92, 95, 178, 181, 187,
synthetic -, 121
w* -, 135
Language Acquisition, x-xii, 1, 3, 5–7, 10, 56, 89, 95, 136–137, 142–143, 149, 160, 162, 176
   child -, 55, 136–137
   genetic theory of -, 51
Language Acquisition Device (LAD), 95, 139, 160
Language Capacity
   in apes, 48
Language Development xii
   late -, 51
Language Faculty, x–xii, 5–13, 15–22, 24, 45–46, 48, 138, 142–143, 153, 155, 157–158, 162–163, 165, 176–177
Language learning child, 136
Language Recovery
   complete -, 51
Langue 156–157
Latin, 135
Layering, 121
Leading idea, 56
Learnability, 99, 136
   mathematical theory of -, 136
Learning
   general mechanisms, 3
   theory, 176
   of exceptions, 132
   systems, 136
Left-to-right automation, 90
Levels
   of abstraction, 60, 97, 131–132
   of analysis, 97
   of description, 42, 97
   of embedding, 42
   of Inquiry, 43
   of Investigation, 38
   of representation, 38, 118
Lexical
   entry, 111
   item, 11, 111, 167
   structure, 121

   theorist,
Lexical Functional Grammar, 169
Lexicon, 87, 92–93, 99, 110–111, 119–120, 136, 165
LFG *see* Lexical Functional Grammar
Linear
   notation, 128
   operation, 128
   order, 163
   theory, 128
Linearization, 128
Linguistic
   argumentation, 59
   category, 117
   data, x, 3–7, 9, 44, 108, 141
   research, 39, 53
   traditions, 63
Linguistics,
   Cartesian -, 64
   comparative -, 65
   department, 36, 67, 76, 78
   generative -, 51, 80
   historical -, 65,
   history of -, 64, 170
   mathematical -, 82, 90, 106, 174–175
   nineteenth century -, 65
   theoretical -, 96, 106, 186
Linking,
   rules, 122, 138
   theory, 122
Literature, 77, 94
Local Properties, 124
Local Phenomena, 122–123
Locality, 122–124, 141
Locally adjacent, 124
Locally bounded, 123
Location, 135
Logic, 12, 115
Logical Form, 48, 111, 120, 137–139, 141
   rules (SI-1), 138
Logical Modalities, 115
Logical Necessity, 8, 109, 115–116, 118

Marked, 112–115, 129, 133–134
Markedness, 132–135, 138
Markedness rules, 138
Market Economy, 48
Markov processes, 89
Markov sources, 41, 90
Mathematical
   ideas, 43, 56
   notions, 142
   object, 43

psychology, 83
reasoning, 79
Mathematics,
  abstract -, 56, 79
  applied -, 22, 42–43
  classical view of -, 43
  foundations of -, 43
  history of -, 48, 79
  intuitionist view of -, 43–44
  intuitionistic -, 43
  modern -, 79
  new -, 79
Max Planck funds, 75
Meaning, vi, 13, 15, 24, 58, 72, 88 fn 5, 143, 157, 175
Mechanical systems, 108
Mechanism, 3, 5, 13–16, 22, 55–65, 96, 120, 131–132, 142, 148–149, 173–174
Medieval Grammar, 64
Memory, 41–42, 90, 93, 133
Mental
  ability, 62
  capacity, 62
  models, 38
  objects, 40
  organ, 5, 7, 13–15, 18–19, 57, 162
  phenomena, 19, 60–61
  representation, 60, 94, 118
Mentalese, 118
Mentalism, 89
Merge 12, 152–154, 162–163, 165, 167–169, 172
Metagrammar, 99
Methodology, 34
Mind, 1, 36, 41, 44, 55–57, 60, 89, 95, 118, 138, 160, 177, 180, 182
Mind/Body Problem, 60–61
Mind/Brain, ix–x, 1–2, 60–61
Minimalism, 11–12, 18, 24–25, 154, 158–159, 162, 186–187
  methodological -, 154, 156, 158–159, 171–172
  pre-, 180
  substantive -, 155, 158–159, 162, 171–172
Minimalist program, 11, 17, 149–151, 154, 158, 163, 167
MIT, xv–xvi, 35–36, 61 fn 5, 67, 74, 78, 89–90, 147, 152, 183, 185
Modalities, 115–116
Modular conception
  of linguistic structure, 5, 16, 87
Molecules, 50, 179
Monism, 60

Montague Grammar, 70, 72, 75, 115
Morphology, 119–121, 123, 133, 156
Morphophonemics, 91, 107, 119, 161
Motion, 38–39, 60, 108, 170–171, 173
Move alpha, 58, 87, 91–92, 96, 98–99, 103, 120, 122, 140
Movement, (*see* also NP-movement, quantifier movement, *wh*-movement) 92, 106, 123, 140, 154
  constraint, 104
  covert, 152
  overt, 152
  rule, 96–97, 104, 140, 154
Mutation, 49

NAFTA, *see* North American Free Trade Agreement
Name, 114 fn 5, 117
Name-like expressions, 93
Native speakers, 89
Necessity
  causal -, 116
  logical -, 8, 109, 115–116, 118
  mathematical -, 116
Negation, 90
Neural Coding, 63
Neurons, 19, 38, 179
Neurophysiology, 36–37
Nineteenth Century, 65
Node-to-terminal-node ratio, 167
Nominalization Transformation, ix, 119, 140
Nominative Island Condition, 103
Nominative NP, 78 fn. 34
Non-local phenomena, 98
Nonrecursive sets, 101
Non-theta-position, 112, 140
North America, xv, 71, 73
North American Free Trade Agreement (NAFTA), 184 fn 41
Norwegian, 129
Notational variant, 96–97
Noun Phrase (NP), 4, 101, 112
  extraction from -, 101, 104
  referential -, 111
NP
  case-marked -, 114 fn 5
  movement, 102, 106
NP-to-VP Filter, 103
Number,
  concept of -, 48
  faculty, 14-15, 47, 176
  intuitions about -, 48
  natural -, 14, 47–48, 176–177

prime -, 48
system, 48, 79
theory, 167–177
Numbers,
  addition of -, 97
  analysis of -, 44
  irrational -, 43
  properties of -, 43

Object, xii, 2–3, 12, 110–111, 143, 152
  identification, 46–47
  impossible -, 118
  in motion, 38–39
  non-existent -, 118
  real-, 118
Obligatoriness, 140
Ontogenetic Mechanism, 55
Ontological commitment, 118
Operationalism, 59
Operator-bound
  case-marked trace, 112
Optimality Theory (OT), 166–167
Orbits of planets, 61
Order, 110–111, 127–128, 163
  constituent -, 119
  free theory, 128, 135 fn 7
  of complements, 111
  word-, 135 fn 7
Ordering,
  constraints, 135 fn 7
  of transformations, 152
Organisms, xi–xii, 17, 24, 46–50, 155, 158, 178–180
OT, *see* Optimality Theory
Output, 19, 89, 103–104, 151, 161. 166–167, 176
Overgeneration
  morphological -, 120
Overt
  Case systems, 135
  elements, 93

Parameters,
  of Universal Grammar, 54
  ordering of -, 54
  ranking of -, 54
Parametrized
  constructs, 50
  theory, 11, 54
Paris, 74
Parsing, 9, 38, 90, 93
Passive, xi, 51, 69
Perception, 2, 108, 183

Perceptual
  categorization, 46
  constancies, 47
  phenomena, 38
  psychology, 45
  world, 46
Performance, 17, 92, 95
  Constraint, 92
  models, 95
  systems of -, 92
Parole, 156–157
Performatives, 34
Periphery, 120, 131–133, 138
Perlmutter's Generalization, 103
Perpetuation of the species, 46
Person, 117
Philology, 65
Philological work, 33
Phenomenology, 95
Philosopher, 30, 33–35, 59, 65–66, 117, 132, 182
Philosophy, 33–34, 36, 63, 67, 77, 159, 171
  ordinary language -, 33
Phonemic analysis, 107
Phonetic
  features, 142, 167
  representation, 137, 139
  side, 139–140
Phonetics, 107, 122, 153, 167
  descriptive -, 40, 72
Phonological representation, 138
Phonology, 82, 88, 106, 121–125, 128, 133–135, 138, 151–152, 166–167, 186
  abstract -, 138
  generative-, 106
  suprasegmental -, 122
Phrasal categories, 87 fn 2
Phrase Marker, 111, 126–128
  reduced -, 126
  three-dimensional-, 127
  union of two -s, 128
  unreduced -, 126
Phrase Structure
  mathematical theory of -, 98
Phrase Structure Grammar, 11, 23, 87, 99, 126, 169
Physical
  entities, 61
  growth, 61
  intuitions, 79–80, 97
  mechanism, 55, 132
  organs, 13, 97
  properties, 62

sciences, 94, 170, 182
system, 60
world, 50, 138
Physically possible systems, 50, 91
Physically real systems, 59
Physics,
　Aristotelian -, 108
　elementary particle -, 56–57
　Galilean -, 25, 66, 94, 108, 170–172
　high energy -, 81
　scholastic -, 108
　seventeenth century -, 63
Physiology, 36–38, 57, 63
Picture Noun, 133, 134,
Pigeons, 44–45
Pisa, xv, xvi, 29, 100–103, 110, 114, 132–134
Planning, 47–48
Popularization, 80–81
Port-Royal Grammar, 63–64
Possible
　circumstances, 116
　grammars, 54, 91, 98
　organisms, 50
　rules, 126
　systems, 50, 91
　transformational grammars, 96
　worlds, 115–116, 118
Poverty of the stimulus 5, 133
Precede, 142
Predication, 46
Prelinguistic notions, 143
Pretheoretical
　analysis, 141
　data, 142
Primates, 45–47, 165, 180
Primitive, 48, 113, 142–143
Primitive societies, 62
Primitive notions, *see* Primitives
Primitives, 139, 141–143
Principles,
　abstract, 11, 40
　general -, xi, 11–12, 22, 24, 151, 153, 158
　locality -, 123
　of grammar, 112
　of organization, 50
Principles-and-Parameters Theory, 11, 16, 23, 147–149, 162, 186
PRO, 103, fn 33, 106, 112–114, 123
Pro-drop languages, 103
Problem solving, 59
Procedures
　actual -, 38
　parsing -, 38

Processing, xi, 41, 149, 153, 182
　models, 41
　systems, 92
Processors, 42
Productive, 45, 57
Productive rules, 120, 133
Projection, 53, 87 fn 2, 124
　feature -, 124
　problem, 53, 89, 136, 141
Pronominals, 93–94, 114 fn 5, 115
Pronouns, 3–5, 93, 114 fn 5
Properties
　abstract -, 58,
　accidental -, 117
　empirical -, 142
　essential -, 18
　invariant -, 116
　linguistic -, 117, 137
　local -, 124
　mathematical -, 90
　metaphysically necessary -, 117
　physical -, 62
　semantic, 128
　structural -, 58, 128
Propositional attitude context, 116
Propositional Calculus, 39
Proximity, 135
Psychoanalysis, 40
Psychological
　interpretation, 118
　reality, 59, 95, 182
　test, 59
Psychologically real systems, 59
Psychology, (*see also* Behavioral, Behaviorist, Cognitive, Developmental, Mathematical, Perceptual Psychology), 24, 36–37, 44–45, 65, 90, 94–95, 106, 149
Pushdown memory, 90
Pushdown Storage Automaton, 42
Pushdown tape, 93

Qualitative differences, 48
Qualities,
　new -, 50
Quantifier,
　branching -, 127
　movement, 138–139
Quark, 58
Quechua, 120
Quine's questions, 116

R-expression, 114 fn 5
Raising, xi, 106, 140, 166

Reaction Time Experiment, 59
Real Time Model
  of language acquisition, 136
Real World, 59, 131, 184
Realism, 57–58
Reality, 3, 59, 95–96, 125, 143, 182
Reanalysis, 125
Reciprocals, 93, 114 fn 5, 137
Recoverability of Deletion, 88
Recursive, 14–15, 22, 53, 152, 162–163, 176
  rules, 47, 121
  sets, 53, 54, 125
Recursively enumerable set, 53, 125
Recursiveness, 121
Redundancy, 56–57, 78, 110–111, 113
Referential
  expression, 112, 115
  noun phrase, 111
Reflexive, 114 fn 5
  affixes, 120
Relational Grammar, 70
Relations of accessibility
  between worlds, 116
Relatives, 55, 103, 129
Renaissance Grammar, 64
Representation
  abstract -, 4, 128
  conditions on -, 120, 137
  levels of -, 38, 88
  logical -, 4
  mental -, 60, 94, 118
  phonetic -, 137, 139
  phonological -, 138
  syntactic -, 101 fn 27
  systems of -, 38
Representational theory
  of neural coding, 63
Research strategy, 108
Restructuring, 127
Revolution
  conceptual -, 67–68, 83
  Galilean -, 94
  intellectual -, 71, 83
  linguistic-, 65
  scientific -, 94, 171
Rhymes, 132
Romance, 106, 130
Roots, 120
Rotation in a plane, 97
Rule
  formal -, v
  global -, 72
  grammatical -, 24, 87, 143

linearization -, 128
of morphology, 120–121
phonological -, 122, 123, 128
schema, 103, 137
structural -, 104
system (system of rules), x
transformational -, 11, 87, 103, 125, 138, 154
Russian, 135

Scattering, 53–54
Schizophrenia, 51–52
Schizophrenic language, 51–52
Scholarship, 64–65, 94
Science,
  history of -, 60, 65
  normal -, 30, 68
  philosopher of -, 30, 65, 159
Sciences,
  Brain -, 10, 18, 20–21, 24–25, 149, 181–183
  cognitive -, 22, 36
  computer -, 36
  natural -, 19, 24, 35, 40–41, 66, 68, 72–73, 77, 81, 94, 104, 108, 172, 187
  social -, 10, 183, 187
Scientific method, 79
Scuola Normale Superiore, xv, 29
Selection, x, 13–14, 18, 46, 49–50, 87, 106 fn 41, 150, 178
Selectional
  control, 49
  pressure, 46
  value, 46
Self-identical, 117
Semantic,
  approach, 115
  notions, 143
Semantics,
  classical -, 72
  descriptive -, 40, 70, 72, 111, 115, 118
  Fregean -, 116
  generative -, 30, 69–72, 74, 88
  model theoretic -, 34, 115
  non-possible world -, 115
  possible world -, 115–117
Semitic, 120
Sentence, 4, 11, 15, 39–40, 42, 49, 88, 93, 99, 114, 116–117, 123, 129, 152, 159, 162, 182
  simplex -, 88, fn 3
Set union, 127–128
SI-1, *see* Logical Form Rules
Simplicity, 7, 158–160
Skinner review, 44

Sloane funds, 75
Snowflake, 150, 153–154, 156, 159, 163
Social systems, 62
Sociobiology, 35
Sound, 13, 15, 24, 41, 72, 119, 129, 133, 138, 142, 156–157, 162
   spectogram, 41
Source, 3, 5, 41, 89, 90, 113, 120
SOV order, 111
Space
   three-dimensional -, 79
Specialization
   of organs, 52
Speciation, 50
Specified Subject Condition (Constraint), 100–101, 133–134
Specifier, 87 fn 2, 119
Speech, 13, 142–143, 163
Speech Act, 34, 95
Spine, 155–156, 159
S-structure, 112, 137–139, 141, 151–152
Standard Theory, 75, 88, 153, 162, 177
Statistical model, 50
Stimulus, 5, 133
Strict Cycle, 88, 99
Stress
   alternating-, 123
Structural Description, 102–103,120, 140
Structural linguistics, 2
Structuralist grammar, ix
Structurally bounded, 123
Subcategorization, 120
Subcategorizational theory, 87
Subcomponents of syntax, 139
Subjacency, 51, 71, 97–102, 104, 123, 137, 140–141
Subject,
   accessible -, 134
   anaphoric, 99
   grammatical -, 143
   lexical -, 103
   missing -, 105
   null -, 103 fn 32
   of a tensed clause, 103 fn 34, 134 fn 5
   overt -, 93
   raising, 140
Subregularities, 133
Successive Cyclic Movement, 123
Successive Cyclicity, 124, 126
Suprasegmental
   phenomena, 122
   phonology, 122
Surface

form, 55
structure, ix, 55
Surface-oriented approach, 93
Survivor Property, 125–126
SVO order, 111
Swedish, 104
Syllable Structure, 122
Symbolic Behavior, 48
Symbolization, 48
Symbols, 12, 40, 42, 44–45, 47–48, 89, 117, 161
Symmetry, 50, 159
Synonymy, 59
Syntactic
   features, 124
   function, 112
   levels, 118
   structure, 48, 87, 89–90, 166, 186
Syntax, 82, 87–88, 100, 106–106, 119–125, 133–135, 137–139, 150, 169, 182

Taxonomy, 68, 94
Tensed Clause, 134
Tensed S Constraint, 100 fn 33
Tensed Sentences, 99
That-trace effect, 103 fn 32
That-trace Filter, 103
Thematic Relations, 88, 106, 110–111, 113, 164
Thematic Role (Theta-role), 111–113, 115
Thematic system, 112
Theorem, 39, 113–115, 125–126, 133, 141–142, 176
Theory
   automata -, 42
   binding -, 100–102, 108, 112–114, 130, 141
   bounding -, *see* Bounding
   control -, *see* Control
   elementary particle -, 56
   evolutionary -, 25, 50, 178–180
   explanatory -, 16–17, 53, 69, 79, 94
   group -, 98
   Information -, 41
   Island -, 100
   linear -, 128
   linguistic -, 7, 11, 16, 23, 30, 53, 69, 87–89, 97–98, 100, 104–106, 124–126, 139–142, 147, 154, 158–160, 177
   linking -, 122
   markedness -, *see* Markedness
   of communication, 41
   of conditions, 100, 134
   of government, 101, 104, 110, 112

of grammar, *see* Grammar
of language, 9, 13, 51, 56, 149
of mathematics, 43
of neural coding, 63
of the algorithm, 43
of the base, 87
of the computation, 37
of the lexicon (*see* also Lexicon), 87, 119
of thematic (theta) roles, *see* Thematic Role
of transformations, *see* Transformations
of universal grammar, 8, 126
selectional -, 87
semantic -, 115, 116
subcategorizational -, 87
syntactic -, 139
trace -, *see* Trace
Theta
  theta-criterion, 110, 112–114, 119
  theory, 165
  theta-position, 112
  non-theta-position, 112, 140
  theta-role, *see* Thematic Role
Thought, xii, 8, 46–48, 156, 163–164, 187
T-marker, 88
Topic, 164, 165
Trace,
  case-marked -, 113–115, 129
  non-case-marked -, 112
  operator-bound case marked -, 112
  proper government of -, 140
Transfer, 152
Transformational
  apparatus, 126
  component, 103, 136, 140
  depth, 140
  derivation, 140
  grammar, 23, 43, 53, 66, 69, 81, 87, 89–92, 96–97, 119, 125–126, 136, 169
  power, 87, 96
Transformational Rules, 11, 87, 103, 125, 138, 154
  cyclic -, 125
  interaction of -, 96
  ordering of -, 96
  structural descriptions of -, 96–97
  theory of -, 87, 125
Transformational Schema, 96
Transformational Theory, 96, 125, 126
Transformations,
  elimination of -, 96
  generalized -, 88
  number of -, 98

scope of -, 96
set of -, 140
singulary -, 88
theory of -, 87, 120, 168
Tree,
  representations, 128
  structures, 42
  three-dimensional -, 128
True statement, 58–59
Truth,
  in all possible worlds, 166
  necessary -, 43, 117
Truths
  arithmetical -, 43
  of mathematics, 43
  of physics, 43
try, 112
Turing Machine, 17–18, 41, 54
Turing Power, 126
Twins, 52

Unbounded
  experience, 54
  phenomena, 122
  phonology, 122
  processes, 123
  properties, 123
  range of expressions, 47–48
  system, 41
  variety, 99
Understanding, 13, 18, 20–21, 35, 38–40
Unexplained data, 70–71
Ungoverned, 114
Uniquely dominating, 127
Uniqueness of human life, 47
United States, 36, 44, 67, 71–75, 184–185
Units
  assembly of -, 38
Universal Grammar, xi, 6, 8, 11, 16, 35, 50, 54–57, 63, 107, 126, 129, 139, 148, 159–160, 162
Universals
  Greenberg-, 119, 135
University of Amsterdam, 73
University of Pennsylvania, 37
Unmarked, 134
Utrecht University, 30

Variable, 4, 94, 100–101, 113–114
  Q-variable, 122–123, 129, 181
Variation,
  genetic -, 51
  genotypical -, 50–51

intraspecific -, 50
Verb, 4, 110, 111
Verbal Structures, 120
Vision, 10, 37
Visual Space, 48
V-movement, 106
Vocabulary, 120
(Vowel) Harmony, 123–124
Vowel Shift, 134
VP-analyses, 93
VP complements, 93
VP-deletion, 106

Warlpiri, 149, 169
Weak generation, 49, 54, 89, 91, 98, 174–176
wh-Island Constraint (Condition), 71, 105
wh-Movement, 71, 99, 101–102, 105–106, 124, 141
wh-in-situ, 165

W* language, 135
Word,
  boundaries, 59
  formation, 120–121
  formation rules, 120
Word order
  free -, 136 fn 7
Wordstrings
  finiteness of -, 124
Word structure, 120
World,
  natural -, 3, 19, 50
  phenomena of the -, 96
  physical -, 50, 138
  real -, 59, 131, 184

X-bar Theory, 12, 87, 92, 98–99, 119, 135, 151–152, 162

Noam Chomsky at Mouton

■ **The Generative Enterprise Revisited**
Discussions with Riny Huybregts, Henk van Riemsdijk, Naoki Fukui and Mihoko Zushi
With a New Foreword by Noam Chomsky
2004. xviii, 196 pages. Paperback.
Approx. € 19.95 / approx. US$ 24.00
ISBN 3-11-018001-4

Noam Chomsky
■ **Syntactic Structures**
With an introd. by David W. Ligthfoot
2nd ed. 2002. xviii, 117 pages. Paperback.
€ 14.95 / US$ 14.95
ISBN 3-11-017279-8

Noam Chomsky
■ **Lectures on Government and Binding**
The Pisa Lectures
7th ed. 1993. x, 371 pages. Paperback.
€ 22.95 / US$ 24,95
ISBN 3-11-014131-0
(Studies in Generative Grammar 9)

Noam Chomsky
■ **Studies on Semantics in Generative Grammar**
3rd printing 1980. Reprint 1996.
207 pages. Paperback.
€ 22.95 / approx. US$ 28.00
ISBN 3-11-015413-7
(Janua Linguarum. Series Minor 107)

Noam Chomsky
■ **Topics in the Theory of Generative Grammar**
5th printing 1978. 95 pages. Paperback.
€ 12.95 / approx. US$ 16.00
ISBN 90-279-3122-4
(Janua Linguarum. Series Minor 56)

Noam Chomsky
■ **Strukturen der Syntax**
Preface by Klaus P. Lange
1973. 136 pages. Paperback.
€ 18.95 / approx. US$ 23.00
ISBN 3-11-015241-X
(Janua Linguarum. Serien Minor 182)

Noam Chomsky
■ **Current Issues in Linguistic Theory**
6th printing 1970. 119 pages. Paperback.
€ 22,95 / US$ 24.95
ISBN 90-279-0700-5
(Janua Linguarum. Series Minor 38)

Mouton
de Gruyter
Berlin · New York

www.deGruyter.de

Please place your order with your local bookseller or order directly from us.
Prices are subjects to change.

WALTER DE GRUYTER GMBH & CO. KG · Genthiner Straße 13 · 10785 Berlin
Telefon +49-(0)30-2 60 05-0 · Fax +49-(0)30-2 60 05-251 · E-mail wdg-info@degruyter.de